W9-ADO-163

Education and Poverty in Affluent Countries

Routledge Research in Education

Education and Poverty in Affluent Countries

Edited by Carlo Raffo, Alan Dyson,
Helen Gunter, Dave Hall, Lisa Jones,
and Afroditi Kalambouka

Routledge
Taylor & Francis Group
New York   London

First published 2010
by Routledge
270 Madison Ave, New York, NY 10016

Simultaneously published in the UK
by Routledge
2 Park Square, Milton Park, Abingdon, Oxon OX14 4RN

Routledge is an imprint of the Taylor & Francis Group, an informa business

© 2010 Taylor & Francis

Typeset in Sabon by IBT Global.
Printed and bound in the United States of America on acid-free paper by IBT Global.

Library of Congress Cataloging in Publication Data

Education and poverty in affluent countries / edited by Carlo Raffo . . . [et al.].
   p. cm.—(Routledge research in education ; 31)
Includes bibliographical references and index.
 1. Children with social disabilities—Education—Developed countries—Cross-cultural studies.   2. Educational equalization—Developed countries—Cross-cultural
 3. Poverty—Developed countries—Cross-cultural studies.   I. Raffo, Carlo.
LC4065.E38 2009
371.826'942—dc22
2009030100

ISBN10: 0-415-99880-8 (hbk)
ISBN10: 0-203-86033-0 (ebk)

ISBN13: 978-0-415-99880-2 (hbk)
ISBN13: 978-0-203-86033-5 (ebk)

Contents

Figure

Tables

Acknowledgments

The editors would first like to thank Ben Holtzman, Jennifer Morrow, and the team at Routledge for believing in our book and providing professional guidance in its production. Secondly we would like to show our huge appreciation for the Joseph Rowntree Foundation (JRF) for supporting our Education and Poverty project and providing permission for elements of the report to be used in this book. In particular we like to thank Helen Barnard at the Foundation for her steadfast thinking and guidance in undertaking the project. Without the support of both her and the Foundation more generally this book would never have come to fruition. In addition we would also like to thank our advisory group—Dr. Leon Feinstein, Professor Howard Glennerster, Ann Gross, Professor Ruth Lister, Diana McNeish, Chris Power, and Ray Shostak—for their invaluable critical friendship.

In undertaking the research for this book we must also thank colleagues from the University of Manchester including Professor Mike Bradford, Professor Fiona Devine, Professor Peter Farrell, Dr. Marianna Fotaki, Professor David Hulme, and Dr. Bernard Walters for their considered thoughts on our conceptual journey and for papers and contributions to our international seminar that was sponsored by JRF. In addition the team would also like to thank all those from beyond the University of Manchester who supported the international seminar through conversations, presentations, seminar contributions, or written comments on our papers. Many of these contributions have now become chapters within the book. Needless to say, however, the views expressed in the book, and any errors or shortcomings it may contain, are entirely the responsibility of the editorial team.

Finally we would especially like to thank Carlo's wife Mandy and all wives, husbands, and partners for their enduring love and support in the production of this book. Without their understanding and tolerance the task of putting this book together would have been that much more arduous.

Part I

Education and Poverty: A Mapping Framework

1 Education and Poverty in Affluent Countries

An Introduction to the Book and the Mapping Framework

Carlo Raffo, Alan Dyson, Helen Gunter, Dave Hall, Lisa Jones, and Afroditi Kalambouka

INTRODUCTION

The education systems of many affluent countries contain a paradox. Although education is seen as the way out of poverty, learners from poorer backgrounds consistently do badly in the education system. International data from the Programme for International Student Assessment (PISA) study of Organisation for Economic Cooperation and Development (OECD) countries shows that this is a widespread problem with deprivation having a negative impact on attainment across all OECD countries (OECD, 2008 a&b). This enduring challenge has led affluent countries, in their different ways and based on different types of research, to advocate particular policies and implement a plethora of targeted 'magic bullet' intervention strategies to deal with the challenge. Growing evidence, however, suggests that these interventions have, in large measure, failed to deliver systemic change and greater equity in terms of educational outcomes. Although there is widespread agreement that poverty and poor educational outcomes are related, there are competing explanations as to why that should be the case. This is a major problem for practitioners, policy makers, and researchers who are looking for pointers to action, or straightforward ways of understanding an issue that troubles education systems across the world. The situation is made more problematic because there are competing explanations and a plurality of positions that researchers have taken with regards to the field of education and poverty. Put simply, researchers often work in domains within the field that share a similar set of philosophical assumptions, whilst practitioners and policy makers too often reach for the action that is closest to hand, without considering its underlying assumptions about why and how poverty impacts on educational outcomes. As a result, the competing explanations of the poverty-education link have rarely been categorised and synthesised. The purpose of this book is to provide within one text a mapping framework for organising these disparate competing explanations, perspectives, and positions. Hence the book provides an opportunity for multi-disciplinary and multi-perspective researchers to respond to the issues at hand in ways that provide a deeper and more critically diverse set of explanations. What we hope this provides researchers and policy makers is a framework of explanations that can be examined in the light of any particular perspective, position, or viewpoint that might be held—a set of ideas against which practice, policy, and theory might be explored and extended. The mapping framework and expert voices contained in the book emanate from a research project funded by the Joseph Rowntree Foundation as part of their Education and Poverty Programme. This project enabled the editors of the book to undertake a review of the field and to invite internationally renowned academics to seminars to discuss and develop our review. We then asked them to develop their own detailed thinking about the link between education and poverty that made reference to our review. As part of the project we also developed some initial thinking about the implications of our review for educational policy. The book is the culmination of this project and it is hoped that our coherent synthesis of explanations, with detailed examples of particular perspectives and approaches that link to policy in the UK, US, and beyond, provide a depth of understanding that will transcend time and be as relevant to understanding future educational interventions and changes in government as we hope it does now. It is perhaps the first time that such a major and significant task has been undertaken, and we hope it will be widely used over time and to inform new studies and policy making.

In order to start engaging fully with the issues at hand we should set out our thinking about certain key terms that underpin the book. In our considerations about how to map the major conceptualisations of the relationship between education and poverty we immediately needed to reflect on how both terms might be defined. Although extensive and detailed debates about the concepts are beyond the remit of the book we do offer some broad working definitions of these terms that reflect explanations that we can work with and that at the same time set parameters for the nature of the book.

WORKING DEFINITIONS OF EDUCATION AND POVERTY

Education and Educational Outcomes

When examining notions of education, the book primarily focuses on young people's experiences of formal education in the primary, secondary, and tertiary sectors in affluent countries, and, more specifically, how these experiences translate into outcomes. Educational outcomes can be both narrowly and more broadly defined. Narrow definitions of educational outcomes generally refer to educational attainments (for example in England by Key Stage [KS] 2, 3, and 4 results, Standard Assessment Targets, and Cognitive Ability Tests). Alternatively they may refer to data regarding enrolment and retention as young people complete their compulsory schooling and progress through further and higher education. Broader definitions of outcomes may also reflect wider notions of valued educational capability and processes that include, for example, creativity, citizenship, social and emotional intelligence, and the development of autonomy and reflect umbrella terms such as educational well-being. Some of these broader definitions of educational processes and outcomes are encompassed in national educational policies in most affluent countries. The book seeks to reflect both broader and narrower notions of education when examining the links between education and poverty.

Defining Poverty

The definition and measurement of poverty is also a highly contested area. Key issues in the definition include the extent to which poverty describes an absolute state or relative inequality. Absolute definitions are based on access to basic resources to sustain life (e.g. food and shelter). Relative definitions are based on indicators of access to goods or activities that are deemed essential or appropriate in particular societies at particular points in time. Absolute poverty is a relatively rare phenomenon in the world's richer countries and consequently most indicators of poverty in such countries are based on relative indicators.

We, in line with many researchers in the field, refer to poverty as people living in households below 60 percent of median income. In order to illustrate this definition we provide some examples of what child poverty looks like in the UK. National statistics in 2004–05 suggest that there are 2.4 million children living in households with below 60 percent of median income. Poverty is also inequitably distributed geographically in the UK with an increased risk of experiencing child poverty being associated with living in particular regions or localities. A study by Hirsch (2004) for the Joseph Rowntree Foundation found that 70 percent of the most deprived areas in the UK are found in the four cities of Glasgow, London, Liverpool, and Manchester. They are home to 128 of the 180 local areas where more than half of families are out of work and relying on benefits. Evidence in such areas suggest that those young people most at risk of living in severe and persistent poverty are those in lone-parent families, whose parents are unemployed or working part-time, in families with four or more children, and with a mother aged under 25. Other groups that are also particularly at high risk of living in poverty in such areas are those from ethnic minorities, disabled people, local authority housing association tenants, and those with no formal educational qualifications. Although these are UK statistics, similar types of at-risk groups experiencing parallel levels of relative poverty and concentrated in particular urban regions reflect the demographic features of many affluent countries, particularly those countries with greatest levels of inequality and heterogeneity.

Although levels of relative poverty may vary between affluent countries, the experiences of living in poverty and their effects on personal, family, and community well-being appear to have some strong parallels. A strong theme is how a lack of resources can generate financial pressures on families that result in a whole number of hardships— economic, cultural, personal, and social. Economically, families may struggle to pay bills, may have limited space in their homes for shared living, may need to undertake two or more jobs to try and make ends meet, and may struggle to provide the basic essentials including heating, clothing, and food. The social, cultural, and personal consequences of economic hardships are equally compelling. These may range from family strife and conflict emanating from not being able to cope financially to a lack of self-respect and dignity about living in poverty in a society that apparently has so much to offer and which the media glamorises as being open to all sorts of possibilities. The concentration of poverty in certain communities also has the effects of fragmenting relationships and networks of support, distancing people ever more from potential developments in their localities and stigmatising those areas and people in those areas as 'unsafe' and at times 'not worthy' of society's support. Poor areas are also sites that attract those who take advantage of the vulnerability that people can feel when made poor—whether these be loan sharks or those peddling drugs to provide apparent 'relief' from the daily grind of poverty. This culture of scarcity can make for a dispiriting existence which impacts on self-confidence, self esteem, and the ability to see further than one's locality and perhaps those immediately around. It is the material, social, economic, and cultural conditions of poverty, their impact on educational outcomes, and the educational policy challenges required to remediate such outcomes that provide the focus to this book.

THE LINK BETWEEN POVERTY AND POOR EDUCATIONAL OUTCOMES

Although the concepts of poverty and education are at times seen as both complex and contested, the link between education (as defined in various ways and in relation to indicators of enrolment, retention, and outcomes) and poverty in affluent countries has been demonstrated clearly (Chitty, 2002; OECD, 2008a). Those young people who live in conditions of poverty, however defined, are more likely not to enrol or be retained in education, are more likely to achieve poorer educational outcomes and in many other ways are likely to demonstrate lower levels of general educational well-being than young people living in relative affluence. Conversely, those not enrolling or being retained in education and those achieving low educational outcomes in either narrow attainment terms or in more general terms of educational well-being are also more likely to then experience poverty. In some affluent countries (e.g. England) these findings are consistent from one generation to the next (Bynner & Joshi, 2002). Other research has demonstrated the link between schools serving poor communities and some of the lowest levels of aggregate educational attainment to be found in those areas (Kelly, 1995; Mortimore & Whitty, 1997; Demie et al., 2002; Bell, 2003). For example, in England the Social Exclusion Unit found that five times as many second-ary schools in the "worst neighbourhoods" had "serious weaknesses" than was typically the case, and children drawn from poorer family origins were more likely to have been in the lowest quartile of attainment in educational tests compared to their counterparts in other quartiles (SEU, 1998). Evidence from the Department for Children Schools and Families in England highlight that deprivation as measured by free school meals (a crude and yet accessible indicator of relative poverty) and the Income Deprivation Affecting Children Index (a neighbourhood poverty index) is strongly associated with poorer performance on average, at every stage of a pupil's school career (Schools Analysis and Research Division, Department for Children Schools and Families, 2009). For example at the Foundation Stage (from age 3 to reception class) in 2007, only 35 percent of pupils in the most deprived areas reached the expected level of attainment, compared to 51 percent of pupils in other areas. A deprivation attainment gap (measured by FSM) is also observed in English and maths at primary and secondary school: in each subject, a gap opens at Key Stage 1 (age 7) and increases by the end of Key Stage 4 (age 16). At Key Stage 4, there was a 29 percentage point gap between FSM and non-FSM pupils in English in 2007, and a 28 percentage point gap in maths. Evidence from the Office of the Deputy Prime Minister (2005) shows that key attain-ment in 2001-2 increases steadily from pupils in schools that are located in most deprived wards to those in schools in most prosperous wards. In the US, Jencks' (1972) comprehensive study showed that whatever type of school chil-dren attended, their educational performance reflected the socio-economic position of their parents. Finally, the OECD's PISA (2001) study, analysing the literacy and numeracy levels of 15-year-olds in developed countries found that for most OECD countries the distribution of educational achievement reflected pre-existing inequalities, with differences between high and low attainment accounted for by socio-economic class and by implication levels of relative poverty (Chitty, 2002). This international evidence clearly points to the fact that young people living in poverty in affluent countries are less likely to achieve educational outcomes than their more affluent counterparts. Perhaps what is more disturbing is the depressing fact that the link between education and poverty has been enduring. As Levin states: " . . . The problems do not seem to be any smaller today than they were in 1970, and the gaps in achievement between poor urban schools and provincial or national averages remain large just about everywhere" (Levin, 2009: 181–82).

Although the evidence for the link between education and poverty is overwhelming, this is not a deterministic relationship—not all young people who experience poverty do badly in education. As we will establish later in the book, there are many young people who demonstrate forms of resilience that moderate the risks associated with living in poverty. In addition there are also examples of policy interventions that have made a real difference in the educational lives of disadvantaged young people that have resulted in real improvement in educational attainments.

In essence, therefore what this book attempts to do is examine the competing explanations for how and why poverty and education are jointly linked and implicated in maintaining disadvantages and underachievement, what policy makers have attempted to do to resolve the situation, and what other policy possibilities exist to improve the situation.

EXPLANATIONS FOR THE LINKS BETWEEN EDUCATION AND POVERTY—AN INTRODUCTION TO THE MAPPING FRAMEWORK

As we have highlighted, the relationship between poverty and educational outcomes is an international phenomenon and one which has attracted much attention. One reason for this is that, although there is widespread agreement that poverty and poor educational outcomes are related, there is much less agreement as to why that should be the case. Competing explanations—in terms of the differential distribution of educational opportunities, the cultures of poor communities, the dynamics of poor families, the quality of schooling in disadvantaged areas, and many more—have been advanced. Policy makers and practitioners are therefore faced with a bewildering array of possible explanations, each of which seems to be supported by equally convincing evidence and argument. It is hardly surprising, therefore, if their interventions often seem to be based on the latest explanation to be advanced, the one which is argued for most fiercely by its proponents, or the one which is most politically convenient.

The purpose of Part I of the book is to review some (though by no means all) of the research literature on poverty and education that emanated from a project undertaken by the authors for the Joseph Rowntree Foundation. We attempt to identify the different ways in which that relationship has been conceptualised and explained and we have organised those explanations into what we call a 'mapping framework.' In other words, we have tried to identify clusters of explanations which share features in common, and have tried to show how these differ from each other and, equally importantly, how they might relate productively to each other.

The scope of our research documented in Part I of the book needs to be clarified. First, it is not definitive. The proposed map of the field is one amongst many that might be constructed, and it is also one which inevitably simplifies what are often complex explanations. We therefore advise readers to use it as a springboard for exploring the primary literatures on which it is based, so that they can come to terms with those complexities for themselves. Second, it is not itself a new explanation of the poverty-education relationship. In mapping out current explanations, we have made no attempt to go beyond them in order to offer something 'better.' Third, it is not a handbook for action. We believe that there are important implications for policy makers and practitioners in our work and we have tried to make these explicit in Part III of the book. However, we have made no attempt to evaluate the different explanations currently on offer in order to identify the most powerful and persuasive ones, or to identify the most promising courses of action. Our view is that there is no 'magic bullet' in this field. Effective interventions in the education-poverty relationship are likely to be multi-dimensional and to demand social action well beyond the remit of education policy—or, indeed, of public policy as a whole. If there is one lesson from our work, it is that single-strand interventions aimed at 'quick fixes' are almost certainly doomed to failure. This multi-dimensionality is reflected in the variety of studies highlighted in Part II. In this chapter we set the scene by developing our 'mapping framework' and in Chapters 2 and 3, we describe the literatures that are aligned to the two major families of explanations—we call them 'perspectives'—that we identified.

DEVELOPING THE MAPPING FRAMEWORK— RESEARCH DESIGN, METHODS, AND ANALYSIS

Our literature review for the Joseph Rowntree Foundation project was in the form of a "conceptual synthesis" (Nutley et al., 2002) of research evidence. According to Nutley et al. the aim of a conceptual synthesis " . . . is not to provide an exhaustive search and review of all the literature published in the field [. . .]. Instead the aim is to identify the key ideas, models and debates, and review the significance of these for developing a better understanding of research utilisation and evidence based policy and practice implementation" (2002:2). Therefore, a conceptual synthesis differs from both traditional narrative reviews of research and from systematic reviews in that it is concerned not only to synthesise the substantive findings from research, but also to identify the conceptual bases out of which they have emerged. We use the term 'conceptual synthesis' as it denotes a broad approach to reviewing research evidence as opposed to a prescribed methodology. However, this approach has a long history which can arguably be traced back at least as far as Burrell and Morgan's (1979) classic account of 'sociological paradigms.' Our particular approach to the synthesis of the literature was to develop a mapping framework that would primarily categorise and classify literature rather than provide new paradigmatic and theoretical models of explanation for the links between education and poverty. Our conceptual synthesis was based on:

- identifying an appropriate level of analysis in terms of the sorts of assumptions which might be surfaced;
- ensuring that the full range of conceptualisations were identified; and
- ensuring that the assumptions of each conceptualisation were identified accurately and that research studies were allocated reliably to different conceptualisations.

However, unlike a systematic review, which demands a comprehensive search for all relevant research reports, our conceptual synthesis depended on locating only key exemplary items. Key in this sense refers to pieces of research literature which are particularly illuminating of assumptions and/or which review the research within a conceptualisation and/or which have been particularly influential in determining the direction taken by research. This literature included research texts, policy papers, evaluations, and various other reports. As we read, we began to develop a provisional mapping framework, and we tested this in a sensitising seminar with a range of academics. As the framework developed, we invited a wider group of researchers and policy makers to an international seminar in order to examine and challenge our framework. We used both seminars to provide advice on key literatures to help refine the framework, and we used the enhanced mapping framework to structure database interrogation, keywords searching and screening criteria, and the development of a database categorising framework (for a more detailed explanation of our methods see Raffo et al., 2007).

STRUCTURING THE MAPPING FRAMEWORK

In mapping out the terrain we wanted to examine how various literatures helped suggest or explain the links between poverty and low educational outcomes. We became aware that there was little agreement about a linear causal effect between poverty and education, and set ourselves the task of organising this complex literature into ways that simplified this complexity.

From our readings the literature appeared to cohere, to a greater or lesser extent, around three different foci:

- Explanations that focus on the individual including areas such as the characteristics of the individual or his/her relationship with family or teachers or peer groups; we have termed the focus of these studies as being at the 'micro-level.'

- Explanations that focus on 'immediate social contexts' that might be located in families, communities, schools, and peer groups; we have termed the focus of these studies as being at the 'meso-level.'
- Explanations that focus on social structures and/or are linked to notions of power and inequality; we have termed the focus for these studies as being at the 'macro-level.'

We use 'micro,' 'meso,' and 'macro' only in the sense defined here. We have attempted to handle the underlying complexities that could be obscured by interrogating particular explanations in terms of the following questions:

- Within the broad identification of the factors linking education and poverty, what *specific* factors are identified and how are these understood?
- Although the fundamental explanation may be located within one particular aspect at the micro, meso, or macro level, are the other levels taken into account and, if so, how? (In Chapter 2 of the book we highlight writers that operate within functionalist integrating approaches.)
- What are the implications of the explanation for the possibilities of changing the poverty-education relationship?

Our reading of these explanations has led us to recognise that there are differences in views of the role of education in producing what we might call the 'good society'—and hence, what counts as 'good education.' In particular, we would like to make a distinction between two broad positions. These are summarised in Table 1.1. While both regard education as a good for the individual and society, they differ in relation to what sort of a good it is and how it is to be produced.

Table 1.1 Mapping the Terrain—Organizing the Education and Poverty Literature

Perspectives and Knowledge Claims about Education	The Foci	Sites—The locations within foci	Purposes of, and Pressures on, the Explanations	Policy Implications
Functionalist	Micro	Individuals, families, schooling, neighborhoods, peer groups, and/or the system(s)	Explanation and/or intervention	Ways of examining the purpose and enhancing the functionality of the education system
Socially Critical	Meso			
	Macro			
	Integrated			

The first, we label as the 'functionalist' position, because it takes it for granted that education plays an important part in the proper functioning of society. When it works well, education is seen as bringing benefits both to society as a whole and to individuals within that society. There is ample scope for debate about precisely what these benefits are or should be, but typically they include economic development, social cohesion, and enhanced life chances for individuals. The problem, as seen from this perspective, is that these supposed benefits often do not materialise in the case of individuals and groups from poorer backgrounds, and this failure calls for explanation and intervention.

Commonly, explanations tend to be offered in terms of dysfunctions at the level of the individual learner (the micro focus), the social contexts within which the learner is placed such as schools, families, and neighbourhoods (the meso focus), the underlying social structures such as class, race, and gender (the macro focus) out of which those contexts arise, or some interaction of these. Examples of explanations that might be said to broadly fit within this category include the correlation between educational achievement and social class explained through language (Bernstein, 1961), values (Hyman, 1967), and parental interest and support (Douglas, 1964). Crucially, however, the assumption is that, if specific (albeit complex) problems in the way education works within society can be overcome, its expected benefits will indeed materialise.

The second position, which we label here 'socially critical,' likewise assumes that education is potentially beneficial. However, it doubts whether its benefits can be realised simply by overcoming specific problems in its contribution to current social arrangements. Those social arrangements are themselves seen as being inherently inequitable, and education in its current form reflects unequal distributions of power and resource. The failure of education to produce benefits for people living in poverty is not simply a glitch in an otherwise benevolent system, but is a result of the inequalities built into society and the education system alike. It follows that, if educational benefits are indeed to be realised, a form of education is needed which is *critical* of existing arrangements and which can both challenge existing power structures and enable democratic development. Examples of explanations that broadly fit into this category includes work that raises wider questions of power, hierarchy, social control, and cultural reproduction (Bowles & Gintis, 1976, Bourdieu & Passeron, 1977), the nature of curriculum design (Jackson & Marsden, 1962), and teaching and learning approaches (Friere, 1970). In addition socially critically approaches have criticised assumptions about issues of representation, identity, and place with regard to the relationship between education and lived experience. Furthermore these approaches can be activist through giving recognition to the experiences of young people, families, and communities and, through local action, legitimate ways of living and making a difference to prevailing social and economic circumstances. Hence many explanations within this perspective focus on the possibilities of radical interventions at the macro and meso level such as tax reforms and investment decisions at the national level and new forms of democratic management and leadership at the school level. Studies often examine either the possibilities of such interventions or the realities of small scale attempts of such interventions.

What we have highlighted in terms of functionalist and socially critical explanations and interventions are familiar, though relatively crude distinctions. In addition although they are partially derived from sociological perspectives, they are not theoretical models of explanation per se, but rather descriptive positions for categorising and classifying the literature on education and poverty. Furthermore these positions, in practice, could be interdependent. For any conceivable construction of 'education,' it is important to know both whether things are working as well as they might and how particular assumptions, values, and patterns of advantage and disadvantage are in-built. It is entirely possible, therefore, to ask both functionalist and socially critical questions of education at a particular time and place, just as it is possible for researchers to do work that draws on both positions. In this respect it is important to avoid easy assumptions. One might be that functionalism necessarily implies approval of the status quo, or that socially critical approaches necessarily relate only to some ideal and unrealisable social context. However, as we shall argue later in the book, one of the fundamental problems of attempts to understand—and take action in relation to—the poverty-education relationship is that explanations drawn from these two positions rarely engage with each other, other than through processes of somewhat dismissive critique (Shain & Ozga, 2001).

A further issue that needs to be borne in mind when reading categorised explanatory accounts or intervention strategies suggested by research is that the relationship between the professional practice of researchers and interventions intended to break the link between poverty and educational experiences and outcomes is complex. The disposition to research and develop interventions, and to work on securing change, is related to personal interest combined with an increasing demand to demonstrate the impact of research on policy and practice. Additionally, the increase in commissioned research by government and agencies means that researchers within both the private and public sectors are frequently involved in project work that is directly related to delivering outcomes. Many researchers do see it as central to their project to engage in practice at the micro and/or meso and/or macro areas of interest. Some involve themselves in data gathering at a macro level so that their work influences national strategy (see for example Feinstein et al., 2004). Others operate at the meso and focus, for example, on schools and both gather data and work with students, teachers, and the community to make changes (see for example Thomson, 2002). And others again operate at the micro level and work with individuals and families in raising and meeting aspirations (see for example Luthar & Zelazo, 2003). There are those who locate their work in the functionalist paradigm and, for example, work on school effectiveness at one or more levels of interest (see for example Muijs et al., 2004) and there are those who work in the socially critical paradigm, and, for example, work on bringing about change through national and local action on inclusion (Anyon,1997). By implication we caution against the possibility of stereotyping any researcher's work on account of the particular types of engagement with policy and practice in the work they are undertake and which we describe in this book.

STRUCTURE OF THE REST OF THE BOOK

In this chapter we have documented a mapping framework for organising the research literature on education and poverty. As we have suggested this mapping framework is a digest of the research literature on education and poverty and organises studies into three levels of explanation: (a) the individual (the micro level), (b) the immediate social context that might be located in families, communities, schools, and peer groups (the meso level), and (c) social structures (the macro level). These levels are also underpinned by two broad perspectives that provide quite different views about the purposes of education: we have termed these functionalist and socially critical perspectives. In Chapters 2 and 3 of the book we provide detailed summaries of the literatures that are underpinned by these two perspectives and together with this chapter provide the structure and evidence base for how the explanations between education and poverty are understood. Readers will note that Chapter 2 on functionalist explanations appears somewhat longer than Chapter 3 on socially critical explanations. We need to stress at the outset that this does not mean we are attaching greater levels of importance to functionalist explanations. Rather, as we highlight above, the number and type of explanations perhaps reflects government concerns (and hence research funding) from across the developed world about the nature of the endemic problem, suggesting starting points for investigation that reflect a functionalist perspective. Chapter 3 provides counterbalancing explanations and we feel that both together reflect the general 'lay of the land' in terms of the number and types of key explanations. Part I of the book should therefore been seen as providing the broad explanatory evidence and framework for the rest of the book.

In Part II of the book we focus on international studies on the link between education and poverty. The part provides an opportunity for internationally renowned authors in the field to develop particular aspects of the framework that link to their own particular philosophical, theoretical, and empirical contexts and interests. So for example in Chapter 4 Pauline Lipman focuses on issues of education and poverty through an examination of the political economy and cultural politics of race in Chicago school policy. In her chapter she argues that education policy is a strategic aspect of an urban agenda producing intensified inequalities and poverty. The Chicago macro context is described and then the chapter focuses on specific urban developments, in particular the drive by financial and corporate interests and the state to make Chicago a first tier global city and the cultural politics of race that regulate, exclude, and pathologize low-income communities of colour, especially African Americans. Lipman then examines three key education policies in relation to the political economy and racial politics of the city: (a) accountability regime and new architecture of stratified education experiences, (b) privatization and marginalization of community participation in schools, and (c) "mixed income" schools linked to "mixed income" communities. Finally she outlines some contradictions and counter trends and grass roots projects for educational equity in this context.

In Chapter 5 John Smyth examines inclusive school leadership strategies in communities made poor based on student and community voice. He argues that Australians have a long history of regarding themselves as egalitarian, and yet he points to mounting evidence suggesting that Australia is becoming an increasingly divided and less tolerant society. Given that there is evidence for the social impact of inequality and poverty, he suggests that this presents a particular set of challenges for schools as social institutions and for educational leadership in particular. The chapter therefore focuses on issues of school leadership in an Australian context and it exposes the inadequacy of dominant deficit school leadership narratives by emphasising the importance of how school leadership should develop understandings of its students and its communities in order to enhance and expand their capabilities. In order to do this he examines how leadership might see communities as important educational assets and resources and therefore develop an ethos of *school-in-community* as well as *school-as-community*.

In Chapter 6 Daniel Muijs examines how school effectiveness research might develop to enhance educational equity in areas of poverty. He argues that school effectiveness research has received a fair amount of criticism—much of it justified—for having contributed to growing inequities by allowing its findings to be (mis)used by policymakers as a justification for policies that have at times have led to socially inequitable outcomes, particularly in areas of poverty and disadvantage. He argues that, this notwithstanding, school effectiveness research can make a positive contribution to research and practice aimed at a more equitable education system to deal with issues of poverty, but that the field needs reorienting and needs to engage with other fields and traditions if it is to do so. He then presents a model for equity-based school effectiveness research and practice.

In Chapter 7 Ingrid Schoon focuses on how poverty and social disadvantage impacts on school motivation and educational aspirations and examines the implications of these for educational policy. In the era of growing knowledge economies Schoon sees that an increasing number of young people aspire to participate in further education beyond the compulsory schooling age and are postponing the step into full-time employment in favour of lengthened education. Certain discourses suggest that the motivation for maximising school achievement results from beliefs that more education improves chances for attaining better jobs, higher wages, and social status. In this chapter, Schoon assesses the premise that extended education leads to success or improved social mobility by comparing transition experiences of young people growing up in families experiencing poverty and those from more privileged backgrounds. Using macro level data collected for two British Cohort Studies following the lives of over 20,000 individuals born in 1958 and 1970, she assesses the role of teenage aspirations in contributing to increasing or decreasing social mobility within different socioeconomic groups. Her findings suggest that young people from relatively poor backgrounds have generally lower aspirations than their more privileged peers, even after controlling for academic ability. Linking aspirations to long-term outcomes and social status in their early thirties, her study suggests that academically able children with high aspirations from poor families are not achieving to the same level as their more privileged peers. These findings are then discussed in terms of contextualized capabilities, differentiating between functional capabilities and actual life chances and opportunities that underlie variations in transition strategies, their antecedents, and outcomes.

In Chapter 8 Ruth Lupton examines how issues of poverty and place have resulted in a raft of area-based initiatives in UK education. She documents how governments in England have demonstrated a history of interventions that top up national policies by area-based initiatives: additional programmes targeted on specific geographical areas of disadvantage and poverty. In education, these interventions can be traced from the Educational Priority Areas of the 1960s to Excellence in Cities in the 1990s, and now the London, Manchester, and Black Country 'challenges.' Lupton explores how these interventions reflect ideas about the role of place and space in education, and reviews critiques of their underlying rationales.

In Chapter 9 Pat Thomson argues that the social and economic situation/situatedness of schools serving poor communities creates obligations and opportunities to contribute to local regeneration. She suggests that this can be accomplished in part through curriculum and critical pedagogies that encourage students to understand their social and material place in the world and how it came to be the way that it is. In making this case she argues for the necessity of some discussion of the purposes of schooling, critical pedagogy, and the official processes of regeneration.

In Chapter 10 Meg Maguire examines the dynamics of poverty, the urban, and education in the UK and its impacts on learner identities and trajectories. She initially explores some of the contradictory elements of poverty and the policy effects of different interventions in the UK. Then she examines how the way in which the urban is positioned in the education policy setting may displace more critical and structural concerns of inequality and poverty. Drawing on two large-scale ethnographic studies of young people's urban transitions, the chapter examines the ways in which experiences of neighbourhood poverty are implicated in the sorts of micro level learning identities that young people make up in order to navigate through their schooling experiences. Maguire ends by exploring how some of these identities may provide some scope to disturb some of the barriers to educational achievement arising out of poverty.

In Chapter 11 Jane Gaskill and Ben Levin draw on a study of urban education in two Canadian cities over the last forty years and outline the forces and dynamics that arise in efforts to improve urban schools. They show how improvement efforts are affected by larger social policies, by debates about the appropriate role of schools, by disagreements about the best place to focus improvement efforts in diverse and poor communities, and by the typically difficult politics around urban education.

The third part of the book specifically focuses on a systematic examination of policy developments in education that have attempted to break the link between education and poverty. It does this by referring to the mapping framework developed in Part I and the more detailed studies in Part II. In Chapter 12 Gunter et al. focus on policy as a process so that its productive possibilities for the state and society can be examined. The chapter constructs and deploys a framework for doing this in order to examine, first, *sources* or where policy comes from; second, *scope* or what policy aims to achieve in ways that are systemic (macro), or focused on e.g. a region (meso), and local or individual (micro); and third, *patterns* or the exercise of power through how policy and strategy intervenes into existing policy practices and culture. In Chapter 13 Raffo et al. use the mapping framework from Part 1, the case studies in Part II and the productive policy possibilities highlighted in Part Chapter 12 to provide an examination of, and commentary on, both universal strategies and also priority education policy initiatives that have attempted to break the link between education and poverty. Illustrative examples are mainly from England and include Excellence in Cities (EiC), Sure Start, and Full Service Extended Schools to name a few. These examples are also supplemented by policy approaches from a number of other countries including Head Start and No Child Left Behind in the US. In the final chapter of the book Dyson et al. focus on how policymakers, practitioners, and researchers might read and use the mapping framework and evidence in Part II of the book. Suggestions for how current and future policy might be developed in affluent countries as a result of such an analysis are provided that build on notions of scope, coherence, and power.

We do hope you enjoy the book and that what we present provides a richness of ideas that will help you develop your thinking further in this most important field.

2 The Mapping Framework, Research Literature, and Policy Implications Within a Functionalist Perspective

Carlo Raffo, Alan Dyson, Helen Gunter, Dave Hall, Lisa Jones, and Afroditi Kalambouka

INTRODUCTION

It might be pertinent at the outset of this chapter to remind the reader what we mean by the functionalist perspective. The functionalist perspective takes it for granted that education plays an important part in the proper functioning of society. When it works well, education is seen as bringing benefits both to society as a whole and to individuals within that society, including economic development, social cohesion, and enhanced life chances for individuals. The problem, as seen from this perspective, is that these supposed benefits often do not materialise in the case of individuals and groups from poorer backgrounds, and this failure calls for explanation and intervention. This chapter examines some of the key ideas in the literature that are underpinned by this position. The ideas and key literatures are organised via a micro, meso, and macro focus as highlighted in Chapter 1. We also have examples of approaches and studies that integrate these levels of analysis.

THE FUNCTIONALIST PERSPECTIVE AND THE MACRO FOCUS

Explanations adopting this focus tend to see the relationship between poverty and education as resulting from underlying social structures—though these are, of course, mediated by factors at the meso and micro levels. A summary of the main approach is provided in Table 2.1.

In the past, macro-level explanations may have focused on relatively stable social structures. In the context of a manufacturing-led economy, relatively clear distinctions between workers, managers, and owners (amongst others) led to an interest in the role of social class in shaping educational outcomes. The different skill levels needed by groups in different socio-

Table 2.1 Functionalism and the Macro Focus

☐ Globalisation has resulted in particular forms of social exclusion for particular individuals and communities. This is reflected in aspects of spatial ghettoisation, health inequalities, high levels of unemployment, poor housing and poor infrastructures for such individuals. Together these factors are linked to, and compound, poor educational attainment.

economic positions might be seen as resulting, ultimately, in differential educational opportunities, expectations, and resources, reflected most obviously in the limited access to secondary education for working class children prior to 1944, and the sharply differentiated tripartite system[1] thereafter.

Although the basic structure of this explanation has remained the same, a theme of particular importance in this literature latterly has been the impacts of globalisation on national and local economies, particularly in relation to changed labour market conditions. Work that has examined notions of globalisation in advanced economies have tended to focus on issues of de-industrialisation, restructuring, and post-industrialisation (Lash & Urry, 1994) and the corrsponding spectrum of opportunities and constraints generated by such transformations. In many respects it is the constraints of these transformations that have been experienced most forcibly by many of the poorest communities, constraints that many theorists have argued can be understood as forms of 'social exclusion' (Byrne, 2005). This term is heavily contested, particularly in relation to notions of poverty and inequality (Lister, 2004). Nonetheless, what the concept of social exclusion enables us to examine are some of the dynamic processes which generate growing levels of societal polarisation that have had a negative impact on the ability of individuals to partake and/or engage with aspects of mainstream society—what some have termed a "deprivation of capability" (Sen, 2000).

The argument is that the simple stratifications of educational and other opportunities associated (rightly or wrongly) with class have now become much more complex. In particular, many young people and communities are now confronting differently-constituted labour markets that reflect the emergence of the post-industrial, where much employment takes the form of either high value-added, knowledge-driven tertiary sector work (for instance, in finance or the new media and cultural industries), or the more mundane, flexible, part-time, and inherently insecure service sector work (Brown, 1999). However various forms of social and economic restructuring have resulted in many of the poorest families and communities being left further behind, with growing evidence that geographical areas are spatially excluding those most disadvantaged into ghettoised locations (Meen et al., 2005). These locations are often characterised by inadequate housing and poor levels of resources, infrastructure, and health provision where educational attainments are frequently at their lowest (Hastings et al., 2005).

In general terms, the conclusion of this work is that social position continues to shape education outcomes, but that it does so in complex ways. Rather than a large section of society facing limited opportunities, different forms of 'exclusion' impact on different groups, frequently interacting so as to compound one another's effects. So, people living in poverty face forms of exclusion which may differ between inner cities, peripheral housing estates, and rural locations, or between different ethnic groups, or between the genders. They may be compounded by health inequalities (Acheson, 1998; Exworthy et al., 2003) transport difficulties, lack of access to financial services, family breakdown, and so on. For those facing multiple exclusions of this kind, the impact on educational outcomes may be far worse than the impact of 'class' alone. We will shortly consider research which explores how these factors operate at the meso level. However, macro-level explanations are distinguished by tracing these factors back to the underlying social processes—notably, the impacts of economic globalisation—from which they are seen to spring.

THE FUNCTIONALIST PERSPECTIVE AND THE MESO FOCUS

These macro-level explanations lead naturally to attempts to explain how, at the meso level, different forms of exclusion impact on educational outcomes. Recently there has been a range of research that has examined (a) some of the socially and culturally mediating impacts that peer groups, the family, and neighbourhoods have had on young people and their understanding of, aspiration towards, and capability within schools and (b) the processes of schooling and delivery of other public services more generally that have aided or constrained educational achievement for such young people.

The main themes in this work are summarised in Table 2.2.

The Impacts of Globalisation on Particular Families and Communities

The Social Exclusion Unit through their Policy Action Team reports (National Strategy for Urban Renewal, 2000) have examined the various barriers to achievement and attainment that individuals, families, and communities have experienced due to poverty generated by the dynamics of globalisation impacting on particular communities in specific locations. These reports together suggest that poor educational outcomes stem from a variety of factors that shape both the nature of schools (see below) and the various socially excluding factors that impact on young people outside of school. These latter factors include the spatial ghettoisation of particular poor neighbourhoods, a lack of jobs and infrastructure in such neighbourhoods and poor opportunities for developing networks of trust within and between communities. In addition, an often cited factor is a lack of

Table 2.2 Functionalism and the Meso Focus

☐ Globalisation has had an impact on the way families and communities living in poverty experience life. Of particular importance is the ghettoisation of particular neighbourhoods with a lack of employment and effective public services, low levels of bridging social capital , a lack of role models for young people, forms of discrimination that are likely to impact on self-esteem and a lack of resources that result in poor health and diet, all of which when taken together impact on the ability of families to support young people with education.

☐ Different neighbourhoods and communities can provide differential levels of social and cultural capital that can obviate some of the material aspects of poverty and provide improved opportunities for educational success for certain groups of young people.

☐ Effective parenting linked to notions of the educational aspiration of parents, educational support and stimulation for young people in the home, secure and stable home environments and participation with school is central to young peoples' educational success. However, such notions are premised on social class, maternal levels of education and material deprivation all of which positively correlate with poverty. In addition schools and teachers often have deficit and negative views about the nature of communities, parents and young peoples' aspirations for education in areas of challenge and poverty.

☐ Schools with particular strategies and approaches can make a difference in areas of 'challenge', However, the extent to which such schools can make a difference is heavily influenced by the backgrounds of the pupils in schools, the constraints that poverty exerts on the schools, the operational capabilities of teachers and the nature of educational markets in such areas.

☐ Improved public sector service delivery can improve families and young people's access and achievement within school but the ability to develop effective multi-agency working is constrained by professional and organisational boundaries.

appropriate role-models within families which may have little or no history of work, and pressure on very poor families to secure an income greater than that available from education and training. These studies have also identified a lack of development of appropriate bridging social capital and cultural capital[2] within peer, family, and communities that have limited the capacity of people to realise their potential at school.

One of the central issues that these studies highlight through their analysis of social exclusion is the behavioural manifestations that social class differences linked to poverty generate amongst individuals and families. Rothstein's (2004) work in the US is an illustration of a much larger body of research that makes clear the links between the way social class and poverty link to educational outcomes. In his analysis of the connection between poverty and poor educational attainment he examines the way the social, cultural, and economic position of a particular social class (see previous section) are mediated at the meso level through individual, family, and community characteristics and the behavioural manifestations of those classes. He sees social groups as being defined by particular factors that then find expression in the contexts of families, schools, communities, and peer groups. His message is that those from a lower social class, and particularly those in poverty, will demonstrate a collection of occupational, psychological, personality, health, and economic traits that have the capacity to predict in a relatively deterministic fashion an average performance in education and other areas of life that is qualitatively different from middle class and relatively well-off families/groups.

NEIGHBOURHOODS AND ETHNICITY

It has long been accepted that particular minority ethnic populations are at greater risk of low educational outcomes (Committee of Inquiry into the Education of Children from Ethnic Minority Groups [Swann Report], 1985; Pathak, 2000). The Department for Education and Skills (2005b) in the UK noted that Black Caribbean and White/Black Caribbean (mixed heritage) pupils are amongst the lowest achieving pupils in the final years of statutory schooling (alongside Gypsy/Roma pupils and Travellers of Irish Heritage) with Indian, Chinese, White/Asian (mixed heritage), and Irish pupils being amongst those ethnic minority groups more likely to gain five or more A*-C (i.e. 'top grade') GCSEs. Amongst those lowest achieving minority ethnic groups, the rates of special educational needs and permanent school exclusions are also higher than for other minority ethnic groups and whites (DfES, 2005b). It has also long-been established that particular minority ethnic groups are likely to suffer from higher levels of poverty and associated problems relative to majority white populations (Dorsett, 1998; Berthoud 1998). As will be discussed later in the chapter, some researchers have sought to locate the reasons for this within the individual, looking to genetic differences to help explain this apparent difference in educational achievement and attainment (e.g. Jensen, 1984). Others have rejected this view in its entirety and pointed to structural factors and stereotyping of ethnic minorities as a major cause for minority ethnic low achievement (Verma, 1985).

Others however have sought to locate and explain this apparent difference through articulating social differences that may exist between groups of different ethnic and racial origins. One such explanation comes from the notions of cultural and social capital differences whereby it is argued that differences in these capitals (alongside other forms of capital) amongst various ethnic and racial groups can result in different enabling or inhibiting factors towards educational attainment. For example, Kalmijn and Kraaykamp (1996) and Carter (2003) explore the way in which cultural capital as related to race could be playing a vital role in the closing gap between black and white students in schools in the US and might explain part of what they see as the black-white convergence in schooling outcomes.

LaVeist and Bell McDonald (2002) suggest that in the US, when whites and blacks (as defined by the authors) from similar areas are compared, white outcomes from education are at the very least the same as if not worse than black outcomes despite 'race' being seen as a key determinant of educational success. They argue that this may have to do with black communities sticking together across the social strata through well-formed social links (to do with race and or/faith) thus offering young poor blacks access to middle-class African Americans and with a consequent higher value placed on education as a way to do better in life. The authors suggest that this increased social and cultural capital can help offer black youth a legitimate example of the benefits of education and can thus serve as an educational advantage. The authors argue that their findings run counter to ideas of black underachievement through identity and culture which argues that many black youths, particularly males, view education as 'acting white.' By way of contrast, their research illustrates a higher level of aspiration towards education amongst African Americans than other accounts such as these suggest.

Patterns of ethnicity differ significantly, of course, between the US and other affluent countries. For example in the UK there are also strong interactions between ethnicity and faith, and some studies have examined the role of faith communities in the development of social capital. Furbey et al. (2006) show that faith communities can contribute substantially to social capital gains in communities which can be seen to lead to higher educational attainment, lower crime levels, improved health, and so forth.

Parenting and Young People's Preparedness for, and Support, in Schools

Central to much writing on the link between education and poverty within a functionalist perspective is the level and type of parenting that young people experience with regards to preparedness for, and support, in schools. The research focuses on both the way parents interact with their children in preparing them more or less fully for schooling and on the way parents and teachers view each other's support for the education of the children under their responsibility.

Desforges and Abouchaar (2003), reviewing the research literature on the relationship between parental involvement in children's education and educational outcomes, highlight a number of findings. First, parental involvement takes many forms including good parenting in the home, the provision of a secure and stable environment, intellectual stimulation, parent-child discussion, good models of constructive social and educational values and high aspirations relating to personal fulfilment, and good citizenship; contact with schools to share information; participation in school events; participation in the work of the school; and participation in school governance. Second, the extent and form of parental involvement is strongly influenced by factors including family social class, maternal level of education, material deprivation, maternal psycho-social health, single parent status, and, to a lesser degree, by family ethnicity. Third, the extent of parental involvement diminishes as the child gets older and is strongly influenced at all ages by the child characteristically taking a very active mediating role. Fourth, parental involvement is strongly positively influenced by the child's level of attainment: the higher the level of attainment, the more parents get involved. Perhaps the most important finding is that parental involvement in the form of 'at-home good parenting' has a significant positive effect on children's achievement and adjustment even after all other factors shaping attainment have been taken out of the equation. In the primary age range the impact caused by different levels of parental involvement (in this extended sense) is much bigger than differences associated with variations in the quality of schools. The scale of the impact is evident across all social classes and all ethnic groups. However differences between parents in their level of involvement were associated with social class, poverty, health, and also with parental perception of their role and their levels of confidence in fulfilling it. In a similar vein, Scott et al. (2006), in their report on a controlled trial of a parenting programme in primary schools, offer evidence of parenting programmes leading to improved standards of parenting and child behaviour at school.

Schools Operating in Challenging Circumstances

There are sets of literatures at the meso level that are specifically located in schools, school markets, and neighbourhood contexts. This broad range of work suggests that particular forms of schooling, school/educational markets, and the particular types of compositional mixes of schools are key to explaining different educational outcomes.

Perhaps the most extensive literature review that examined international research evidence on school improvement in socioeconomically disadvantaged areas was conducted by Muijs et al. (2004). They start by acknowledging that schools in difficult and challenging circumstances have received increasing policy, and to some extent research, attention and that these schools 'must exceed' what might be termed as 'normal efforts' because of the increased socioeconomic problems in the wider areas they serve. In their review, a number of themes emerged including the following:

- a focus on teaching and learning—academic focus is more prevalent in effective low-socioeconomic status (SES) than in effective high-SES schools
- leadership—effective leaders exercise indirect but powerful influence on school effectiveness, particularly through distributed forms of leadership

- creating a positive school culture—these include developing a blame-free culture, continuity in approach, setting high expectations, developing coherence, and open communication, minimising the high staff turnover and enhancing teachers' beliefs in the effectiveness of proposed interventions.

Finally, the authors stress that it is not enough to create improvement, but it is crucial that every effort is made to sustain the improvement.

Amongst the strongest advocates of market initiatives in England are scholars such as James Tooley who argues that market approaches to education "bring in delivery mechanisms that are responsive to what parents and students require, meet the needs of all, including the most disadvantaged, and succeed in raising educational standards" (Tooley et al., 2003:5). Alongside advocates of full market forces in the field education, there are also those who argue that quasi-markets are better placed to improve costs and efficiency of state provided services such as education (Le Grand & Bartlett, 1993). Bradley and Taylor (2002) suggest that quasi-markets in education have resulted in parents taking advantage of choice with schools with 'good' exam results improving their enrolment numbers viz-a-viz other local schools with lower results. However Gorard's (1997) review of market reforms suggests that "reforms are likely to be both less effective than originally suggested by some, and less damaging than feared by others" (Gorard, 1997) .

Many writers have also examined the school social context as it impacts on the ability of schools to drive up improvements or minimise drop outs (Crowder & South, 2003). For example Hallinger and Murphy's research in the US (1986), while acknowledging school effectiveness variables, go beyond the school effectiveness perspective to stress the importance of school social context and how certain variables vary according to this context. Reflecting some of the above literatures on the differential nature of parental engagement with young people and with schools, they highlight how parental involvement, parental expectations, and attitudes to education and preferences on curriculum may vary according to the social context of the school. In particular they found that the school's social context influenced the breadth of the curriculum, the allocation and use of instructional time, the instructional leadership role of the principal, the nature of the school reward system, and the type of expectations embedded in school policies and practices. The implications for intervention are that well-publicised school effectiveness factors should not be treated in a homogeneous way but should be applied with consideration according to each school's specific social setting.

There have also been other studies that have examined schools in challenging circumstances that sensitise school improvement and effectiveness studies to issues of context and mix. For example Lupton's study (2005) summarises the distinctive features of the contexts of high-poverty schools and illustrates how these contexts impact on the processes and practices of the schools. In terms of the distinctive features of these schools in high-poverty contexts, Lupton argues they are characterised by unpredictability in the working environment. She argues that although these schools are differentiated, they have in common many things not shared by schools in less disadvantaged areas: low prior attainment; poverty manifesting itself in poor health and diets, lack of uniforms, equipment, and parental contributions for enrichment activities. Lupton also argues that these schools tend to have an emotionally charged atmosphere with children often sharing this with teachers and as such, the teachers she interviewed talked of 'mothering' and 'caring' for the children and the comparison with 'social work' was also made (Lupton, 2005:594–5).

In addition these contexts impacted upon teachers' recruitment, retention, and behaviour. For example schools in challenging contexts had difficulties in staff recruitment and retention due to not only the context but the perceived underperformance of the school and bad local press. There was evidence of pressures on teacher performance whereby daily 'firefighting' would divert attention away from teaching and learning and could lead to lowered expectations of themselves as teachers as well as of the pupils. Work by Thrupp (1999) points to how particular mixtures of young people in schools from different socioeconomic backgrounds can suggest 'tipping points' where schools either struggle to achieve educational success or make improvements. This is complemented by Levačić and Woods (2002) (see also: Woods & Levačić, 2002), who looked at the differences in the rate at which schools improved their exam results between 1991–1998. Their analysis revealed that two variables were found to have the most impact on examination improvement—(a) a low concentration of social disadvantage relative to other local schools (this is the most influential variable in explaining improvement in exam results over time) and (b) starting from a low base level of exam results. They also argued that schools with high levels of social disadvantage were likely to be dually handicapped as their relative social disadvantage tended to get worse over time.

A growing body of research has highlighted how the needs of particular young people and families in the poorest contexts appear to require schools to operate as part of multi-agency partnerships. A multi-agency approach to tackling poverty offers the justification that problems that are complex and multi-faced need multi-agency partnership solutions that can harness the strengths and expertise of several different welfare perspectives (Atkinson et al., 2005; Milbourne et al., 2003). Such an approach has been characterised as an attempt to offer 'joined up solutions' to 'joined up problems' (Milbourne et al., 2003). Multi-agency working to tackle poverty-related issues in educational settings commonly include collaborations among departments, organizations, and professionals from the educational, social work, and health sectors. Examples in England on a large scale include the Education Action Zones, Health Action Zones, the New Deal, Centres for Excellence, Sure Start, *Connexions*, the Children's Funds, and Children's

Table 2.3 Functionalism and the Micro Focus

☐ The individual is seen as having 'choice' in an era of globalisation. The opportunity to shape one's path with regards to education suggest the need to enhance particular forms of social capital that might bridge young people into experiencing and hence valuing education. This approach recognises the importance of appropriately developed and culturally embedded mentoring programmes in order to provide opportunities for broadening networks of influence for young people.

☐ Some research focuses on notions of constrained inherited capability and intelligence that pre-ordains an individual's ability to succeed in society. This provides few opportunities to ameliorate the position an individual has due to the inherited capabilities with which he/she is born. This approach has been heavily criticised methodological, theoretically and morally.

Trusts and Extended Schools. Many of the studies that have examined multi-agency partnerships have tended to focus on those issues that either assist or hinder the development of multi-agency working. These can be categorized in the following ways:

- Critical success factors include the need for managers to have very clear and unambiguous ideas of the kind of the programme to be established; team members to have a professional predisposition to bottom-up approaches that assists them to enable and empower disadvantaged communities, and non-hierarchical, flat management structures based on mutual respect. (Bagley et al., 2004; Millbourne et al., 2003)
- Hindrances include the tensions between collaborative and competitive approaches and the consequent pressures for organisations to act in their own interests by, for example, pursuing higher places in educational league tables (Machell, 1999, Millbourne et al., 2003). Difficulties are also highlighted in terms of networking and cultural capital brought from previous interpersonal partnerships (Milbourne et al., 2003). Related to these issues is the difficulty of practitioners to operate at a level that is highly sophisticated and to juggle demands that are beyond their traditional professional roles (Anning, 2005; Engestrom, 2001).

THE FUNCTIONALIST PERSPECTIVE
AND THE MICRO FOCUS

Explanations that are located at the micro level are summarised in Table 2.3 and include concerns about identity and its links to actions taken by young people in a world of choice possibilities (Giddens, 1991; Beck, 1992) and the notions of hereditary differences particularly located around IQ (Herrnstein & Murray, 1994; Rutter, 2003).

The Individual, Identity, and Choice

Issues of individual identity and choice have been examined by sociologically-informed researchers. They reflect a view that the emergence of a 'risk' society with complex and uncertain pathways to adulthood generates a plethora of choice options. Here the discussion is about how the dynamics of globalisation that have compressed time and space and that have broken down the structuring influences of traditional bureaucratic capitalist organisations (Sennett, 2003), community organisations, the church, and extended families, have resulted in greater opportunities for young people to shape their life chances. However, these potential life chances come with an attendant and associated array of extended risks and opportunities. The result of this for young people is that they are viewed, and view themselves, as being personally responsible for their actions. Their actions will then be reflected via the networks of influence of which they choose to be a part and that will then shape ultimately how and whether they get on in education. These arguments suggest that notions of social class have declined and class identities have been dissipated and replaced by 'individualised social inequality' (Beck, 1992:88). The implications of this for education are described below:

> Schooling means choosing and planning one's own educational life course. The educated person becomes the producer of his or her own labor situation, and in this way, of his or her social biography . . . Depending on its duration and contents, education makes possible at least a certain degree of self-discovery and reflection. The educated person incorporates reflexive knowledge of the conditions and prospects of modernity, and in this way becomes an agent of reflexive modernisation. (Beck, 1992:93)

Perhaps the most important set of studies that have examined the impact of poverty and disadvantage on identity and choice amongst young people has been research that has examined skills formation, career choices, and the transition experiences of young people as they progress from adolescence and schooling to adulthood and work. For example Brown (1999) and Coffield (2000) see skills formation as being more about the development of the social capacity for learning, innovation, and productivity than it is about the development of purely technical skills. As this chapter highlights earlier, the social capacity of learning skills in various informal and formal contexts can be closely aligned to the development of social and cultural capital. This is a process that creates an embedded cultural 'know-how' that is also enhanced by the resources accrued by individuals from others through their high trust social relations in varied networks of influence (Ball, 2003). In addition, and reflecting some of the insights developed by Rudd (1997) and Archer and Yamashita (2003), research has shown that life chances for young people can be both constrained and enhanced by the informal learning and identity-forming experiences developed through networks of relations that are central to an individual's life experiences (Raffo & Reeves, 2000; Raffo, 2003). In addition there is evidence that 'turning points' (Hodkinson et al., 1996) in young people's lives can occur when there is a coming together of various new networks of experiences which provide a weight of evidence, influence, and support that then creates a new confident understanding for the individual with the capacity to inform new actions.

These examples suggest that the ability of individuals to meet the changing structural demands of globalisation are dependent on the quantity and quality of access to appropriate material and symbolic resources and information. However for those in disadvantaged situations the reality is that social relations are often linked to high risk situations, (for example a lack of employment opportunities or stable home environments) without appropriate material and symbolic resources such as income or adult role models to support them. The challenge for on-going policy development in this area therefore is one of elaborating how particular systems and institutions, such as school careers curricula and *Connexions*, can develop practices that are sensitive to how young people develop their various 'capitals' and how these can be enhanced to enable more effective choices about education to be made.

Genetics and IQ

In contrast to the above research that locates change and development in young people via individual choice and experience, a differently constituted body of research suggests that the link between education and poverty can be traced back to individual genetic and inherited differences. The explanation for low educational success of such theories is that young people who do not succeed educationally are those that have inherited poor cognitive capabilities such as low IQ and dysfunctional behavioural traits. The correlation between education and poverty is premised on the notion that those in poverty are more likely to show low cognitive and psychological capabilities which, in turn, are associated with them in living in poverty. Poverty is concentrated in particular areas because there is a tendency for the reproduction of such inherited traits and capabilities between people of similar genetic makeup who live in such areas. The work of Jensen (1984) perhaps most strongly articulates this theory. He argues that there is such a thing as "g" which means general intelligence. This, he asserts, can be measured through particular forms of tests. Jensen's work is particularly provocative as he argues that tests which measure 'g' show different levels of general intelligence amongst different ethnic groups. Jensen argues that evidence is overwhelmingly supportive of 'g' but that there are two main reasons why this may not be politically or socially acceptable:

- it doesn't allow for the possibility of raising children's intelligences
- it doesn't offer readily acceptable explanations for race/ethnic groups differences in tests scores.

The latter work of Herrnstein and Murray (1994) and their thesis in their book *The Bell Curve* is strongly linked to Jensen's perspective. They argue that intelligence exists and is accurately measurable across racial, language, and national boundaries. Intelligence is one of, if not the most, important correlative factor in economic and social success in general in America, and is becoming more important. According to this school of thought, intelligence is largely (40 percent to 80 percent) genetically heritable and there are racial and ethnic differences in IQ that cannot be sufficiently explained by environmental factors such as nutrition, social policy, or racism. They argue that nobody has so far been able to manipulate IQ long term to any significant degree through changes in environmental factors, and in light of their failure such approaches are becoming less promising. Finally they argue that as a country the US has been in denial of these facts, and in light of these findings a better public understanding of the nature of intelligence and its social correlates is necessary to guide future policy decisions.

It terms of legitimacy and claims to knowledge, both these studies and the particular perspective underlying them has been heavily criticised methodologically, statistically, and morally. For example Holtzman (2002) sets about assessing the claim by Jensen and Herrnstein and Murray that educational low/underachievement is due to hereditary class differences in IQ. He suggests that the reality is much more complicated than this picture would have you believe. He suggests that interactions of genes occurs with those of other genes and that a wide variety of environmental factors and thus inherited social class differences are a myth perpetuated by and acting as a justification by ruling groups for their power and privilege. Holtzman explains the principles of genetics and how genes function to show it cannot explain the perpetuation of complex traits: "inherited genetic factors cannot provide the explanation of social organization" (529).

THE FUNCTIONALIST PERSPECTIVE AND
INTEGRATING EXPLANATIONS

There are perspectives that are more integrating in their analyses. They may, for example, start at the micro level but interlock with factors at the meso and macro level. Here much of the work focuses on bio-psychological perspectives that focus on human and self development and the interactive influences of genetics and environment in the contexts and relationships within which this development is enhanced or constrained. This is summarised in Table 2.4.

Table 2.4　Functionalism and Integrating Explanations

☐ Integrating literatures start from a developmental psychological viewpoint and then build levels of theory on how particular variables at different levels of experience away from the individual create risk or resilience in the lives of young people and consequently their ability to actively engage with education.

☐ Research highlights particular risk factors such as family characteristics linked to issues such as maternal depression, violent neighbourhoods or negative peer group socialising. Some research identifies moderators to risk particularly the development of a warm caring relationship with a significant adult or within a caring community. Other studies examine the way factors experienced at a distance from the lives of families such as educational qualifications are then mediated through particular forms of lived experiences for those families that then result in particular levels of educational achievement for young people associated with those families. Various macro, meso and micro level variables are then examined within an integrated theory often refereed to as a bio-ecological systems theory that synthesises many of the different risk and protective factors.

☐ Such studies are complemented by the early child development research that focus on the importance of these issues in early childhood and that recognise aspects of neurobiology. This reflects the more sophisticated work undertaken by geneticists who have examined the environmental impact on genes and in particular how poor environments can biologically alter capability..

Risk, Resilience, and a Bio-Ecological Systems Framework

Writers from within a developmental psychology research perspective are suggestive of an integrating approach. Although primarily concerned with an examination of those risk factors that impact on the micro and in particular the individual psychological development of young people, they are clear that many of these are both mediated and moderated by factors associated with a meso focus located in families, peer groups, and the community more generally. There are, for example, certain attributes associated with poverty that are experienced at first hand by the individual. The literature refers to these as proximal factors and they are exemplified by issues such as stressed parenting and experiences of community violence that are likely to create risk for individual development. At the same time certain research writings within this perspective highlight how certain protective factors such as caring and warm adult relationship can at times moderate some of these risk factors.

The motivation for much of this work is to find ways of developing intervention strategies that might create resilience in young people facing adverse situations. Writers have identified a number of distal (at a distance from the individual and not directly experienced by the individual) and proximal (experienced directly) risk factors that either by themselves or concurrently influence differentially the general self development of young people and by implication the probability of their educational success. At the same time as describing the links between risk and individual vulnerability much research also examines those variables (and the interventions that might generate those protective variables), that create resilience against risk. So for example the 'at risk' factors include both distal and proximal factors such as:

Proximal:

- Community violence
- Maternal depression and anxiety disorders possibly linked to potential drug abuse
- Parental divorce/bereavement
- Negative peer group socialising influences
- Parental stress related to economic well-being, e.g. housing, access to resources
- Particular processes in families and disturbed family functioning—hostile family environments, effects of maltreatment, ineffective parenting, unresolved discord, insufficient child monitoring and supervision, and lack of close relationship with one or both parents
- Racism and discrimination in the lives of ethnic minority families (this can also operate as a distal factor in relation to broader patterns in society)
- Low individual IQ
- Personality traits, temperaments, and disorders
- Gender
- Risk, agency, and self-development

Distal:

- Negative neighbourhood influences
- Levels of social isolation for families in particular communities
- Inner-city deprivation

An example of a study that examines the proximal risk factors associated with parental mental health issues and poverty is provided by Ellenbogen and Hodgins (2004). This research explores the impact on children's psychosocial functioning of parents with high levels of neuroticism (e.g. anxiety, anger, or depression) who live in poverty. Their results suggested that high neuroticism in parents living in poverty and with major affective disorders (mental disorders that primarily affect mood and interfere with the activities of daily living) is associated with inadequate parenting practices and the creation of stressful family environments. These factors are subsequently related to psychosocial problems among offspring, that then result in poor educational engagement for those young people.

Other studies, rather than focus on the impact of proximal risk factors *per se,* instead focus on the mediators of risk and, in particular, how distal factors can be mediated by proximal factors. So, for example, Feinstein et al. (2004) examines how parental educational qualifications can act as a distal factor with regards to the future capabilities of young people in families. He demonstrates how qualifications can act as a risk for young people if parents lack them, or be protective if parents have them. He then makes the links between distal factors and the various family characteristics that manifest themselves as proximal factors, such as parental attitudes and capabilities in supporting young people with their education. These proximal factors are then seen as key influences in the way young people can, or want to interact, with education.

Others studies, instead of focusing purely on risk, examine how childhood resilience factors can moderate risk. Luthar and Zelazo (2003), for example, examine a number of proximal factors at the meso level that can moderate and help protect young people against some of the risks highlighted above. Their main finding is that resilience rests, fundamentally, on relationships—particularly in families, peer groups, and schools. For example, during childhood years, early relationships with primary caregivers affect several emerging psychological attributes and influence the negotiation of major developmental tasks. Accordingly, serious disruptions in the early relationships with caregivers—in the form of physical, sexual, or emotional abuse—strongly impair the chances of resilient adaptation later in life. They are clear that good relationships are built on warmth and support on the one hand and appropriate control and discipline on the other. In the context of families, these skills/attributes are important aspects of parenting and there is a recognition that these skills may be difficult to sustain in the face of major life risks such as chronic poverty and ill health. In addition, where communities are at risk of violence or discrimination, resilience for individuals and families may only be fostered if these are clearly combated to ensure physical and emotional safety. However it is also the case that the community can provide protective factors when a child's own parents are, for whatever reasons, partially or wholly incapacitated.

Others again suggest that certain distal and proximal risk factors are so endemic in areas of chronic poverty that there are few possibilities for protective factors to mediate or moderate positively. The focus in these studies tends to be at a macro and meso level. For example Cauce et al. (2003) in their work noted that the riskier the setting the fewer protective factors are likely to be present. They point to areas of concentrated poverty in inner-city US where studies have explored the level of observed or experienced violence, individual and peer group dysfunctional behaviour, high risk sexual behaviour or substance abuses, and poor educational outcomes. For Cauce et al., the very nature of deprived inner-city neighbourhoods, the dangers they pose, and the sheer grind of daily living under the onslaught of poverty-related stress strongly militates against the development of parenting skills and other protective factors.

These examples of studies that examine risk and resilience focus on the macro, meso, and micro either separately or in a more integrated way and are complemented by other studies that emanate from within an ecological systems approach that attempts to model the linkages between the systems at various levels as they impact on the individual. Bronfenbrenner's theory (1979) defines complex "layers" of environment, each having an effect on a child's development. This theory has recently been renamed "bioecological systems theory" to emphasize that a child's own biology is a primary environment fuelling her development. A good example of the use of Bronfenbrenners' bioecological approach is Eamon's (2001) review of the effects of poverty on children's socio-emotional development. She suggests that the nested structures of the ecological environment proposed by Bronfenbrenner's model provide a useful framework for examining theories of the effects of economic deprivation on children's socio-emotional development. She highlights that within the microsystem of the home, stress-coping theory and family process models frequently are used to explain the socio-emotional developmental effects of poverty. The stressful life events or chronic strains caused by economic deprivation appear to affect children's socio-emotional functioning by eroding parental coping behaviours, creating psychological distress and marital discord, and resulting in parenting practices that are uninvolved, inconsistent, emotionally unresponsive, and harsh. Her review suggests that practitioners such as teachers and social workers who work with low-income families and children with socio-emotional problems should assess parental psychological distress, coping behaviours, the quality of the marital or partner relationship, and parenting practices to assist in selecting appropriate interventions. In addition she highlights how parent-child interactions may not always account for the relation between poverty and children's socio-emotional functioning. Hence poverty may result in children's socio-emotional problems by impeding or influencing peer relations, attending low-quality schools, or being exposed to unsupportive school environments. Her review of research in this area suggests that increasing support in parents' social networks and communities may decrease parental psychological distress and improve parenting practices.

Assessing the child's exposure to violence and associations with dysfunctional peer interaction also provide information for intervening at the individual, family, or community level. Consistent with Bronfenbrenner's conceptualizations, researchers and social workers frequently recognize that developmental processes may be contingent on a particular culture or subculture, including shared beliefs and knowledge, and on available economic resources and opportunities. Social policies that increase access to economic resources and good quality housing, neighbourhoods, schools, nutrition, and health care are likely to enhance processes in the more immediate system levels and result in better developmental outcomes. Historical and life events, and individual change across the life span, also have important influences on child development. Although chronic poverty has detrimental effects on children's socio-emotional development, income loss appears to be particularly disruptive to parent-child interactions. Social policies that educate families concerning these risks and ensure families have access to mental health services and economic resources may help to stabilize the parent-child interactions that appear to have detrimental effects on the socio-emotional functioning of both younger and older children.

Genetic and Environmental Interfaces

More sophisticated models associated with genetics are represented in new work that crosses the boundary between the individual and the environment and examines the interface between biological processes and environmental factors that generate psychopathological responses.[3] Of particular interest here is what Rutter (2003) refers to as gene-environment interaction, which refers to genetically influenced differences in individuals' sensitivity to particular environmental factors, and gene-environment correlations, which refer to genetically influenced differences in individuals' exposure to particular environmental factors. His view is that until very recently, much genetic research was concerned with partitioning population variance into effects attributable to genes and those due to environmental influences, with the implicit assumptions that these effects summed to 100 percent and that no others could be involved. According to Rutter, both sets of assumptions are mistaken. Segregating genes (i.e. those that vary among individuals) and specific environments do not account for all variance. Biological maturation (genetically programmed by genes present in all people) may influence resilience. In other words, both normal and abnormal psychological development will be influenced not only by genetic and environmental factors acting independently and additively but also by a combination of these factors. Examples of this include notions of neuroplasticity[4] where there is structural and functional re-organisation of the brain in response to environmental inputs such as experiences of violence. For example there is much evidence that environmental factors over time can influence children's inherited attributes including IQ and individual temperaments. Hence young people living in unsupportive and poor stimulating environments are likely to see their IQ diminish over time. There is a view therefore that heritability does not imply intractability but that risk factors associated with certain environmental elements can have very negative influences on apparently heritable traits. DiPietro (2000) sets about evaluating the current state of knowledge that relates to early child developments in brain research and in particular the potential misuse of such information. For example she suggests that by focusing too heavily on using science results in early academic and science enrichment programmes as a particular indicator of childhood development, what this obscures is the potential effects of other factors such as the relative burden of poverty. An emphasis on intellectual functioning therefore misses the most compelling evidence on the role of early social environments in mediating the establishment of neural networks that regulate children's responses to stress and the capacity for self-control and self-regulatory and coping behaviours.

This work is supported by Locurto (1988) who illustrates the potential malleability of IQ drawing on adoptive family studies. He argues that studies from psychology and science have neglected issues around the malleability of IQ and evidence shows that IQ is malleable to some extent but argues that some paradoxical problems exist. To illustrate this point he argues how people have become taller over time or how people on average do better on IQ tests over time to show at least simplistically evidence that genes change over time. Locurto argues against simple environmentalism on the one hand and simple hereditary arguments on the other. He asserts that available evidence on the interaction of environmental and genetic factors is not entirely clear. Evidence, he suggests, currently shows that approximately one third of the influences on IQ are neither genetic nor environmental. Instead they are viewed by Locurto as being more complex and possibly linked to within-family differences.

Early Childhood Development Perspectives

There are various literatures that have specifically focused on early childhood development in the context of dramatic transformations in the social and economic circumstances under which families with young children live. Much of this literature reflects the US Committee on Integrating the Science of Early Childhood Development report "From Neurons to Neighborhoods: The Science of Early Child Development" (Shonkoff & Phillips, 2000). This report draws together research findings from neurobiology, behavioural sciences, and social sciences and covers the period from before birth until kindergarten. It includes efforts to understand how early experience affects all aspects of development—from the neural circuitry of the maturing brain, to the expanding network of a child's social relationships, to both the enduring and the changing cultural values of the society in which parents raise children. There is a recognition of the scientific gains that have generated a much deeper appreciation of (a) the importance of early life experiences, as well as the inseparable and highly interactive influence of genetics and environment, on the development of the brain and the unfolding of human behaviour; (b) the central role of early relationships as a source of either support and adaptation or risk and dysfunction; (c) the powerful capabilities, complex emotions, and essential social skills that develop during the earliest years of life; and (d) the capacity to increase the odds of favourable development outcomes through planned interventions.

What the general findings suggest is that there are four overarching themes that link into numerous core concepts of development. These themes are that (1) all children are born wired for feelings and ready to learn, (2) early environments matter and nurturing relationships are vital, (3) society is changing and the needs of young people are not being addressed, and (4) interactions among early childhood science, policy, and practice are problematic and demand rethinking. Perhaps most importantly there are a number of implications for how poverty intervenes in these four themes and hence influences development and educational achievement and success. With regards to the first theme, what the literature suggests is that development in the early years is both highly robust and highly vulnerable. In other words what happens during the first months and years of life matters a lot, not because this period of development provides the blueprint for adult well-being, but because it establishes either a sturdy or a fragile foundation for what follows. However, there are also clear signs that these early development opportunities are strongly associated with social and economic circumstances that are predictive of subsequent academic performance.

With regards to the second theme again there are risks associated with poverty. As highlighted in previous sections of the report that focus on explanations generated within a functionalist perspective, poverty can generate parental stress and mental health problems and can locate families in demoralised and violent neighbourhoods. Circumstances characterised by multiple, interrelated, and cumulative risk factors impose particularly heavy burdens during early childhood and are most likely to incur substantial costs to both the individual and society in the future. In addition there is evidence from behavioural and neurobiological sciences that document a range of environmental threats associated with poverty that impact on the central nervous system. In addition the third theme of social and economic transformations are posing serious challenges to the efforts of parents and others to strike a healthy balance between spending time with their children, securing their economic needs, and protecting them from the many risks beyond the home that may have an adverse impact on their health and development.

SYNTHESISING THE LITERATURE FROM A FUNCTIONALIST PERSPECTIVE—IMPLICATIONS FOR POLICY AND PRACTICE

Explanations that focus on the dynamics that generate social exclusion highlight how certain individuals, families, and communities are marginalised and potentially made poorer by a lack of access to education. There are structural barriers that result from a lack of resources for neighbourhoods and for individuals and families that live in those neighbourhoods. This lack of resources is linked to unemployment or poorly paid employment and is exacerbated by the poor infrastructures of health, housing, and transport in such neighbourhoods. This perspective is suggestive of the need for educational intervention strategies to deal with barriers to educational access, aspiration, progression, and opportunities for lifelong learning. By enabling educational success, young people, families, and communities experiencing the greatest levels of disadvantage and poverty will be provided with opportunities to develop and demonstrate capability and therefore access the new opportunities that globalization brings to the UK. In addition we have described explanations that have highlighted the risk factors of experiencing poverty at the meso level for families, communities, peer, and ethnic groups and some of the challenges that schools and other public services in such areas experience. At the individual micro level there has also been an exploration of identity and the role of individual choice as well as the constraining ideas of inherited individual capabilities. Perhaps most interesting have been explanations that have attempted to integrate the macro, meso, and micro around notions of risk and resilience with approaches that advocate a bioecological systems approach and one that integrates neurobiology, behaviour, and social sciences through a focus on early childhood development.

What these explanations suggest is the need for a range of interventions at the macro, meso, and micro levels. These are summarised in Table 2.5.

With regards to the macro issues highlighted, the evidence appears to point to the need for strategies that would maximise the opportunities for wealth-creation inherent in globalisation, whilst minimising the sharp polarisations which globalisation seems to entail. This seems to imply particular sorts of national economic development policies, complemented by local strategies in the more economically-vulnerable areas. These might well be accompanied by redistributive and 'safety-net' policies, such as child poverty reduction strategies and financial support mechanisms for young people and their families. In addition at the meso focus of analysis, the

Table 2.5 Functionalism Interventions

Level	Functional Interventions
Macro	Local and national economic development strategies
Meso	Support for parents and parenting as knowledge and developable skills
	Multi-agency working to support individuals, families, and communities
	Improved school effectiveness in areas of poverty and disadvantage
Micro	Choice, identity, and transition in post-industrial contexts
	Recognition and development of moderating positive and productive relationships within communities and schools for at risk students
	IQ and environmental factors

difficulties of providing appropriate parenting for those families living in poverty is suggestive of the need for effective family support. Whether current models of parenting classes and parenting networks are appropriate is a moot point. However, as the child development literature suggests, interventions might profitably focus at the pre-school and early school ages.

The evidence points to a need both to develop the appropriate values and norms in young people for the importance of education and to help parents provide support for education. It is also clear from the risk and resilience studies that interventions which create protective factors for young people in their immediate social context or create opportunities at a distance that help to moderate various immediate risk factors can be implemented at various stages in a young person's development. What this literature suggests is that young people do have agency and can construct paths that enable the developments of new identities and, consequently, of what they want to achieve from life and through education. The various research studies point to those factors that appear to influence this agency. For example, close, warm, adult relationships or role models are seen as being protective for individuals experiencing a number of risk factors. These could be in the guise of effective teacher/student relationships, through close mentoring roles, or via the aspirations of parents. What these relationships can do is enable young people to re-imagine their identities, desires and choices with regards to education. There are also indications that identities developed through being part of positive networks of support, influence, and reciprocity are also important frameworks for explaining the differences in experiences and response that particular individuals and neighbourhoods make to living in poverty. Providing young people with supportive networks might well be part of a wider set of strategies to develop social capital in neighbourhoods of disadvantage.

This body of research also highlights how environmental factors can have an impact on inherited attributes such as IQ. There seems to be good evidence that an enriched environment with sustained levels of stimulus and support for young people can, over time, improve IQ, and that, conversely, deprived environments with low levels of stimulus and support can reduce IQ levels. It seems that living in poverty is likely to result in impoverished environments that are insufficient to maintain IQ levels. The policy implication is that young people living in such environments might need to be targeted for enriched and sustained opportunities for enhanced and stimulating experiences to compensate for environmental deficits.

In addition, there are factors at the meso level that reflect the multifaceted nature of the some of the problems that young people and their families face. They point to the need for public services, including education, to work in a multi or inter-agency way so that joined up solutions are developed with families and young people that deal with their holistic concerns. However there are also issues about the nature of schools, schooling, and educational markets in areas of disadvantage that are also potentially creating problems for educational success for young people and their families that live in poverty. These include the need to examine compositional mixes of pupils in schools, the types of neighbourhoods that schools are located in, the effective leadership styles and approaches that succeed in schools in challenging circumstances, and the teaching ethos and curriculum provision that most successfully retains and generates educational success in such schools.

NOTES

1. The **Tripartite System**, known colloquially as the grammar school system, was the structure by which Britain's secondary education was organised between the 1944 Butler Education Act and 1976. Secondary schools were divided into three categories, Grammar schools, Technical schools, and Modern Schools. Pupils were allocated to each according to their performance in the Eleven Plus examination.
2. Cultural capital: forms of knowledge; skill; education; any advantages a person has which give them a higher status in society, including high expectations. Parents provide children with cultural capital, the attitudes, and knowledge that makes the educational system a comfortable, familiar place in which they can succeed easily.
3. Pyschopathological responses are behaviours or experiences which cause impairment, distress, or disability, particularly if it is thought to arise from a functional breakdown in either the cognitive or neurocognitive systems in the brain.
4. Neuroplasticity (variously referred to as brain plasticity or cortical plasticity) refers to the changes that occur in the organization of the brain, and in particular changes that occur to the location of specific information processing functions, as a result of the effect of learning and experience.

3 The Mapping Framework, Research Literature, and Policy Implications Within a Socially Critical Perspective

Carlo Raffo, Alan Dyson, Helen Gunter, Dave Hall, Lisa Jones, and Afroditi Kalambouka

INTRODUCTION

The socially critical position assumes that education can both challenge existing power structures and enable democratic development. This suggests that education in its current configuration should not be seen as an unproblematic good and its benefits cannot be taken for granted as either neutral or benign. On the contrary, many commentators on educational policy and practice, as it has historically evolved, suggest that education is variously implicated in creating, reproducing, and enhancing inequality. They suggest that education was never developed to be enabling and educative for all young people in a manner that might challenge existing social structures. This chapter documents some of the key explanations of the link between education and poverty from this socially critical perspective. At the outset we need to state that most of the explanations and suggested interventions from such a perspective appear to be at the macro and meso level. At the macro level research focuses on global economic structures and power inequalities that result in poorer educational outcomes for certain class, gender, and ethnic groups. Meso level analysis tends to focus on the possibilities of changed power relations in the classroom or between school and community or on reviewing 'emancipatory' curricular interventions. Although much of the writings from a socially critical perspective focus on the social, there are some strands in the literature where the main level of analysis is on the individual and at the micro. Certain radical developmental psychologists have worked on the interface between a focus on the individual and the impact of community but often in response to what they see as a conservative bias in much mainstream developmental psychology (Holzman, 1997). In addition, there is the work by Davies (2006) and Youdell (2006) which draws on the philosophical work of Judith Butler focusing on the way in which the individual pysche develops. They argue that identities are heavily shaped by external power relations which constrain or enhance the possibilities that individuals can achieve. Their ideas suggest that educators and policy makers need to take responsibility for the way in which taken-for-granted practices and discourses can limit individuals' life chances. Some of these ideas are taken further in the meso section below. Given that studies at this level of conceptualisation are limited and, when they do focus on education and poverty, tend to leach out into other levels of analysis, we have decided not to have a separate section in this chapter that focuses exclusively on a socially critical perspective at the micro level. We do, however, document some of the key implications of micro level social critical perspectives in the final section of the chapter.

THE SOCIALLY CRITICAL PERSPECTIVE AND THE MACRO FOCUS

The summary of the key points is in Table 3.1.

Education as Integral to Reproducing Social Disadvantage and Poverty

Maguire's (2006) re-examination of studies in education and poverty from the 1960s and beyond offers an illuminating recent statement within what we have called the 'socio-critical' perspective. Essentially, education is seen as a 'classed' phenomenon where the curriculum, the preparedness, and support of young people for such a curriculum and the way the curriculum is structured and implemented though schools offers advantages to the middle classes at the expense of the working class and the poor. It therefore reflects the existing inequalities in society rather than offering a way out of those inequalities. Maguire quotes Williams (1973) on the way education is implicated in social reproduction:

> Yet we speak sometimes as if education were a fixed abstraction, a settled body of teaching and learning, and as if the only problem it presents us is that of distribution . . . when this selection of content is

Table 3.1 Socially Critical Perspectives and the Macro Focus

□ An identification of global and national social and economic structures that determine educational provision and achievement.

□ An examination of how power structures impact on the lives and educational experiences of particular groups.

□ Critical analysis of functional policy interventions such as choice and the market.

---

examined more closely, it will be seen to be one of the decisive factors affecting its distribution. (Williams, 1973:145)

Maguire is characteristic of work in this perspective in concluding that the role of education in society is not about equality and social justice but rather about normalising exclusion and failure for some and success for others.

Maguire and other researchers within this perspective take a somewhat different view on the relationship between globalisation and education than do commentators from a functionalist perspective. Globalisation is not just a problem—and a source of social problems—to be managed so that education can produce its intended benefits. Rather, as Lipman (2004) has noted, education is explicitly tied to global economic competitiveness and into the "normalising discourse"—the network of language and ideas that present the effects of globalisation as inevitable—that sustains globalisation. Lipman quotes Rizvi and Lingard (2000) who suggest that educational policy is linked to national economic planning with the skills of a nation highlighted as being important to attract capital to specific places. Curricula are more and more being directed towards the economy, particularly those for the working class or poor, in the US through a variety of school-to-work programmes or in the UK through enhanced vocational programmes in schools and post-16 colleges. Ideologically it is being linked through human capital development discourses that define education as workforce preparation. As Ozga (2000) notes this 'economising education' is placing more and more emphasis on standards and testing that are eroding the concept of education. Morrow and Torres (2000) argue:

> The overall effect is to shift education towards competence-based skills at the expense of the more fundamental forms of critical competence required for autonomous living and active citizenship. (47)

Lipman, in challenging the prevailing "truth" that capitalist globalisation and neo-liberal policies are necessary and inevitable, continues by suggesting that education policy is the product of specific economic and social agendas rather than being a necessary outgrowth of an inevitable economic and social order. Although neo-liberal social policy is presented as the inexorable result of the logic of economic imperatives, it is in fact the result of an "ideological convergence—most notable in the English-speaking world—upon neo-liberal educational recipes as a specific response to globalisation and international competition" (Morrow & Torres, 2000:45).

Other critical studies examine the power dynamics within particular places and at particular times that manifest themselves structurally, economically, and culturally on particular groups of people and on how they experience education. For example Jean Anyon's (1997) book *Ghetto Schooling* shows that concentrated poverty and racial isolation result from issues of power that link to a long historical evolution, in part the product of political and corporate decisions about which the urban poor had no say. She takes as her focus Newark, New Jersey, the third oldest major city in the US and among the first to experience industrial decay and a majority black population. The degree of racial segregation evident by the 1960s in Newark meant that, more than ever before, urban children were other people's children, not worthy of educational investment. Anyon's recommendations for present-day reform focus on a renewed war on poverty. She feels that if we are to eliminate ghetto schools, we must ultimately "eliminate poverty" itself (164). Such radical proposals, befitting her structural analysis, are redolent of William Julius Wilson's suggestions at the end of *The Truly Disadvantaged* (1987). Like Wilson, Anyon contextualizes educational reform by demonstrating through her analysis that educational inequality is inseparable from class and racial inequality. The history she details explains how poverty has come to be so concentrated in hyper-segregated inner cities and their schools.

Challenging Education Policies of Choice, Standards, Middle-class Values and the Market as Ways of Enhancing Educational Outcomes in Areas of Poverty

Smith and Nobel (1995) in their discussion of poverty and schooling in Britain in the 1990s discuss the way in which educational access, opportunities, and outcomes in education are unequivocally biased against poorer members of the UK. They argue that the language of 'choice,' 'standards,' and the 'market' that dominates education policies favour the middle class. The work of Harris and Ranson (2005) complements this view. They assert that 'choice' and 'diversity' are unlikely to reduce the gap between disadvantage and achievement. They suggest "that not only will 'choice' continue to reproduce the inequities of the neo-liberal marketplace and strengthen the traditional hierarchies and boundaries of class, race, and gender, but also that 'diversity' signals a return to clearly segmented education provision with selection as the central allocation mechanism" (572). Instead they propose what Apple (2001) calls 're-positioning' whereby every endeavour should be made to try to understand policies and practices from the viewpoint of those who have the least power.

Gewirtz's (2001) study takes a slightly different approach in critiquing strategies that hope to reform 'the culture of achievement' by changing attitudes (of teachers and parents) and effectively making working class and poor parents emulate their middle class counterparts thereby eradicating class differences in education. The paper looks at what is involved in normalising middle class educational values, attitudes, and behaviours and in particular points to approaches that appear to be part of this re-socialisation package:

1. Promoting active consumerism in the education market place (e.g. the English government's education website gives advice on how to 'choose' a school through the use of league tables and other published data).
2. Promoting parental 'policing' of schools (intervening when necessary).
3. Re-making parents as 'home-educators' (possessing and transmitting appropriate forms of social capital).
4. Investing in social capital with self-confidence and social networks identified as the characteristics useful to exploit the education system to their best advantage.

Gewirtz critiques this package by arguing that in a hierarchically ordered, competitive society, education is a positional good and there is therefore insufficient room for everyone to be a winner. She points out the contradiction of policies such as the widening opportunity rhetoric alongside policies that reinforce inequities in hierarchical local educational markets. Second, Gewirtz argues that such policies fundamentally miss the point as to why many working class parents are not like archetypal middle class families— "Poverty, and the stress, ill-health and poor living conditions associated with it, make it difficult for large sections of the population to prioritize education" (374). Third, Gewirtz is critical of the perceived need to universalise middle class values, particularly in the way such values (a) enhance the "instrumental, self-promoting, competitive, individualist manner of the active consumer" (374); (b) reinforce the policing of schools; and (c) constantly construct children as learning at home. Fourth, she argues that lone-parent working-class mothers in particular straddle two very contradictory roles expected of them by New Labour policy—to get paid employment and yet to be active parents in education. Finally, Gewirtz argues against the moral authoritarian overtones of policies intended to re-socialise working-class parents and that perpetuate a deficit model of working-class parents. Within current policy discourses working-class parents, she argues, are passive. The way for parents to be active in this structure is through individualist, choice-based consumerism rather than through collective, political variants of active parenting.

A Re-examination of Ethnic Disadvantage, Poverty, and Educational Underachievement—Critical Race Theory

The socially critical perspective of critical race theory (CRT), which first arose as a counter-legal scholarship in the US in the 1970s (Ladson-Billings, 1998), has been an important contributor to theoretical and empirical debate in education for over a decade in the US (Ladson-Billings & Tate, 1995). Although writers within a functionalist perspective are also interested in the problems surrounding race and ethnicity, CRT attempts a more radical view of the way in which racism is at work in society and its institutions within the education system. CRT posits racism as a normal and natural part of everyday society in the US (Ladson-Billings, 1998), the UK (Gillborn, 2005), and other Westernised countries. Ladson-Billings (1998) suggests that in the US, racial categories have fluctuated over time but two polar categories have remained, that of black and white and that these cultural rankings have persistently told us who is white and as she points out, more importantly, who is not white. Ladson-Billings adds here that who is and who is not white is not merely a matter of biology or individual construction, but rather is decided through different political, economic, social, and cultural circumstances. Mexicans, for example were once considered 'white' but through shifts linked to the above factors, have now moved out of the 'white' category (1998, 8).

In essence, critical race theory seeks to problematise the fundamentals of 'whiteness' rather than simply to look at racism in order to better understand issues of race, race inequity, and racism in education and society more generally. Gillborn (2005) argues that the notion of 'white supremacy' used by CRT goes beyond the narrowly defined notions of white supremacy as associated with small racist/fascist-type explanations or organisations. He argues that 'white supremacy' here refers to the more normalised and taken for granted notions which are much more powerful and wide-ranging

With regards to using CRT in examining education policy in England, Gillborn suggests the need to challenge the view that all policy-making has the best of intentions for all members of society. Gillborn sets out to explore the active role that education policy has had in maintaining and extending race inequality and oppression. He does this by exploring three central tenets to education policy. Firstly he explores the priorities of education policy (i.e. who or what is driving it), secondly he explores who are the beneficiaries (i.e. who wins and who loses), and finally he looks at outcomes in terms of the effects of policy. With regard to educational policy priorities, Gillborn argues that "Regardless of the political persuasion of the incumbent political party, therefore, race equity has constantly to fight for legitimacy as a significant topic for education policy-makers. This is a key part of the way in which education policy is implicated in white supremacy" (2005, 493). With regard to educational policy beneficiaries, Gillborn refers to the concern to drive up standards through national testing and how year on year there has been an improvement in those 16-year-olds gaining higher level exam qualifications. However, he notes that students from minority ethnic backgrounds have not always shared equally in these gains. He suggests that 'black' students in particular now find themselves even further behind white students than they were during the 1980s. Gillborn also refers to groups such as Indian or Chinese students who tend to perform better on average than their white counterparts and explains how these groups are used to deny that racism takes place. With regard to outcomes, Gillborn suggests that different patterns of educational achievement can at least in part be traced to different processes within schools. For example, black children are more likely to be excluded than whites and setting (a form of selection) by ability, currently favoured via policies, tends to position black children disproportionately in the lower sets. Gillborn argues that inequity after inequity occurs that in many ways renders success almost impossible for particular groups such as black children.

THE SOCIALLY CRITICAL PERSPECTIVE AND THE MESO FOCUS

A Different Take on Schooling—Emancipatory Curricula and Pedagogies and Democratic Leadership and Engagement

For critically orientated researchers, education practices and systems are not simply less than optimally effective in responding to the needs of learners from poor backgrounds; they are deeply implicated in maintaining the poverty-education relationship, and hence in reproducing the very problem which they are seeking to solve.

In this situation, writers within a critical perspective are interested not so much in 'improving' education as it currently stands, as in changing the way in which it embodies unequal power relationships. Typically, this means that they seek to define forms of educational practices and systems which problematise and challenge those relationships. In other words, they work for forms of 'critical' or 'emancipatory' pedagogy, curricula, and leadership. Freireian pedagogies, for example, aim to challenge conventional hierarchies and to re-define a range of features of educational processes, including non-hierarchically based teacher-student relationships and a curriculum which enables learners to recognise and challenge existing power structures. In Freire's work (1972) education becomes a tool for the emancipation of the oppressed and a means of developing consciousness so that reality can be transformed. Learning becomes based upon the lived experiences of learners and focused upon actions arising out of dialogues with others that have the capacity to transform lives.

Table 3.2   Socially Critical Perspectives and the Meso Focus

---

□ An account of the lives of people in neighbourhoods and communities.

□ Studies that have emphasised more radical and democratic approaches to running classrooms and schools that have challenged and changed existing power relations through for example the way teachers and pupils interact and the way school governance relates more directly to community needs.

□ Interventions that focus on community radicalism in answering back and creating equitable educational opportunities.

Fielding (2006), in his attempts to radicalise debates about the personalisation of education, articulates the need for education, and particularly the management and leadership of that education, to be concerned first and foremost with the personal and then to examine the functional as a way of maximising the personal. He sees the personal as being manifested in fulfilling interpersonal relations, social justice, and in pursuit of 'the good life.' The functional are all the administrative, curricular, management and leadership, and teaching arrangements within schools that are put into place to achieve the personal. In terms of possible actions to achieve the personal he recommends two requirements:

> . . . the first is that they have within them, individually or in combination, reference to normative structural and organisational change that insists not only on the integrity of the ends and means, but also on the actual experience of persons in community as the ultimate arbiter of their legitimacy; the second is that their advocacy of personal and interpersonal flourishing not only acknowledges and understands the persistence of power, but also sets in place arrangement that guide its egalitarian realisation. (Fielding, 2006:8)

In articulating such a position he reinforces the need to develop opportunities in schools for authentic student voices that might enable staff and students to work and learn in partnership; for schools to provide "discursive and dialogic spaces" for staff, students, and the wider community to discuss and develop practice; for the emergence of democratic public spaces in schools where teachers can derive mutually supportive engagement, companionship, and enquiry, and to problematise the inevitability of school leadership and hierarchical systems of control, power, and authority. Fielding's work is complemented by Pat Thomson (2002) in her research on Australian schooling where she speaks of the need for a commitment to a pedagogic process which creates opportunities for learning and for individuals and communities to 'answer back' through the development of critical literacies[1] as a means of enabling them to defend and develop their localities. Part of this work arises out of the Disadvantaged Schools Programme (DSP) in Australia, which was launched in 1974 and lasted until 1990 (Connell et al., 1992).

Re-interpreting Disadvantaged Neighbourhoods

There have been studies that have examined more critically the nature of neighbourhood and the deficit connotations of neighbourhood that is both implicit and explicit within functionalist perspectives. Put simply, functionalist perspectives see disadvantaged neighbourhoods as presenting self-evident problems, which call for policy interventions. Critical researchers, on the other hand, are interested both in the processes of globalisation which create such neighbourhoods (as we saw above) and in the way the characteristics of these neighbourhoods come to be constructed as problems within particular sets of social arrangements and the ideologies which sustain those arrangements. Problems of these kinds cannot be 'solved' unless those underlying processes, arrangements, and ideologies are themselves changed.

So, for example, there are researchers who have examined the way geographical forms of exclusion (Sibley, 1995) are emerging both in terms of where people live and where children and young people go to school. These forms of geographical exclusion result in children and young people who live in areas of poverty as being constructed as abject and/or considered out of place in specific contexts and in specific schools. Bauder (2002), for instance, uses the notion of cultural exclusion as a way of highlighting how young people from disadvantaged neighbourhoods with different reputations (based in part on the ethnic and class make-up of these neighbourhoods) are steered towards particular training and opportunities in education. Likewise, Gulson (2005) has suggested that particular forms of neighbourhood redevelopment, linked to various area-based educational interventions that have focused on developing aspiration towards careers afforded by these developments, have had a debilitating effect on the educational identities of young people and communities in poorer surrounding areas. At the same time, other social groups, which possess the necessary personal resources, are able to do well out of the new situation, selling their skills for ever-increasing amounts on the labour market. Inevitably, they too congregate in certain parts of the city, contributing to an overall polarisation which was compounded by further divisions along ethnic grounds. In addition Bauder (2002) approaches the notion of neighbourhood effects through reference to the ideological underpinnings of the notion of neighbourhood effects. He suggests that the idea of neighbourhood effects implies that the demographic context of poor neighbourhoods instils 'dysfunctional' norms, values, and behaviours into youths, thus triggering a cycle of social pathology. It is argued that neighbourhood effects are part of a wider discourse of inner-city marginality that stereotypes inner-city neighbourhoods. In effect, this leads to what Bauder sees as essentialist conceptions (fixed traits that do not allow for variations among individuals or over time) of neighbourhood culture among employers, educators, and institutional staff which then further contributes to the neighbourhood effects phenomenon.

Some of these ideas are complemented by Mirón's (2006) work. At one level Mirón is concerned with social representation in relation to the way in which social researchers represent poverty and the quality of schooling. His view is that by overemphasizing the continual links between them, the probability that education and poverty will continue to 'enjoy' strong associations is likely to increase. Mirón recommends that more attention needs to be paid to the theoretical problem of representation (or labelling) of poor education and the material conditions of poverty. He believes that the question of *how* poor underachieving students, particularly in inner city and rural environments, are portrayed through possible racial, gender, class, and sexuality stereotypes is relevant. Perhaps of greater consequence are the largely unintended policy consequences that such stereotyping may induce.

Parenting, Schooling, and Developing Young People's Resilience in Disadvantaged Communities

Much of the literature within a functionalist perspective highlight deficits or differences in parenting styles amongst families living in poverty that result in a lack of preparedness for, and support in, schools for young people. However there are studies that examine how parental engagement in pupils' education can be differently positioned to that underpinning much of the functionalist discourse. For example Lawson's (2003) study addresses teachers' and parents' perceptions of the meanings and functions of parental involvement in their children's education. Analysis revealed that teachers and parents can have different perceptions of parental involvement. In his study of schools and families in one low-income, urban community, the author suggests that parental involvement can mean different things to teachers who tend to be more 'schoolcentric' as opposed to parents who can be more 'communitycentric'. In many respects teachers' prevailing orientations toward parents suggested that they were seen as having poor parenting skills and capabilities with regards to education. This orientation contributed to a fairly systematic silencing of the strengths, struggles, and 'communitycentric' worldviews evident in the parents' explanations. The author argues that parental involvement is a limited and limiting concept in low-income ethnically concentrated communities because the notion is largely the domain of teachers within a narrow schoolcentric view. Lareau's (1987) study asks similar questions, particularly in relation to what schools ask of parents and the variations in teachers' expectations of parental involvement in elementary schooling. Their research suggests that there are a variety of factors that affected parents' participation in their children's education—parents' educational capabilities, their view of the appropriate division of labour between teachers and parents, the information they had about their children's schooling, and the time, money, and other material resources available in the home.

Lareau argues that "the differences in social, cultural, and economic resources between the two sets of parents help explain differences in their responses to a variety of teacher requests to participate in schooling" (1987:81). As schools tend to favour the school-family relationship model more likely to be accessed by the middle class parents, those parents have an advantage over working-class children and parents. If schools were to promote different types of school-family relationship, maybe 'middle class' ways of doing things may not act as a 'social profit'. Middle class relations according to Lareau are not intrinsically better; rather they are just tied more closely to the school's aims and objectives. Lareau argues that the standard of a school's expectations should be problematised as not neutral. She states that "these results suggest that social class position and class culture become a form of cultural capital in the school setting" (82) and argues that it is unfair that all schools ask the same from all parents regardless of social class and yet not all cultural resources are valued equally in contributing to this.

In addition to critical studies that focus on poor parents' particular perspectives of, and approaches to, schools viz-a-viz teachers, there are also radical and critical approach to what are viewed as the victim blaming and labelling of families, communities, and young people as being poor, in deficit, or at risk that are contained in many of the studies within a functionalist perspective (Cooper & Christie, 2005; Lister, 2004). These studies suggest that this type of labelling has a tendency to pathologise families and young people and hence to do more harm than good (Franklin, 2000). In contrast they highlight the diversity of competencies, attitudes ,and behaviours that reflect varying bonding social capitals, support, and engagement activities, and different and yet equally prized set of values that have enabled forms of community activism against the material odds of poverty and inequality. At times these actions are strategic and at times they were ways of coping or fighting back. Together they are suggestive of the varying personal, political, everyday, or strategic actions that are proactively taken by young people, families, and communities dealing with poverty.

Within the field of education there is a recognition that such a perspective is suggestive of how young people actively make use of the social resources, peer networks, family, and the informal economy to variously act out forms of emancipation, resistance, and accommodation to education (Hodkinson et al., 1996; Willis, 1977). A recent and important study provides a critique of deficit notions of parenting and pathologised notions of risk and danger for young people in poor neighbourhoods (Seaman et al., 2006). This study set out to develop an understanding of these issues by examining the experiences and perspectives of parents and young people living in four areas of disadvantage in the West of Scotland. Two linked studies explored the ways parents and young people in ordinary families acted together and separately to cope with adverse environments. The study highlighted the following pertinent issues:

- Most parents and young people saw school as a haven from risks (although there were reports of bullying), but some parents spoke of schools not involving them enough in issues concerning their children.
- Most parents said they maintained open and democratic styles of parenting which respected young people's views and opinions. Children usually confirmed this. Discussion between parents and children was

normally the cornerstone of discipline and when negotiating rules, parents encouraged their children to be open about their activities.

- Parents had high aspirations for their children and expected their children to move away from the area as adults to optimise their educational and employment prospects.
- Many of the children had high educational aspirations but opted for traditional non-professional jobs, often gender-related (e.g. girls: beautician, hairdresser; boys: joiner, mechanic).
- Parents and young people recognised the importance of education and qualifications for success in the adult jobs market and access to more interesting and better-paid jobs. However, many had access to a limited supply of advice and guidance when it came to new forms of work (such as creative and media occupations) or jobs not traditionally entered into by people from disadvantaged backgrounds (such as medicine or law).
- For some, limited income and well-learnt avoidance of debt could also affect their capacity to meet the costs of entering Higher Education and taking on student loans.

SYNTHESISING THE LITERATURE FROM A SOCIALLY CRITICAL PERSPECTIVE— IMPLICATIONS FOR POLICY AND PRACTICE

From a socially critical standpoint, the relationship of research to policy and policy-makers is problematic for two reasons. First, the relationship between poverty and education is not the result of one or more specific functional problems which can somehow be 'fixed.' It demands, at one level or other, a change in underlying structures and power relations, whether this be in the classroom, in the relationship between disadvantaged groups and public policy, or in fundamental social structures. The sorts of interventions which policy-makers and practitioners have at their disposal may well be inappropriate for these sorts of changes.

Second, if current education practices and systems at various levels are implicated in the maintenance of inequality, then policy and policy-makers are part of the problem rather than part of the solution. Rather than providing policy-makers with options, therefore, writers have, to some extent, to stand outside the policy process, offering critique and, ultimately, hoping to engender or support movements which will wrest control of policy from its current owners and deliver it to those who are disadvantaged by current arrangements. In education and social systems which are unequal, policy is inevitably produced, the critical perspective argues, by the powerful in order to serve the interests of the powerful. Almost by definition, therefore, policy interventions which actually exist are precisely the sorts of policies which need to be changed. This is an issue to which we shall shortly return.

A summary of socially critical approaches are in Table 3.3.

In practice, many writers from within a socially critical perspective simply maintain their distance from questions of alternative policies and policy processes. It is possible to deduce from their critical accounts some implications about what alternative policies might be, but these are rarely made explicit and the question about how such policies might come into being is rarely addressed. A second group, including Freire and the advocates of critical pedagogy, advocate a sort of 'revolution from within.' They accept that large-scale structures of power are difficult to shift, but hold on to the possibility that small-scale changes of power are more feasible, at the level, for instance, of interactions with individual learners, or changes in individual schools and classrooms. They tend to speak, therefore, to the radicalised teachers and school leaders who might be able to bring about such changes, and to hope that these will accumulate into something more large scale.

A third group is prepared to work within existing power structures, but in the belief that they are not quite so fixed as they might seem, and that political processes are available which are capable of changing them. There is, for instance, a good deal of work currently emerging from the US which draws on a tradition of community activism and civil rights work to suggest that popular movements can be created which may be capable of changing the control and direction of policy.

For example, Jean Anyon's view of reform in the US leaves no doubt that as disadvantaged urban education's failure is rooted in social and historical context, so must its reform be. Hence fundamental interventions are theorised at the macro level, deal with the causes rather than just the symptoms difficult to change and require forms of political association that may take time to bring about. However she also recognises the need to act at the meso level and she articulates interventions that are located at this level, are more amenable to change, deal with symptoms rather than causes, and focus on issues associated with the renewal of school leadership, improving teaching and learning in schools, and developing full-service schooling. In her latter work, Anyon (2005) continues to rehearse her explanatory reasons for educational failure by suggesting how current economic policies are geared to the wealthiest in US society and why changes must be made if we are

Table 3.3 Socially Critical Interventions

Level	Socially Critical Interventions
Macro	Human rights, social justice and democratic agendas
Meso	Community activism
Micro	Small scale changes in the location and exercise of power

to eradicate urban poverty, especially among the most vulnerable groups, African Americans, and Hispanics. She argues that without changes in economic policies, we can never hope to see meaningful education reform. At the same time, however, she points the reader in the direction of how to effect social change. For example, she offers an extensive review of the civil rights movement along with other well-known movements in US history which have done, or are doing things, to make a difference. Unlike the second group of socially critical writers referred to above, she recognises that the efforts of small groups cannot bring about the widespread support necessary to significantly impact public policy. Instead she suggests that established groups should form coalitions with other groups with the same purpose or similar goals and work together. She is optimistic that when groups come together with strong support to make demands on our political system changes occur. Communities that seek changes in urban education must, she argues, demand equity by drawing attention to the inequities of urban schools in contrast to suburbia. Change is a slow process, but change requires action. Sit-ins, bus-ins, and boycotts of corporations are a few examples of taking action.

Gewirtz's (2001) position suggests that education could be based on different principles from those that currently focus on middle class values. She argues that we need to look at the damaging effects of the competitive, instrumental, and 'pushy' nature of middle class educational norms rather than to simply endorse them. Secondly, Gewirtz suggests the need to sort out the disparities of wealth and power and the hierarchies that structure schools and employment that are largely responsible for differences between classes. Finally she explores the need to develop decision-making structures and curricula which engage with, and give voice, to the diverse experiences and views of working-class children and parents as well as the middle classes.

Although we remarked earlier that conventional policy interventions are by definition the wrong sort of interventions, it can be argued that, even within the socially critical perspective, this is not entirely the case. In other words, it is possible to identify at least some interventions which seek not simply to 'improve' this or that aspect of educational systems, but to redistribute power within those systems. Such examples will always be susceptible to critique, but may offer a useful counterweight to the position that everything done in and by the current system is equally oppressive. Current examples might include student councils, the local governance of schools, the increasing capacity on both sides of the Atlantic for local groups to establish and manage their own schools, the ability of learners to chart their own way through alternative learning pathways, and the involvement of local communities in shaping education services through regeneration initiatives, locally-commissioned children's services and extended schools. To these can be added countless school and classroom practices which are in some way participatory or emancipatory. The implication of all these is that changing the distribution of power within education systems may be a matter of shifting complex balances rather than of large-scale reversals of existing patterns.

NOTES

1. Critical literacy is a critical thinking tool that encourages readers to question the construction and production of texts. Using critical literacy tools, readers consider inclusion, exclusion, and representation in texts; relate texts to their own lives; and consider the effects of texts. Critical literacy is not simply a means of attaining literacy in the sense of improving the ability to decode words, syntax, etc. In fact, the ability to read words on paper is not necessarily required in order to engage in a critical discussion of 'texts,' which can include digital media (movies), art, and many other means of expression. The important thing is being able to have a discussion with others about the different meanings a text might have and teaching the critical literacy learner how to think flexibly about it. Critical literacy primarily deals with issues of language and power and the ways in which texts work to position readers in particular ways. It is also concerned with examining the positions from which we read the word or the world. In some cases critical literacy involves taking social action to change inequitable ways of being.

Part II
International Studies on Education and Poverty

4 Neo-liberal Urban Education Policy

Chicago, A Paradigmatic Case of the Production of Inequality and Racial Exclusion

Pauline Lipman

INTRODUCTION

In this chapter, I take a socially critical approach to urban education policy. My analysis focuses on Chicago, a paradigmatic case of neo-liberal urban restructuring and neo-liberal education policy in the US. In the summer of 2004, two significant events occurred in Chicago. On June 24, the city's mayor, Richard J. Daley, announced the *Renaissance 2010* school plan to close 60–70 public schools and open 100 new schools, two-thirds to be run by private organizations or companies and staffed by non-union teachers and school employees. The plan was proposed by the Commercial Club of Chicago, a venerable organization of the most powerful corporate and banking CEOs and civic elites. On July 16, the mayor presided over the opening of Millennium Park, a 24.5 acre, half-billion dollar public-private venture, a 'world class' park, sculpture garden, and performance space on Chicago's lakeshore. The park is the crowning jewel in a reconstructed downtown of corporate towers, tourism, and leisure. These two, seemingly unrelated events exemplify the intersection of education policy, economic restructuring of the city, and the cultural politics of race. Both events were important milestones in a neo-liberal urban agenda developed and driven by the most powerful corporate and financial interests in the city in collaboration with the mayor and key city officials.

However, this agenda has not gone uncontested. In May 2002, 14 people, mostly mothers and grandmothers, staged a 19-day hunger strike for a new high school in a large Mexican immigrant community. The hunger strike was propelled by a seven-year struggle for a college preparatory high school in the community. In fall 2005, a $63 million state-of-the-art high school campus housing four separate college preparatory schools opened. One of the schools, the High School for Social Justice, is part of a small emerging group of social justice-oriented schools in the city. They exemplify a counter trend of education activism and critical pedagogy in Chicago and other US cities.

In this chapter I argue that Chicago's education policies are strategically related to the political economy of the city and the cultural politics of race. I contend that the restructuring of public (state-funded) education is implicated in the production of increasing economic, social, and spatial inequality and injustice. My intention in focusing on a specific case is to illustrate the relationship between neo-liberal urbanism and the production of educational and social inequality in urban contexts. Thus my analysis is located at the macro level. Clearly, neo-liberal policy is path dependent, shaped by institutional histories, political structures, and relations of social forces in specific contexts, but a similar set of political and economic processes are driving the restructuring of cities globally (Smith, 2002). In other words, we can learn something from the Chicago case about how education policy is related to neo-liberal urban development. Because I examine the educational and neighbourhood effects of these policies, the chapter is also located at the intersection of macro and meso level analysis.

With Anyon (2005), I assume that the roots of poverty lie outside schools, in economic and social policies that maintain low wages, lack of affordable housing and healthcare, inadequate transportation to work, etc. More broadly, poverty is rooted in capitalist economic relationships, supported by the state, that maintain enormous profits and the accumulation of wealth by a tiny minority at the expense of the majority. Neo-liberalism is "capitalism with the gloves off" (McChesney quoted in Apple, 2001:18); it intensifies exploitation and impoverishment (Davis, 2006). In this chapter, I argue that education policy is complicit in the neo-liberal restructuring of cities and thus in the reproduction of poverty.

THE CHICAGO CONTEXT

Like many European and North American cities, over the past 25 years Chicago has been transformed from declining industrial city to headquarters of transnational corporations, global financial markets, business services, upscale living, and tourism. Working class neighbourhoods and public housing complexes have been replaced by condominium developments and retail and leisure spaces for the upper middle class, dramatically redefining the urban landscape. This growth agenda is driven by political, economic, and cultural processes at multiples scales: (1) post-Fordist restructuring of capitalist economies, (2) neo-liberal restructuring of cities and its intersection with radicalised policies of marginalization, and (3) global competition among cities for real estate investment, highly skilled labour, and key productive sectors. The transformation of Chicago reflects a global process of urban transformation. In this case, powerful corporate and financial interests in league with the state aim to restructure the city along neo-liberal lines and to make it a first tier global city, a command centre of the global economy (Sassen, 2006).

Brenner and Theodore (2002:351) argue that "cities have become strategically crucial geographic arenas in which a variety of neo-liberal initiatives . . . have been articulated." 'Roll-back' neo-liberal policy (Peck & Tickell, 2002) in the 1970s reduced federal funding for cities, pushing city governments to reduce funding for public services and to disinvest in public institutions and infrastructure. As cities have moved to reliance on real estate taxes and securities derived from housing markets as key source of revenue, 'roll-out' neo-liberal policy (Peck & Tickell, 2002) favors municipal tax laws that subsidize real estate development. Driven by market ideologies, roll-out neo-liberalism also favours public-private ventures and privatization of public services as a way to make up for federal funding shortfalls. These policies shift governance and ownership of public institutions and spaces to private interests (Smith, 2002).

Neo-liberal globalization has also weakened connections between urban and national economies and encouraged global competition among cities for investment, tourism, highly-skilled labour, and production facilities, including the business services that drive globalization. Marketing cities through projects like Millennium Park and through housing and schools has become a hallmark of urban development. Downtown luxury living and gentrified neighbourhoods, as well as new 'innovative' schools in gentrified communities and choice within the public school system, are located in this inter-city competition (Lipman, 2004).

Gentrification has become generalized as a pivotal capital accumulation strategy (Hackworth, 2007). An economically marginal process in the 1950s into the 1970s has become, "a central motive force of urban economic expansion, a pivotal sector in the new urban economies" (Smith, 2002:447) in the global North but also in the global South. It transforms whole city landscapes into gentrification 'complexes' of consumption, recreation, culture, showcase parks such as Millennium Park, and schools as well as housing. Gentrification fuses transnational, national, and local capital and is facilitated by public-private partnerships that use public funds for private development. Billions of dollars of real estate investment have turned Chicago's downtown area into a glamour zone of corporate and luxury residential hi-rises, retail, and cultural venues. Local tax financing policies, particularly tax increment financing, that siphons off taxes to support infrastructure improvements for land acquisition and real estate development, have facilitated gentrification of working-class neighbourhoods, displacing residents and small businesses. The Chicago Housing Authority has demolished about 19,000 units of public housing, displacing the mainly African American residents. Using public subsidies, developers are constructing mixed-income developments in their place. This process has gained legitimacy through a discourse of pathology that demonizes people of colour and Black urban spaces in particular (Haymes, 1995; Lipman, 2008). The result of gentrification and displacement is a crisis in affordable housing that is driving low-income and working-class people to the fringes of the city and beyond.

Like much of the industrialized capitalist world, neo-liberal economic restructuring in the US has resulted in a highly stratified labour market and increased economic inequality. The new barbell-shaped labour force of high-paid, high-skilled and low-paid, deskilled jobs (Skinner, 2004) includes a significant sector of excluded labour. In Chicago African Americans, Latinos, and immigrants are disproportionately located in low-paid jobs and African Americans, in particular, have been locked out of the new labour force. This is reflected in income disparities which, according to the 2000 census, widened between whites and both African Americans and Latinos in Chicago in the 1990s; nearly 30 percent percent of Chicago's African Americans and 20 percent percent of Latinos lived in poverty in 1999 (Mendell & Little, 2002).

Inequality is exacerbated by Chicago's global city agenda. Sassen (2006) describes global cities as concentrated expressions of the contradictions of wealth and poverty that characterize neo-liberal globalization. They are marketplaces of global finance, strategic sites of innovation, coordination, and competition for the global production of goods, services, and financial speculation. Thus they disproportionately concentrate highly paid professionals (primarily white men) but also legions of low-paid service workers (primarily immigrants, women, and people of colour) who provide much of the labour for globalization and for retail and personal services for the luxury class. These social contrasts are expressed in new forms of social segregation and dislocation and glaring disparities in the use of, and access to, urban space along lines of class, race, ethnicity, and immigrant status. The global city is thus a spatially polarized landscape epitomizing the core dynamics of power and inequality, wealth and poverty that typify neo-liberal globalization. These contradictions define Chicago.

MY RESEARCH

I have been studying Chicago school policies since 1997. In addition to analysis of policy documents and school district data, from 1997–2001, I conducted in-depth qualitative studies of four elementary schools to examine the political economy and lived experiences of accountability and educational stratification (Lipman, 2004). Since Renaissance 2010 was announced in 2004, I have observed and participated regularly in meetings of school district officials, local schools, parents, community organizations, and teachers, as well as press conferences, protests, and public hearings related to the plan. My analyses draw on these data, collaborations with local community organizations and teachers concerned about the effects on schools and communities, and archival documents and policy positions related to school policies, housing policy, gentrification, and community economic development. I also draw on collaborations with scholars in urban policy and planning.

CHICAGO'S EDUCATION POLICIES

With almost a half million students, Chicago Public Schools (CPS) is the third largest school district in the US. The student population is 85 percent low-income and 91 percent students of colour. The trajectory of Chicago school reform over the past 20 years has gone from local democratic community control, to centralized authority and accountability, toward an education market of public school choice and privately-run, publicly-funded charter schools. In the following sections I discuss three key education policies in Chicago in relation to the political economy and racial politics of the city: (a) accountability and a new architecture of stratified education, (b) privatization, and (c) 'mixed income' schools linked to 'mixed income' communities. The latter two policies are related to the Renaissance 2010 Plan.

THE 1995 SCHOOL REFORM: ACCOUNTABILITY AND STRATIFIED EDUCATION

Chicago has a long history of failure to educate African American and Latino students (Orfield, 1990). Persistently high dropout and failure rates and low reading and math levels are indicators of deeper inequities in what is taught, how it is taught, and who has access to what kinds of knowledge. Driven in part by a grassroots social movement, Chicago's 1988 School Reform Law established elected Local School Councils comprised largely of parents and community members with power over the school budget and hiring and firing of the principal, or school head. The 1988 reform was seen as the most dramatic democratization of local public school governance in the US (Bryk et al., 1998). The goal was to draw on the grassroots political power and perspectives of parents and communities to instigate change.

Although there was progress in some schools, in a reverse, in 1995 Chicago's corporate-style mayor took control of the city's schools and consolidated power in his appointed school officials and corporate-dominated Board of Trustees. The school system's new leaders established a regime of centralized accountability based on high stakes standardized tests and sanctions for failure. As a result, since 1997, hundreds of schools have been put on probation under the control of the central school administration. In some years, over one-third of all schools were on probation. Thousands of students were retained in grade, some for as many as three years, and required to attend mandatory summer schools or Academic Preparation Centers with a basic reading and math curriculum—all based on their scores on a single standardized test. The students affected by these sanctions have been almost entirely low-income students of color, mainly African Americans and Latinos.

Results have been mixed. Some schools' test scores improved significantly, some very little. Since 2002, the district's elementary school test scores went from 40 percent to 60 percent of students meeting or exceeding state standards, but high school test scores remained essentially flat (Interactive Illinois Report Card, 2008). There are persistent, large disparities in test scores between whites, on the one hand, and African Americans and Latinos, on the other, and 33 percent of all students drop out before 12th grade. In one African American community only 25 percent of African American males finish high school. Teacher turnover in high-poverty schools also increased (Anderson, 2006). In my study of four elementary schools, I found that a focus on test preparation in low-scoring schools resulted in a diminished curriculum and educational triage (Lipman, 2004). I also found that the focus on meeting accountability goals based on standardized tests undermined bilingual education and substantive projects to improve teaching and learning. Accountability policies fostered a culture of blame with students, parents, teachers, and administrators all blaming each other for low test scores. This discourse of blame and deficiency is part of a broader shift of responsibility for inequality onto parents, students, schools, communities, and teachers. At one point school district heads tried to implement a parent report card as a way to quantify this responsibility. At the same time, the school I studied in a more affluent and whiter community was relatively insulated from accountability pressures and was able to continue its richer, more conceptually based curriculum and less regimented educational culture.

Simultaneously the school district developed a new architecture of stratified 'educational options,' including highly selective college preparatory magnet high schools (in new or refurbished buildings), selective elementary schools, and high status International Baccalaureate programs alongside vocational high schools, public military high schools, and middle schools for children age 12–14 (run jointly by the US military and the school district), and scripted direct-instruction basic education schools. These differentiated experiences produce disparate academic identities and significantly differential access to knowledge. Beyond these 'options,' most students (about 85 percent) attend general high schools, many of which are considered by students to be 'schools of last resort.'

Mapping the new schools onto the social geography of the city reveals a clear pattern (Lipman, 2004). The new magnet college prep schools are located in upper income, gentrified, or gentrifying areas. They are key anchors in the gentrification process, essential to attract investors to real estate projects and upper middle class buyers to gentrifying neighborhoods. For example, a billboard advertisement looming over a condominium development proclaims it is in 'the Bell School district'—an elementary school with a new gifted program. At the same time, military, direct instruction, and vocational high schools are all in low-income African American and Latino neighborhoods.

In *High Stakes Education* (Lipman, 2004), I argue the 1995 school reform is a strategic element in making Chicago a global city through (a) accountability and standards as tools to ensure employers and investors that Chicago is preparing students with the basic skills and disciplined dispositions needed in the low wage workforce, (b) selective schools to attract highly skilled knowledge workers and to attract investors and buyers to gentrifying areas, and (c) military schools and regimented basic skills schools that discipline and regulate African American and some Latino students who are defined by capital and the state as 'dangerous' in the global city.

According to the CPS website, Chicago has the most militarized public school system in the US in number of students involved and in total programs: five public selective enrolment military high schools run jointly by the school system and the Department of Defense with another planned for 2009, 10 military academies inside high schools, and 20 cadet corps middle school military programs. Over 10,000 students participate in the Junior Reserve Officers' Training Corps program (JROTC), a high school program modelled after the post-secondary military officer training program in colleges and universities. The military schools are located overwhelmingly in low income communities of colour with under-resourced schools. Military schools are structured around obedience to a hierarchy of command enshrined in the cadet system, modelled after the military chain of command and incorporate military perspectives in the curriculum. For example, the Rickover Naval Academy High School curriculum includes "Sea Power," "Military History," and "mini-boot camps." It does not include African American, Latin American, or Asian History although the school is 58.8 percent African American, 19.8 percent Latino, and 5.3 percent Asian and 60 languages are spoken. Students wear military uniforms, salute, practice military drills, and have the option to attend summer "survival training" camps. Other US urban school districts with large enrolments of African American and Latino students, including Philadelphia, Atlanta, and Oakland, also have public military schools.

I argue that the regimented practices associated with high stakes accountability, scripted direct instruction, and military schools are racially coded signifiers that these students and, by extension their communities, need regulation and control. Schools in low-income neighbourhoods of colour are the least in charge of their own destiny. In the schools I studied, accountability was experienced as a form of colonial governance that publicly signalled that the communities affected have neither the knowledge nor right to debate and act together with educators to improve their children's education. I argue that education policies that regulate and punish schools in African American communities contribute to their representation, and especially Black youth, as undisciplined and pathological, contributing to the normalization of their containment, criminalization, and exclusion from the labour force and the city.

In sum, despite new opportunities for some students, structural racism and entrenched class advantages/disadvantages are compounded by accountability and differentiated schools to produce greater disparities in teaching and learning. This mirrors the effects of accountability policies in the US nationally (Hursh, 2008) and in the UK (Gillborn & Youdell, 2000). Differential access to knowledge has crucial consequences for one's life chances in a knowledge economy in which one's access to high quality education can be decisive. While some students are on the college prep track, the majority are on the low-wage or military track.

RENAISSANCE 2010: PRIVATIZATION AND DISPLACEMENT

The plan for Renaissance 2010 (Ren2010) was proposed in June 2003, in a report called "Left Behind" by the Commercial Club of Chicago (CCC) (Education Committee of the Civic Committee, 2003). The report calls for a complete overhaul of the school system to break the 'monopoly' of public education and install the values and mechanisms of the market. It blames teachers unions and local school councils for school failure. Chicago's Mayor announced Ren2010 at a CCC event. A new public/private partnership, the CCC's Renaissance Schools Fund and Chicago Public Schools, jointly selects the new schools and evaluates them. School district leaders, the mayor, and the CCC contend that Ren2010 will create options and choice, promote innovation through competition, and increase efficiency.

Since Ren2010 was announced, it has provoked public controversy and opposition from parents, teachers, students, and community members. They claim it destabilizes schools by increasing student mobility, harms low-income and homeless children in particular, weakens unions, eliminates democratic governance of schools (Renaissance 2010 schools do not have Local School Councils), and is part of an agenda to privatize education and gentrify low-income communities of colour, displacing the present residents. All the closed schools have been located in low-income communities of colour (Greenlee et al., 2008). A consistent theme in every round of school closings is that the plan is devised without genuinely consulting the low-income communities of colour that are affected. The opposition has been partly successful, preventing the closing of some schools, but the overall plan has moved forward ahead of schedule and become a model that cities across the US are using.

Under Ren2010, the CEO and Board of Education may close schools that are 'failing,' underutilized, or for other reasons determined by the Board. The accountability regime laid the groundwork by establishing and normalizing a system of ranking and sorting schools and empowering top school officials to take unilateral actions. This was a necessary condition to identify schools to be closed with little local school input, and to turn them over to private operators. Teachers, school administrators, and parents contend that schools in African American communities in particular were 'set up for failure.' In addition to being historically under-resourced, under the

1995 accountability policies they were forced to adopt 'disastrous' direct instruction and other externally imposed programs, and over the past few years they have had cuts in resources and staff (Lipman, Person, & KOCO, 2007).

While it is too early to assess results, some things are clear. Most of the new schools are charter or contract schools operated by private agencies using public funds. From 2004 to spring 2008, CPS closed, phased out, or consolidated 47 schools and opened 82 schools claimed as part of Ren2010. Of these, 60 are privately-run charter or contract schools and 3 are military schools. The data so far show that students in charter schools in Chicago do no better academically than students in regular public schools, but charter schools and public schools are so varied that these comparisons are not very robust. Several charter schools offer a college preparatory curriculum in areas of the city where there were few such offerings, or are culturally centered (e.g., Afrocentric) schools initiated by community groups. A few have been started by teachers based in exploratory learning, single gender leadership development, or social justice. However, most are corporate-style charter school franchises or are sponsored by corporate law firms, corporate CEOs, venture capitalists, branches of the US military, or Latino organizations allied with the mayor and his political organization and policies. The overall thrust is a market of privately run educational ventures.

Parents have become competing education consumers in a market that is not neutral. Markets advantage those with more economic, social, and valued cultural capital (Ball, 1994). This is supported by evidence from education choice markets internationally suggesting they benefit middle class 'consumers' and increase inequality (Whitty, Power, & Halpen, 1998; Ball, 2003). Unlike public schools which must accept all students within their attendance area, when a Ren2010 school opens, there is no guarantee that children from the closed school will be able to attend it, even if it is replaced with a public school, nor is there a guarantee they will find a school in their neighbourhood. My data show parents scrambling to navigate complicated application processes for multiple schools and searching for schools in their neighbourhoods.

School closings intensify the already serious problem of student mobility which is extremely high in Chicago and urban schools in the US (Rumberger & Larson, 1998). Research on student mobility indicates that elementary school students experience both social and academic problems that have a significant negative impact on their classroom success (Tucker, Marx, & Long, 1998). Some students in Chicago's African American Midsouth area attended four schools in three years due to closings and transfers in a precursor to Renaissance 2010. School closings have forced high school students to attend schools out of their neighbourhoods creating an extremely dangerous situation. In 2006, violent conflicts broke out in several schools with students transferred from closed schools into other neighbourhoods. These included a shooting at one school, beatings, and fights

(Lipman, Person, & KOCO, 2007). This was widely reported in the media. One school closing required children as young as five to walk over a mile to their transfer school. There is also a burden on receiving schools, many of which are already overcrowded and are unprepared for an influx of new students (Lipman, Person, & KOCO, 2007).

Charter and contract schools are a form of public-private partnership that opens up public education as a source of direct capital accumulation. Their employees are not members of Chicago Public School unions and the schools are not required to have democratically elected local school councils. A major theme at the many community meetings I have attended is that decisions to close schools and create new schools are made without participation of the communities and schools affected. In place of democratic deliberative bodies, new unelected charter school boards and the CCC's Renaissance Schools Fund make decisions for teachers, students, and communities. This is an erosion of the public sphere and part of the de-democratization of public life that, along with public-private partnerships and marketization of public services (e.g., charter schools, characterizes neo-liberalism generally [Harvey, 2005]).

MIXED-INCOME SCHOOLS

A pervasive theme in the community meetings I have attended is that the city is using school closings to drive out low-income African Americans and support gentrification by opening new schools of choice to attract middle-class residents. A review of closed schools (Greenlee et al., 2008) shows that some were actually improving on the district's measures and some assessments that the schools were underutilized erroneously included non-instructional space. These data support opponents' contentions that schools were closed selectively based upon their location in gentrifying areas. In fact, Greenlee et al. (2008) show that most of the Ren2010 schools are in communities in various stages of gentrification.

The initial target of Ren2010 was the African American Midsouth community. In the initial plan, 20 of the 22 schools in the Midsouth were targeted for closure. The plan was defeated by fierce community resistance. The Midsouth is also the site of intense gentrification, as reflected in two indicators: rate of increase in housing prices and rate of house sales (Lipman & Haines, 2007). Under the Chicago Housing Authority's Plan for Transformation, 28 buildings, housing over 28,000 people in a two-mile stretch in the Midsouth have been imploded. The land on which they stood—near Lake Michigan, public transportation, a major expressway, and two major universities—is an enormously valuable commodity. Private developers are investing almost $2 billion to develop the area where five public housing high rises stood. As investment firms planned the first redevelopment, a consortium of interests (universities, philanthropic organizations, banks, the mayor's office, the city housing authority, and the school system) coalesced to engineer the plan. The CEO of a leading corporate founda- tion and member of the Midsouth planning team described the connec- tion between schools and development: "It's [Midsouth] a great physical location, so close to the lake and downtown. It's a delicate balance to pull something like this off. You can't do it just with the housing and retail development. You have to get the third leg and that's the schools" (Olsze- wski & Sandovi, 2003:1).

Closing schools and then reopening them is a cultural as well as material spatial practice. The new schools, offering a selection of options, including some run by prestigious universities, signal to future middle-class residents that the area is being 'reborn' for them. This is a class- and race-inflected process. African American areas to be gentrified and schools to be closed are constructed as dangerous and pathological, justifying the displacement of the residents, dismantling their communities, and the replacement of their schools with new mixed-income schools, even when they are marketed to both white and African American middle-class homeowners. Good schools and 'options' within the public school system are strategically important in 'space marketing' cities (Harvey, 2001) in the global competition to attract investors to gentrification projects and to sell them to new middle-class residents.

Mixed-income schools in newly redeveloped mixed-income communi- ties are a key part of this strategy. Chicago's Plan for Transformation is one of the most extensive revamps of public housing in the US. Under the 1992 HOPE VI Housing Act, public housing was transformed from a social benefit for low-income families to a market-based project. Its fundamen- tal premise is that poverty is the result of social pathologies (crime, drug addiction, poor parenting, lack of work ethic, low academic performance) produced by high concentrations of (radicalised) poor people isolated from middle-class values (Bennett, Hudspeth, & Wright, 2006). The solution is to dismantle public housing complexes and replace them with vouch- ers in the private housing market or mixed income communities. "We are trying to turn dysfunctional neighbourhoods into healthy mixed-income communities," said the CEO of the Chicago Housing Authority (Olsze- wski & Sandovi, 2003:1). Susan Smith summarizes the principle critique of this project, "The social construction of racial segregation portrays urban deprivation as a moral problem, deflecting attention away from the power structures creating and sustaining the inequalities dividing black and white [Americans]" (1993:136).

This logic has been extended to Ren2010 mixed-income schools as a solution to educational failures of low-income schools. The CEO of Chicago Public said, "No other school system in the country has pursued this link between community revitalization and school development" (Olszewski & Sandovi, 2003). The claim is that mixed-income schools will result in better behaviour and academic achievement of low-income students because they will be positively influenced by the behaviours, values, and motivation of their middle-class peers (Kahlenberg, 2001). Apart from the problems with a discredited culture of poverty thesis and lack of strong evidence for the claims of mixed-income schools (Lipman, 2008; Lipman & Haines, 2007), a larger concern is the degree to which mixed-income schools and housing will actually serve low-income families and children.

Unlike public schools which must accept neighbourhood children, many Ren2010 schools accept applications city-wide, limit enrolments, use selection procedures, do not reserve seats for displaced students, may not offer the same grades as the closed school, and set admission deadlines—a factor that disadvantages low-income families who have less certainty about their housing. Informal selection mechanisms also benefit middle-class school consumers who deploy their cultural capital and social connections to secure places for their children through school choice plans (Ball, 2003).

Plans for mixed-income housing and schools prioritize middle-class families, and marketing schools to these 'consumers' is taken for granted (Raffel et al., 2003). In Chicago, most displaced public housing students have been relocated to schools academically and demographically similar to those they left, with 84 percent attending schools with below the average district test scores and 44 percent in schools on probation for low test scores (Catalyst Chicago, 2007). Research on HOPE VI developments elsewhere suggests a similar pattern with public housing children not attending the new schools because of displacement (Raffel et al., 2003). Research in Chicago indicates that just 18.3 percent of approximately 27,000 displaced residents of Robert Taylor Homes, will have housing in the new mixed-income development complex that is replacing the public housing development (Venkatesh et al., 2004).

CONCLUSION

I have argued that the Chicago case illustrates that urban school policies can be understood in relation to neo-liberal strategies of capital accumulation and, in the US context, the cultural politics of race. The close involvement of powerful corporate and financial interests intertwined with local government indicates the strategic role of education in this agenda. School policies are integral to the development of a labour force which is highly stratified, to gentrification as neo-liberal urban economic strategy, and to the disciplining and control of African American youth, many of whom are seen as superfluous in the new economy and 'dangerous' in the global city. Chicago instantiates economic and social processes that are reshaping cities globally.

Although this may be the main story, it is a narrative dotted with complexities and contradiction and nuanced by counter-agendas and spaces of agency and resistance. In the case of Chicago, education is a focal point of social struggles for economic and social justice and for the right of working-class and low-income people of colour to live in the city. The militarization of schooling, through military schools and other forms of regimentation and coercion, including an oppressive high stakes testing regime, are also producing their opposite. Teachers and administrators, working in the cracks of neo-liberal policies, are initiating schools and education projects that are explicitly oriented to social justice and critical education praxis. The hunger strike for the High School for Social Justice with which I introduced this chapter is just one example. Two others are illustrative of a larger trend nationally. In one 'failing' high school, teachers used district mandates to create learning communities to develop a social justice academy. In another community, teachers and community activists seized on Ren2010 to propose and develop a public social justice high school. Yet, these projects face not only the constraints of accountability and centralized control, but the ideological weight of deeply ingrained neo-liberal education practices and assumptions. Chicago exemplifies the interconnections of education, poverty, and race, and contestations over the future of the city.

5 Inclusive School Leadership Strategies in Disadvantaged Schools Based on Student and Community Voice
Implications for Australian Educational Policy

John Smyth

INTRODUCTION

There is a fundamental and possibly irreconcilable disjuncture or disconnect in Australia between the political or policy level approach to the linkage between education and poverty, and the context of enactment or lived experience at the level of disadvantaged schools and their communities (see for example: Smyth, 2005; 2006; Smyth & McInerney, 2007a; 2007b). This is a disconnect that does not sit easily with the historical egalitarian philosophical underpinnings of what it means to be an Australian (as developed in the next section).

The effects of this reconciliation failure flow through in dramatic form into the way in which the educational leadership relay operates on schools—the implicit messages it gives, and the language within which it is encased. When the official policy process is embedded in a set of views derivative of Frederick Hayek (1976) that in effect say that "disadvantaged groups are little more than failures in the marketplace" (Davis, 2008:50), then what we have amounts to a victim-blaming, deficit, and pathologizing view. This is an unhelpful approach to schools, students, and communities that have already been deeply scarred by the effects of globalization and de-industrialization. In this chapter I do not want to dwell excessively on a critique of the neo-liberal policy views that have enchanted and gripped Australia regardless of political party for the past 30 years, although a certain amount of analysis is necessary. Rather, I want to focus on the more hopeful and optimistic possibilities that exist in some schools and communities, while being extremely mindful of the limitations of what can be done locally to tackle what is at essence a deep structural issue. My approach will pay heed to and be somewhat mindful and illustrative of Raffo et al.'s (2007:xiv) point that "it may be that the best hope lies in grassroots movements in schools, classrooms, and communities." It is not that schools and communities are in any sense policy-free zones so much as they can be astute at finding and working what I have highlighted elsewhere (Smyth, Angus, Down, & McInerney, 2008), drawing from Evans & Boyte (1986) as 'free spaces,' within which they construct a socially critical agenda for themselves.

Another feature of the Australian context is the unswerving and possibly immovable ideological commitment to a paradigmatic approach that is not only 'scatter gun,' incoherent, and opportunistic in its futile search for 'magic bullet' solutions to the problem I will come to in a moment, but which is also mired in a deeply flawed economic trickle-down approach, that says in effect that what is good for the economy will ultimately be of benefit to those who have been pushed furthest to the margins of society.

To clarify the position of this chapter somewhat: it will adopt a socially critical approach by trying to come at what are *macro level* issues (how poverty is created and sustained by social and economic structures), and it will attempt to do this (without any guarantees of success) from the vantage point of the *meso level* (more immediate level of communities, families, schools, classrooms, students, and peer groups). The attempt will be to try and flesh out some of the features of what a grassroots socially critical approach might look like that holds out some hope of dislodging what is proving in the Australian context to be an unworkable and ineffectual functionalist approach to educational inequality and disadvantage, largely based on neo-liberal ideas of the market, school choice, accountability for performance, measurement, and testing, targeted interventions, partnerships with business and corporate interests, and other like-minded ideas.

AN AUSTRALIAN EGALITARIAN SENSIBILITY

To understand educational leadership in contemporary Australia and what it means for the increasing proportion of the population being swept into the gradient of being 'put at a disadvantage,' we need to understand something about the Australian national identity and what is happening to it.

To many outsiders and to a segment of the population itself, Australia gives the outward appearances of being a prosperous country, and in many respects it is, as Mark Davis (2008) reflects in the title of his book *The Land of Plenty*. Like many other settler societies, Australia is a place that has been built on a dream which as Davis argues "goes to the roots of what it means to be Australian," a dream that is "half-known, half-understood by all Australians" (2008:1) whether they be recent arrivals or long-term residents. This uniquely Australian ethos obtains its most recognisable expression in the vernacular of the 'fair go' (Smyth, Hattam, & Lawson, 1998), which as Davis puts it is "at the centre of the Australian social contract and [is] deeply embedded in the self-understanding of Australians"

(2008:1–2). This "ethical project," as Davis refers to it, is central to the Australian ethos. It constitutes the egalitarian notion "that one person is as good as another, irrespective of background" (2008:3). Davis' argument is that this legacy goes back to the founding of modern Australia, and the fact that what Australia offered was "the chance of an escape from nineteenth-century Europe and especially Britain, with its industrial squalor and workhouses, intractable class differences and rapidly worsening inequality, brought on by economic laissez-faire" (2008:3). According to Davis, the Australian ethos was not something that just happened by accident—it occurred over generations of struggle and progressive reform secured by "rebelling miners, small farmers, unionists, feminists, judges, [some] politicians and intellectuals" who all contributed to a sense of social justice around the protection of the "small from the powerful" (Davis, 2008:3). Yet, as Davis (2008) says, "for all of its achievements," the Australian project is "still dreaming of what it might become" and in recent times there is a certain "wary[ness] and defensive[ness]" as "longstanding principles of fairness and unique traditions of egalitarianism have been undermined by recent decades of reform" (Davis, 2008:5). In other words, the project that is "the Australian dream" is "only half-complete, and now finds itself facing a moment of uncertainty" (Davis, 2008:5).

These larger contextual forces operating upon Australia, shaping it to become what it is, and in turn, working as a relay have profoundly shaped what is happening to educational leadership.

The ascendancy of the broad New Right agenda in Australia was not something that happened quickly or catastrophically—it occurred slowly and systematically over several decades and on many fronts, and as Davis argues, it was really a "war of ideas":

> . . . a war on Keynesianism, a war on the welfare state, a war on the left, a war on environmentalism, a war on Aboriginal land rights, a war on non-governmental organizations (NGOs), a war on feminism, a war on received notions of social justice. (Davis, 2008:39)

Although it is far more complicated than I am able to go into here, this multi-frontal war of ideas, warehoused by international predator organizations like the World Bank, the IMF, and the OECD (see Smyth & Shacklock, 1998:56–63), was aided and abetted by local think tanks and organizations like the Business Council of Australia that were fed and sustained through ideas and alliances developed with the UK and US. The New Right ideas of the market, individualism, choice, competition, and the ideals of private enterprise took on the form where they were the only game in town, and schools and their leadership were front and centre in that war.

The earlier reference to 'market failure' gives us a glimpse into why and how neo-liberal polices of markets, the sovereignty of the consumer, choice, competitive individualism, league tabling, naming and shaming, and the accountability and audit strategies that flow from all of these—have been able to be so successfully lodged in the public imagination and populist media discourses. Once we philosophically dispense wholly or in part with collective responsibility for correcting the grossly tilted so-called 'level playing field,' then it is not at all hard to see why these policies have had such a self-fulfilling effect in areas like education, where logic suggests they ought to be anathema. They simply appear to be so natural and commonsensical—or at least until they are exposed for the fraud they are!

Both federal and state governments in Australia have had a 30-year insatiable infatuation with neo-liberal marketized policies in the social policy area generally and education in particular. Neo-liberal ideals have completely saturated education through strategies, rhetoric, and policies of educational leadership. In Victoria the neo-liberal marketized ideas of the so-called 'self-managing' or entrepreneurial school were carried to one of their most extreme and grotesque forms anywhere in the world under the program of 'Schools of the Future.'

In a real sense, therefore, what we have is a major widening contradiction—a mythological past that is being sustained around an incomplete but still largely aspirational egalitarian sensibility, while living out a reality in which neo-liberal ideas are having the effect of excluding more and more Australians, particularly the young non-middle class who can see no place for themselves in this fiction. While there is not the space to elaborate on this fully, recent Australian census statistics reveal that only a little over half (58 percent) of young people from the least advantaged backgrounds are completing schooling to the end of year twelve in Australia. This contrasts with 71 percent of their more affluent peers who are enjoying the social and economic benefits that flow from completing their education (Lamb & Mason, 2008). This is occurring despite continuing government rhetoric about the need to raise school completion rates to 90 percent by 2020 (Council of Australian Governments, 2006). In addition we have the situation where in excess of 30 percent of Australian children are attending private schools—a process that has been exacerbated, encouraged, and accelerated by the former Howard government through its inequitable funding regimes (Connors, 2007; McMorrow, 2008), and that shows no signs of changing under the Rudd Labor government. This is clearly indicative of the working of a user-pays policy in which those who can buy their way out of public education on the basis of fear that their off-spring might not be positionally advantaged if their parents deny them a 'supposedly' superior private school education (Smyth, 2008). What are we to make of all this? At a superficial level we could argue that the increasing class bifurcation in Australia, along with the solidification of the school as a middle class institution, is having the effect of alienating many who are coming to regard it as an irrelevance, even against their own self-interests. This is an argument that of course, warrants further detailed investigation beyond what is possible here.

SOMETHING ABOUT THE CURRENT
AUSTRALIAN CONTEXT

Against this contemporary glimpse of Australian identity, the recent Australian background against which this chapter is written is one of policy rhetoric by the newly elected Labour government that seems to be a continuation or even a hardening of the eleven-year educational policy directions of the former conservative coalition government of former Prime Minister John Howard. The approach towards education, and educational disadvantage in particular, seems to be incoherent, and when it does have a discernable direction, it presents as being overwhelmingly muscular and victim-blaming in its tenor—which is to say, it regards schools and teachers as primarily responsible for poor performance in disadvantaged schools.

Actions that seem likely to be directed at schools in the most disadvantaged communities comprise a combination of measures to target these schools with packages of inducements, for example, a program to parachute the 'best and the brightest' of young teacher graduates (Tomazin & Smith, 2008; Tomazin, 2008) into the most disadvantaged schools with the 'toughest classrooms' and to pay them significantly higher salaries. There are also other actions aimed to bear down on these schools and communities with quite punitive intent. For example, federal government proposals have been mooted that are highly reminiscent of the UK's discredited 'naming and shaming' of schools that would produce data enabling comparisons of schools based on league tables (Gough, 2008a), in which under-performing Australian schools would be closed, their staff and principals replaced, and with schools being forced to merge with more 'efficient schools' (Grattan, Tomazin, & Harrison, 2008). Another illustration is the pilot plan to quarantine the welfare payments of Aboriginal and other disadvantaged families so as to "fight truancy" (Carney, 2008) by forcing welfare parents to ensure that their children attend school (The Age, 2008).

Indicative that the federal government is bent on continuing the policies of educational marketization of its predecessor, the Rudd government has hardened the policy lines by insisting on 'greater transparency' of data (Power, 2008; Gillard, 2008a; Gillard, 2008b) and public provision of information about student and school performance, even if that means the creation of league tables that further denude schools in disadvantaged areas of their most attractive and mobile students. When challenged about this, PM Rudd unashamedly responded that if parents "walk with their feet, that's exactly what the system is designed to do" (Kelly, 2008).

Interestingly, in the Australian context, the federal government has no direct role in running schools per se although it does channel the bulk of the funding to run schools to state governments. The federal government is able to ensure compliance with its views by making money to the states contingent on them enacting certain things, and one of the carrots on offer is clearly 'greater transparency' in return for more cash to disadvantaged schools (Kelly, 2008:21).

The centrepiece of the federal government's policy strategy dubbed the 'Education Revolution' in the run up to the November 2007 election, was a strategy to provide a computer for every year 9–12 student, which meant that at best it was limited to being a 'digital' revolution (Australian Labor Party, 2007) that never held out much chance of tackling the deep structural issues confronting disadvantaged schools and communities, or as one commentator put it, "free computers don't make an education revolution" (Davidson, 2008:17).

The latest educational policy development trajectory, seemingly made on the rebound from a trip to New York by deputy PM and Education Minister Julia Gillard, is a move to centrally involve the business and corporate sector in disadvantaged schools. It seems the Minister was mightily impressed with New York Chancellor of Schools Joe Klein's success in getting big business into schools (Nason, 2008). This was an idea that was quickly picked up by cash strapped Australian states, and Victoria was quick to see the potential of getting themselves off the fiscal responsibility hook, as well as seemingly having disadvantaged schools given access to much-needed role models to provide motivation as well as job conduits for students in areas with high levels of protracted inter-generational unemployment. All manner of fanciful possibilities started to run wild, like "Fast-food giants may be welcomed in schools" (Tomazin & Rood, 2008), headlines proclaiming "Gillard wants business in schools" (Gordon, 2008), to suggestions that the way to fix disadvantaged schools was to engage media and consulting firms to give such schools a much needed "image makeover" (Gough, 2008b).

This necessarily quick snapshot of the Australian situation, for that is all it is, gives a glimpse of a lack of coherent government policy in respect to schools in the areas of most protracted poverty. Much of this still has to come to policy fruition. If there is a theme or pattern here then it is the populist and media-driven view that the market will fix the problem, that if necessary the government will get muscular with recalcitrant schools, that school choice will in the end win out in its own Darwinian way (heavens knows what that means in the context of the complete collapse of the paradigm in the September 2008 global financial crisis), and when bolstered by the 'big end' of town with its hype about competition, diligence, compliance, punctuality, presentation, and image management, then disadvantaged schools will somehow enter an enchanted wonderland where all their problems will magically evaporate. It is nevertheless important to reiterate that it is still very early days, and that much of the detailed policy work has yet to be done by the Rudd Labor government. It is only really possible to point to the policy rhetoric (see for example Ministerial Council on Education, Employment, Training and Youth Affairs, 2008) and the accompanying media blitzkrieg that is a harbinger of the stick and carrot educational policies that will inevitably follow.

This capture of the Australian imagination by the neo-liberal agenda and the view of school leadership (Smyth, 2008) that has flowed from it have produced an effect. The intractable issues of poverty, disadvantage, and low educational achievement have become more rather than less protracted for the most disadvantaged young people (Australian Council of Social Service, 2007; Callahan, 2008; Cleary, 2008; Megalogenis, 2007; Miletic, 2007; Nicholson, 2007; Smith & Turley, 2007) even with all the incoherent attempts to plaster over the cracks.

All of this is by way of saying that we need to look elsewhere for leadership and direction with ideas about ways of working the nexus between education and poverty.

LOOKING TO THE 'BOTTOM UP' FOR SOME COHERENT IDEAS

Behind the recent educational policy rhetoric just described lies a personal view of the overall direction of educational policy in Australia that has not been formed quickly or rashly, but rather comes out of careful reflection and writing about it over 30 years. I long ago reached the conclusion that the only real hope for disadvantaged schools, notwithstanding the huge structural issues surrounding them like health, unemployment, substance abuse, violence, degraded housing and school facilities, lies in galvanizing leadership across a broad set of alliances and coalitions (some of them within governments), to listen to, support, and properly resource ideas that derive from within these schools and communities themselves, rather than being orchestrated from a distance. Not only do indigenous ideas have more chance of working because of local ownership, but they can also be used to force governments to discharge their constitutional responsibilities towards communities that have been blighted and marginalized through circumstances not of their own making. Sometimes it is possible to garner support from those parts of government that are closer to the scene of the action and to that extent may have something of a social conscience towards the conditions being experienced by residents in local proximity.

Shields (2004) has provided an interesting and useful organizing category around which to speak about an alternative and more inclusive view of educational leadership that exists in varying degrees in the Australian context in ways that speak to social justice in the process of overcoming 'pathologies of silence.' The pathologizing silences that have to be worked against in the Australian context are:

- the managerial school and exclusive concern with structures and governance;
- social class and educational disadvantage;

- the exclusion of schools, teachers, and communities from the reform process;
- race, Aboriginality, and ethnicity;
- punitive and retributive processes that fiscally damage schools;
- the pervasive ideology that 'private' is best and 'public' is second rate.

Over the past decade (1997–2007), along with a team of Australian colleagues, I have conducted 25 multi-sited ethnographic studies (Marcus, 1998) with 6 grants from the Australian Research Council, across three states (South Australia, Western Australia, and Victoria) and the Northern Territory around schools in contexts of disadvantage. Often these have been schools in which the majority of students come from backgrounds of social and economic disadvantage—often in excess of 90 percent of the students.

As I take this opportunity to step back from these studies and look afresh in a way I have never done before, one thing that strikes me as being most consistent are the themes and patterns in the ways in which educational leadership at the school and community level has operated against the grain of the official policy discourses alluded to earlier in this chapter. Our research, which is illustrative of more inclusive approaches, has yielded various organizers and rubrics, which exist as archetypes in varying degrees in the lives of actual Australian schools. These include the socially just school (Smyth, Hattam, & Lawson, 1998; Smyth, Hattam, McInerney, & Lawson, 1999; McInerney, Hattam, Smyth, & Lawson, 1999), the pedagogically engaged school (Smyth, 2003a; Smyth, 2003b; Smyth & McInerney, 2007b; Smyth, 2007a), the relational school (Smyth, 2007b; Smyth, Angus, Down, & McInerney, 2009; Smyth, Down, & McInerney, 2008), the dialogical school (Hattam, McInerney, Smyth, & Lawson, 1999), the socially critical school (Smyth, McInerney, Hattam, & Lawson, 1999), and the student-voiced school (Hattam, McInerney, Smyth, & Lawson, 1999; Smyth, Hattam, Cannon, Edwards, Wilson, & Wurst, 2000; Smyth & Hattam, et al., 2004).

There are a number of 'generative themes' (Freire, 1972) that cascade across these archetypes, some of which we have tentatively grouped elsewhere under the shorthand of 'new storylines' (Smyth et. al., 2008:149–65; Smyth et. al., 2009:127–40) that provide a substantive basis for a more inclusive approach to leadership around student and community voice, including:

- knowing the community, regarding the community as a valuable resource,
- taking asymmetries of power seriously,
- having high levels of trust in a context of safety to take risks,
- a preparedness to confront and deal with controversial issues,

- having the courage to be innovative,
- speaking back to entrenched interests,
- regarding students' lives as being part of the curriculum,
- supporting and fostering indigenous leadership,
- having a genuine affection for disadvantaged students,
- being prepared to 'cut slack' and bend rules for students,
- acting as a buffer for teachers against damaging policies,
- working out how to strategically turn outside policies back on themselves,
- creating a culture in which it is safe for the school and community to be reflective,
- findings ways to celebrate working class identity,
- challenging deficit narratives,
- teaching students and community how to 'speak back' to injustices,
- providing students with an expanded range of experiences, and
- a willingness to engage in political action when necessary.

In the space available I want to provide a partial glimpse, from actual schools, into what some of the trajectories of *three* of these heuristics have to say about the more inclusive approaches to educational leadership in contexts of disadvantage, that inhere in this list of bullet points. While the three archetypes I deal with below are meant to be indicative, I provide reference to the full range of archetypes so that the reader can follow up on the others if desired.

The Socially Just School: (which appears variously as a school known as The Pines [Smyth, McInerney, Hattam, & Lawson, 1999b], The Gums [Smyth et al., 1998b], and Wattle Plains [McInerney, 2003; 2004]) has a view of leadership in which there is a central unswerving passion and commitment to making the school work in the interests of the 'least advantaged.' In practical terms this means placing teaching and learning for all students at the centre of everything they do—and not being distracted or deflected by issues of accountability, performance measurement, league tables, standards, image and impression management, sorting and sifting, choice, and marketization—all of which have little or nothing to do with the central mission of student learning.

This is a school in which the leadership prides itself in the way in which teachers are continuous learners, amongst themselves, and with their students, parents, and colleagues in other schools. They learn *in stitu*, and funding and resources are made available for this (Smyth et al., 1998b:101). As a consequence, the whole school gets to understand what is crucial about local circumstances and how ideas from elsewhere might be adapted to help make sense of and grapple with difficult and intractable issues of inequality. There is a preparedness, too, to organize the school around a pervasive process of fostering a culture of debate and innovation (Hattam, Brown, & Smyth, 1996) around what best serves the interests of students. In a real sense, the school is committed to being a 'dialogical school' or as one informant put it: "You can't get away with being a bastard, being a blocker here" (Smyth et al., 1998b:105). In other words, the emphasis is on debating the issues of how to improve the life chances of students, not labelling them as deficits or as being personally worthless. Such schools position themselves as places in which people "feel safe in putting out ideas because they are debated on their merits" (Smyth et al., 1998b:102). The school is a 'moral community' in the sense of being passionately engaged in an exploration of ideas and practices that make a difference in the lives of children.

These are schools that do not shy away either from gathering 'data,' but it is data of a kind that provides *them* with the informed basis upon which to make decisions and to take actions consistent with their overall philosophy. For example, in pursuing their mission of providing a more enriching set of artistic learning experiences for students, finding out that 70 percent of students did not know what a sculpture was, provided the information to enable the school to secure the funding to have a 'sculptor-in-residence' for a period so as to work with the students to create a sculpture court in the school.

These are also places that have a strong sense of 'staff cohesion.' By this they mean activities in which people get to see in a practical way the skills, resources, and assets that reside in the school and the community. For example, the teacher who described himself somewhat self-deprecatingly as a 'failed artist' but who passionately pointed out to his colleagues that the drab and dull appearance of the external walls of the school building impacted negatively on the students, and who went about organizing the teachers, students, and parents (and local hardware supplier to provide the paint) to make a continuous mural of the curriculum on the walls of the school buildings.

The Student-Voiced School: (developed out of backward mapping from the stories of 209 young people, 80 percent from disadvantaged backgrounds, who had given up on school and left before completing [Smyth et al., 2000; Smyth & Hattam et al., 2004]). The overwhelming point made by these young people is that school and educational system leadership was deeply disrespectful of their lives, class background, and aspirations. By this they meant, they were excluded from having a real say in what, how, where, and when they learned, and often schools bore down on them relentlessly and without regard to their real needs, interests, or backgrounds. The consequence, without putting too fine a point on it, was that these young people regarded schooling as being antagonistic and irrelevant to them and their lives, so much so they were prepared to walk away from it.

In instances where schools were able to reinvent themselves around young lives, inclusive leadership took the form of giving students an authentic voice; negotiating curriculum and learning around students' lives and interests; connecting what goes on in classrooms to popular culture; providing flexibility around students' out-of-school lives especially around work and family caring commitments; taking students' emotional lives seriously; creating an atmosphere of trust in which school policies around issues like behaviour, dress codes, school attendance, and use of banned substances involve young people in their formulation and understanding of their rationale. In other words, many young people from contexts of disadvantage engage in adult-like behaviours outside of schools, many of them risk-averse, but in schools they are treated in child-like ways.

The Relational School: (See for example, Mango High School in Smyth & Fasoli, 2007.) This is an archetype of a school in which the leadership positions itself in ways in which students have 'relational power.' That is to say, what is placed at the centre is how people deal with one another, how the school leadership team models this with teachers and students, and how teachers in turn employ this approach with students, and students in turn in their dealings with each other. As one assistant principal put it, this involves "knowing the kids and their homes," and where they are coming from with all of its colourfulness and tragic fragments. There is a real sense in which teachers have to genuinely like these young people, reinforcing the view that learning is a highly contingent activity. As this leader put it, here "the kids learn you first, then they learn your subject." These students quickly learn which teachers are prepared "to go the extra mile for them," and can spot those teachers who are "going through the motions" and they "switch off the teachers they don't like" (Smyth & Fasoli, 2007:281). The kind of leadership necessary here is of a kind that is committed to making these students 'powerful people' (Smyth & Fasoli, 2007:281) in the sense that they have agency and the school reinforces a worthwhile image of them as human beings, rather than disparaging them or their backgrounds. It is this relational power that is such a crucial site for identity formation and which provides the affirmation necessary to improve the life chances of these young people.

CONCLUDING REMARKS

As a way of drawing this together theoretically before concluding, it is possible to argue that the ideas about more inclusive educational leadership in disadvantaged contexts has implicit within it three big ideas, as shown in Figure 5.1.

First, there is a crucial over-riding imperative to confront issues of power and to challenge asymmetries in ways that involve deconstructing hierarchies, whether they are of class, gender, race, ethnicity, or of an artificially constructed organizational type. Unless this occurs in the kind of schools being spoken about here, then what gets to be perpetuated is the situation Kohl (1994) captured in the title of his book *I Won't Learn from You.* Confusion arises as a result whereby a refusal to learn gets to be mislabelled as underachievement or failure, neither of which is the same as non-learning, especially in contexts of disadvantage!

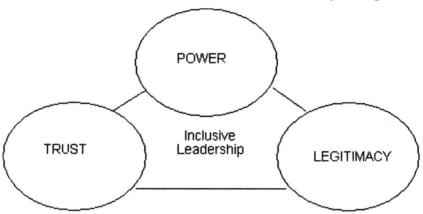

Figure 5.1 The three big ideas of inclusive leadership.

Second, there is an imperative to authentically deal with issues of trust that have become severely corrupted and corroded as a consequence of welding schools onto the economic and neo-liberal project. At the moment schools in Western education systems have an overwhelming and unshakable emphasis on educational policies that are extremely distrustful. Power put it most perceptively when he said that a society that becomes over-reliant on accountability has basically "lost confidence in itself":

> When this happens a society tries to tell reaffirming stories, it makes explicit what was implicit and it creates more and more formal accounts which can be checked. An anxious society invests heavily in evaluative practices of self-affirmation and new industries of checkers are created. It is not so much a loss of trust that has occurred but a desperate need to create it through the management of formal appearance . . . all this checking makes a certain style of management possible, one that is now firmly established. The problem is not evaluation and assessment as such, but the belief that with ever more of it, real excellence can be conjured into existence. The opposite is almost certainly the case; increasing evaluation and auditing are symptoms of mediocrity rather than its cure. (Power, 1996:18)

Third, there is the issue of legitimacy which is really at heart about affirming the correctness of perspectives and actions. In this case, it means acknowledging that it is not only permissible, but crucial to involve students and their families in decisions about their futures, even when all around is very different from the views of the middle class institution of schooling. Bringing about fundamental life changes involves leading schools in these circumstances in ways whereby young people and communities are put in the centre of the frame, and everything that follows is about providing them with experiences that add to and enrich the range of opportunities available. In other words, it is about the institution of schooling being sufficiently mature and secure to allow its limited view to get out of the way, to acknowledge the legitimacy of cultural trajectories different from its own, and in the process advance the interests of *all* of its young charges.

This chapter started by highlighting the policy disconnect alluded to by Raffo et al. (2007), and then moved to show something of how this has worked in the Australian context. It has also shown the inherent shortsightedness of approaches developed at a distance, of their inability to garner credibility, and their lack of potency in making in-roads into the education-poverty nexus. While being extremely mindful of the severe limitations of what is possible without challenging the underlying structural conditions that produce and sustain inequality, the chapter pointed to some hopeful philosophical and practical commitments necessary to make a closer connect with the existential reality that lies at the centre of disadvantage and poverty.

ACKNOWLEDGMENTS

The ideas contained in this chapter came from two Australian Research Council funded projects: "Enhancing school retention: school and community linkages in regional/rural Western Australia" (Linkage Grant, 2005–2007), and "Individual, institutional and community 'capacity building' in a cluster of disadvantaged schools and their community" (Discovery Grant, 2006–2008).

6 Effectiveness and Disadvantage in Education

Can a Focus on Effectiveness Aid Equity in Education?

Daniel Muijs

INTRODUCTION

School Effectiveness has been a key goal of education in many countries for a number of years now, and has also become a burgeoning international research field, with studies in countries ranging from Hong Kong to Chile (Teddlie & Reynolds, 2000). There has long been policy interest in the field, with school effectiveness units being common in Local Authorities in England, for example. However, the influence of school effectiveness on education has been controversial, with many arguing that the emphasis placed on outcomes by proponents of school effectiveness has had negative equity consequences. This chapter will explore to what extent this is the case, and whether research on poverty and equity in education can benefit from effectiveness research. I will also consider the extent to which effectiveness research needs to be adapted to develop a better understanding of the processes that operate within disadvantaged educational contexts.

Effectiveness, defined rather unhelpfully by Webster's dictionary as "the quality of being effective," is essentially about finding the best way to meet a particular goal. A clearer definition used in engineering, is that effectiveness is the degree to which a system or an organisation's features and capabilities enable it to meet its goals. This definition has three main elements, all of which lead to contestation in education. The first element is the organisation. In most extant research this has been defined as the school, though most research has shown that actually what happens in the classroom is key here (Muijs & Reynolds, 2001). One could argue that system more correctly refers to the education system, but, as I will argue later, one can also define this as being a community or environment. The second is the goals of the organisation. In most school effectiveness research this has been quite narrowly defined as cognitive outcomes, in particular test achievement, though studies looking at pupil well being, self-concept, and attitudes to school also exist (e.g. Opdenakker & Van Damme, 2000). This narrowness is a weakness, though it has to be remarked most research shows quite clearly that schools have a stronger impact on cognitive than on non-cognitive outcomes, even attitudes to school, so this focus is not without logic (Creemers, 1994; 1997). The final element is features and capabilities, or those factors that enable an organisation to reach its goals. This is the key element in effectiveness research—finding out what it is that organisations do to be optimally effective in reaching their goals. In school effectiveness research this has typically taken the form of looking at variables that are correlated with better student outcomes taking intake characteristics into account. Therefore, a key characteristic of effectiveness research is its instrumental focus, which has been described as value-free, even though in the practice of research this is of course an impossibility, as all researchers approach their work from within a certain values framework. In practice, most effectiveness studies take an input-process-output model as their starting point, with pupil characteristics as the input, results as the outcome, and school factors as the processes. Most studies have been correlational and cross-sectional, a clear limitation of the field (Teddlie & Reynolds, 2000).

It is therefore clear that within the framework presented earlier, school effectiveness research can be situated towards the more functionalist approaches, focussing on working within rather than trying to change systems, and that it operates very much on the meso and micro levels, with relatively little attention to the macro level other than as covariate factors within which schools operate.

As such, one would not inherently see any great contradictions between the goals of alleviating poverty and disadvantage and their educational outcomes and the field of educational effectiveness. Effectiveness can be defined to look at a range of goals or outcomes that we may want to achieve, such as equity, or the advancement of particular disadvantaged student groups, and it is clear that one could see effectiveness research as helping to achieve key goals in helping to alleviate educational disadvantage. However, in practice there are very few links between the fields of effectiveness and poverty, and it is fair to say that effectiveness research is frequently regarded with some hostility in these areas. How has this situation come about, and to what extent is it justified?

STRENGTHS AND WEAKNESSES OF EFFECTIVENESS RESEARCH

What is clear is that this is not a result of a lack of effectiveness research in disadvantaged contexts. From the start of the effectiveness movement much of the research has been conducted in disadvantaged settings. Edmonds (1979), one of the founders of school effectiveness research, for example, was driven to research effectiveness in order to improve the educational conditions of impoverished students in inner-city New York. In this he was reacting to pessimistic voices claiming that schools did not impact significantly on educational outcomes following the seminal Coleman (1966) study. Subsequently, it is fair to say that the majority of research in school effectiveness has taken place in schools serving disadvantaged communities in a variety of mainly Western European, Australian, and North American cities; to this extent we probably know more about effectiveness in public (state) schools serving urban disadvantaged communities than we do about any other type of school (Teddlie & Reynolds, 2000). This bias towards disadvantaged schools is if anything even stronger in the related discipline of school improvement (Muijs et al., 2004). This would obviously suggest that school effectiveness and improvement research would play a key part in improving equity in education.

However, the extent to which this research base can usefully inform this area is not that clear. It quickly became obvious that compiling lists of factors present in high performing schools, which anyway were merely the result of correlational research, was not the same as being able to improve schools in similar circumstances (Muijs, 2006). In many cases it is hard even to distinguish causality from the correlational factors with any confidence. The research base in many cases was less strong than the prescriptions based on it, and the factors found often too general to usefully inform practice. For example, it is not clear what shared vision, or strong and purposeful leadership from a headteacher look like in practice. The tendency to move very quickly from research to prescription in this as in other areas of educational research (such as leadership) is particularly problematic in this regard, and it has been said, not entirely without foundation, that there are more papers and articles providing summaries of school effectiveness research than there are actual research studies (Alexander, 2001). Furthermore, many researchers concerned with equity working outside of school effectiveness believe that the preoccupation of the field on improving schools internally was both insufficiently radical and too simplistic to address the underlying problems afflicting disadvantaged communities (Ainscow et al., 2008).

The quantitative, correlational nature of effectiveness research provides a further reason. There is a tendency in this type of work to amalgamate data, which can lead to groups of students, for example smaller minority groups, not being considered separately but lumped together with other students. This is clearly problematic in the light of the well-known issues of disadvantage and discrimination that particular groups may face. This can lead to effectiveness research understating the diversity of urban contexts and the issues particular groups of students may face. Given sufficiently large samples and advances in statistical methodology this does not now need to be the case, but in practice it frequently still is. That this has in some cases led to hostility to not just effectiveness research, but quantitative methods more generally is deeply unfortunate.

The main problem, however, probably lies in the (mis)use made of the concept of effectiveness by policy makers. As Goldstein & Woodhouse (2000) amongst others have pointed out a range of government policies have been justified under the aegis of school effectiveness, often aimed primarily at stronger accountability and greater central control of school and classroom processes. It is also clear that some, though by no means all, effectiveness researchers have been involved in formulating central policy. The problem here is that many of these policies, while purporting to be based on research, are not in fact supported by the school effectiveness knowledge base, going well beyond actual research findings (a particularly egregious example of this being the 'clock' in the National Numeracy Strategy documents, specifying the exact amount of time to be spent on different activities within the Literacy hour that was produced early on in the Labour government's tenure and was supposedly based on research on effective teaching [Muijs & Reynolds, 2001]). Some policies that have resulted, such as the emphasis on competition between schools, have the potential to harm the education of the most disadvantaged students in particular (Ainscow & West, 2006). Other policies, such as the inspection and accountability regime in England, are likewise not based on School Effectiveness Research, though they are often seen as part of the school effectiveness movement. In this case, notwithstanding the criticisms of the inspection regime, subsequent research, in particular the work of Sammons (2007) has shown a positive impact of inspection on school improvement, particularly in disadvantaged areas.

A myopic focus on schools is another issue in effectiveness research that hinders its impact on work on equity and poverty in education. Effectiveness research itself points to limitations in this regard. The percentage of the variance in pupil performance that is attributed to schools is only around 10–30 percent depending on study and context, so any school intervention would per definition appear limited in its possible outcomes (Teddlie & Reynolds, 2000). Nevertheless, the critics of effectiveness research tend to make an error here as well, in that the remaining 70–90 percent of variance tends to be attributed without further thought to pupil background characteristics. This is erroneous. For starters, some element of innate ability is likely to account for at least some of the variance. While overly deterministic account of 'g' have been roundly discredited, genetic research tends to show that most characteristics can be accounted for by both nature and nurture, with most estimates being around 50 percent for each (Plug & Vijverberg, 2003), and there is evidence that cognitive functioning would contain a genetic component alongside the strong nurture component largely explained by social background (Payton, 2006; Behrman & Taubman, 1989). A further proportion of the variance in performance, and one that is frequently overlooked, is simple measurement error. In much educational research, and indeed much social scientific research more generally, measurement error takes up a far higher proportion of variance than is often recognised. An example of this lies in the use of test results as an outcome measure. As anyone with experience in teaching will testify, tests are often inaccurate measures of whatever it is they purport to measure, and are subject to a variety of random factors such as test takers' mood, physical condition at time of test taking, and levels of test anxiety, as well as more systematic sources of error such as question formats and inadequate sampling of the knowledge domain. The situation is probably even more serious when measuring internal constructs like self esteem, where the concept itself may arguably not exist outside of the test developer's remit. Even seemingly obvious variables like gender will typically show a couple of percentages of measurement error due to such factors as faulty data input. Therefore, the actual proportion of variance attributable to student background is likely to be significantly less than 50 percent rather than the 80 percent that is often attributed to it. This figure is also more in accordance with findings from studies where social background measures have been included, as typical correlations with educational outcomes tend to be around 0.3 to 0.5 depending on the measure used. Correlations are usually highest with mothers' education level and lowest with poor proxy variables such as free school meal eligibility, which, with its two-level classification can at best be described as a somewhat inaccurate proxy measure of poverty rather than of SES as it is often portrayed. Therefore, while it is clear that social background has a strong impact on educational outcomes, the impact of social background is not as great as sometimes is believed, and not much greater than the impact of schooling (Sammons, 2007).

As mentioned above, while schools can certainly have an impact, this impact is limited to approximately 30 percent of the variance in pupil outcomes. Therefore, even if we found all the factors that make schools more or less effective, we would still not be able to affect more than 30 percent of the variance in pupils' outcomes. It has therefore become increasingly clear that a narrow focus on the school as an institution will not be sufficient to enable work on more equitable educational outcomes to progress (Muijs, 2006). Interventions will need to impact more directly on pupils' environment and life chances. Work with the community is essential, if expectations are to be raised and social and cultural capacity built, as is work on health and socio-psychological inhibitors. It is important that this factor is realised by policymakers and practitioners, and educational researchers do the field a disservice if they don't make this clear to them. This realisation is certainly growing in research and practice, and has led to the development of full service schools and extended schools which aim to integrate services. The evidence on the effectiveness of these programmes is as yet unclear. Studies in the Netherlands, US, and the UK have often tended to show that the overall impact of such programmes is limited to individuals rather than having sustained community impacts, though there is increasing evidence that achievement gaps may be smaller in extended schools, notwithstanding the difficulties experienced in developing programmes in which organisations with very different goals and cultures collaborate (Muijs, 2007; Cummings et al., 2007; Van Veen & van den Bogaert., 2006). Interestingly, the English governments extended schools programme postdates a lot of this work and is therefore a good example of policymakers going ahead with programmes and initiatives without recourse to existing evidence. What is clear is that if inequity is to be addressed community work is essential, though the top-down English model may not be the most suitable for this, as US work that has used a more bottom-up approach which actually involves the community in developing solutions has shown. However, these wider programmes likewise need to be based on trials and evaluated for effectiveness as stringently as is the case for school programmes before promoting them nationally.

WHAT CAN EFFECTIVENESS RESEARCH CONTRIBUTE TO EDUCATION IN DISADVANTAGED CONTEXTS?

The impact of schools and classrooms differs not just over subjects, with those subjects least affected by tutoring and experience in the home more strongly impacted by school (e.g. the school effect on maths is stronger than that on English), but importantly in the context of equity, differs depending on the social background of the students as well. The school effect, as demonstrated in research on the Gatsby project, is up to three times higher for pupils from low SES backgrounds than for those from higher SES backgrounds, and therefore the school has a far stronger role in terms of helping or hindering (and it often is hindering) the progress of students from disadvantaged groups than is often realized (Muijs & Reynolds, 2000). In a large-scale study of mathematics teaching in primary schools we carried out a number of years ago, for example, correlations between teacher behaviours, measured using a direct instruction framework, and outcomes were on average twice as strong in schools with a high percentage of pupils eligible for free school meals as in schools with a low percentage of pupils eligible. Similarly, correlations of teacher behaviours with both achievement and attainment tended to be stronger in schools with a high proportion of students with low achievement scores (Muijs & Reynolds, 2003). Therefore, school and teacher effectiveness research should be able to at least inform research and practice in education in disadvantaged contexts. In what ways can it do so, and why would effectiveness research matter? Two key elements are important here. The most obvious one is to look at some of the actual findings of school and teacher effectiveness research, which may help inform policy and improvement efforts in this area. The other is to take account of some of the underlying premises and methods used in effectiveness research.

One such consistent finding from not just effectiveness research, but from meta-analyses of educational interventions more generally, is that what matters is what happens in the classroom. As mentioned earlier, this is especially the case for students from disadvantaged backgrounds. Classroom level variance in student outcomes is typically twice school level variance, and learning and teaching are key factors therein. There-fore, interventions in teaching and learning have the potential to improve the educational outcomes of disadvantaged students more strongly than do other interventions in school. This is especially the case for pupils from disadvantaged backgrounds. However, this does not mean that any inter-vention has a similar impact, and especially it doesn't mean that every intervention has a similar impact on students from more advantaged and disadvantaged backgrounds.

One study of schools that had moved off the list of poorly perform-ing schools in New York found that the common denominator for all of them was a focus on students' academic achievement. All had developed new instructional strategies (Connell, 1996). Teddlie and Stringfield (1993) found that in ineffective schools in Louisiana heads focussed less on core instructional policies than in effective schools, while separate studies of effective and high performing schools in low-income areas in Quebec and Texas produced similar findings (Henchey, 2001). In one large-scale review of reform programmes in the US, a strong instructional focus was com-mon to all the most effective programmes, many of which have tradition-ally focussed on schools in low SES areas (Herman, 1999). There is some evidence that an academic focus is actually more prevalent in effective low SES than in effective high SES schools, and, more generally, that effective low SES schools have more limited and short term goals than their high SES counterparts (Teddlie, Stringfield, Wimpelberg, & Kirby, 1989). Other researchers have likewise stressed that a focus on teaching and learning can be encouraged by training staff in specific teaching methods at the start of the school's improvement effort (Joyce, Calhoun, & Hopkins, 1999; Hop-kins & Reynolds, 2001).

Research findings show that compared to students from middle and high SES backgrounds, low SES students need more structure and more posi-tive reinforcement from the teacher, and need to receive the curriculum in smaller packages followed by rapid feedback (Ledoux & Overmaat, 2001). They will generally need more instruction, and be more responsive to exter-nal rewards (Teddlie et al., 1989; Teddlie & Stringfield, 1993). While mid and high ability students do not benefit from praise unrelated to the task, there is some evidence that low achievers do benefit from non-contingent praise, due to the low self-esteem of many of the students (Brophy, 1992). Pupils from lower SES backgrounds have been found to benefit from a more integrated curriculum across grades and subjects (Connell, 1996). Connect-ing learning to real-life experience and stressing practical applications have been found to be particularly important to low-SES pupils, as has making the curriculum relevant to their daily lives. This may diminish disaffec-tion as well as promoting learning (Montgomery et al., 1993; Henchey, 2001; Hopkins & Reynolds, 2001). According to Mortimore (1991) effec-tive teaching in this type of school should be teacher-led and practically focussed, but not low-level or undemanding. Creating consistency in teaching approach is important for pupils from low SES backgrounds, and has been found to be related to improved outcomes (Mortimore, 1991).

In their study of schools in high and low SES areas, Teddlie & Stringfield (1993) found that in effective low SES schools there was more emphasis on basic skills, and less on extending the curriculum than in effective high-SES schools. A survey of 366 high-performing schools in high poverty areas found that they had focussed more strongly on maths and English by extending teaching time and changing the curriculum so there was a stronger emphasis on basic skills (Barth et al., 1999). A Dutch study found that in effective schools with high numbers of underperforming ethnic minority students there was a strong emphasis on basic skills and a strongly structured curriculum (Ledoux & Overmaat, 2001), and one American study looking at the implementation of the New American Schools school reform reported that some (though by no means all) teachers in a poor urban district felt that some of the designs lacked the structure and basic skills emphasis needed in those contexts (Berends, Bodily, & Kirby, 2002).

Other authors, however, claim that pupils from low SES backgrounds are more capable of higher order thinking than is often supposed, and should be exposed to a curriculum that is as rich as that of their advantaged counterparts, built around powerful ideas and focussing on metagcognitive skills (Leithwood & Steinbach, 2002). Interestingly, one school improvement project that chose to narrow the curriculum by aligning it to a basic skills test used by the region (the Iowa Test of Basic skills) failed to result in improved performance after two years (Philips, 1996). Further evidence comes from an American project in which the curriculum of a highly selective private school was transplanted to two high poverty schools in Baltimore (with a large amount of professional development and support through a school-based coordinator), leading to strong improvements in achievement in both schools, as well as improvements in attendance (McHugh & Stringfield, 1998). Programmes stressing an advanced skills curriculum were found to improve the achievement of high poverty ethnic minority students in another US study (Borman, Stringfield, & Rachuba, 2000). A danger with focussing on basic skills in schools with a low SES intake is that by offering them an impoverished curriculum social divides could be exacerbated rather than diminished. A study of 26 high achieving impoverished schools in Texas showed that both direct instruction and constructivist teaching strategies were employed in these schools, neither seeming inherently more effective (Lein, Johnson, & Ragland, 1996). A similar finding was reported by Ledoux and Overmaat (2001) in their Dutch study of effective schools using a mix of traditional and constructivist methods. Interestingly, in two well-executed studies in the US and UK, improving schools were found to have emphasised arts (Connell, 1996; Maden, 2001).

While a focus on teaching and learning is crucial, the conditions must first be in place in which effective teaching can occur. Maden and Hillman, (1993) found that improving schools had all put clear discipline procedures in place and were focussed on creating an orderly environment. In particular in disadvantaged areas it is crucial to have effective discipline in place. However this does not mean that schools should be excessively disciplinarian. Valuing pupils and making them feel part of the school 'family' are also characteristics of effective schools, as is pupil involvement in setting up the rules (Connell, 1996; Lein et al., 1996).

In terms of pedagogy, results are actually pretty clear. There is clear evidence that Direct Instruction methods have to be a significant part of teaching if pupils from socio-economically disadvantaged areas are not to lose out. Studies have consistently shown that Interactive Direct Instruction can aid student progression and can do this better for disadvantaged than advantaged students, thus helping to close at least a little bit of the achievement gap. In our own research on the Gatsby programme, we found, for example, that effective teaching according to a Direct Instruction model explained between 50 percent and 75 percent of the classroom level variance in performance (Muijs & Reynolds, 2002). The larger percentages were found among pupils from disadvantaged backgrounds, the effect being twice to three times as high for them. Direct instruction has its strongest impact on pupils from low SES backgrounds, as is shown by research across a number of contexts, including the UK, the US, the Netherlands, and Belgium (Sammons, 2007; Houtveen et al., 2004). In Hattie's (2003) meta-analysis this was found to be one of the most strong educational interventions, while Dutch research has likewise found this to be more effective in improving the performance of disadvantaged pupils than constructivist and more so-called learner-centred approaches (Houtveen et al., 2007). By contrast, the research on constructivist teaching methods shows mixed results at best, and there are few studies that focus specifically on disadvantaged students (Muijs and Reynolds, 2005). This is seen as likely to result from the fact that constructivist approaches and others that tend to rely on pupils discovering more for themselves, or even in collaboration with peers, by their nature require pupils to draw more strongly on their prior knowledge and experience. What this means in effect is that they rely more strongly than Direct Instruction methods on pupils' cultural and social capital, found to be strongly related to parental SES. Thus, this type of approach may well exacerbate rather than decrease SES differences, even if it has overall benefits, and is therefore highly problematic in terms of equity. This does of course not mean that there is no possible alternative to Direct Instruction methods. Methods such as peer tutoring and collaborative small-group work, for example, have strong evidence behind them as well. Rather, what it does mean is that when we look at those alternatives we need to take full account of equity considerations and analyse the effectiveness of these approaches on that basis rather than just jump on popular bandwagons or teaching methods which have too often been developed and promoted without their equity impact factored in.

Another important effectiveness finding in terms of helping disadvantaged pupils in schools is the importance of consistency. As researchers such as Creemers and Kyriakides (2006) have pointed out, higher levels of performance from disadvantaged pupils in particular accrue where they can experience consistency in terms of approaches to teaching and pedagogy, a consistency they may well not experience in the home. Again, this has not always been a popular message, as consistent approaches to a certain extent entail curtailing the individual freedom of the classroom teacher. From this perspective, a focus upon equity in terms of educational outcomes has implications for teacher autonomy and freedom; accordingly if equity is our key concern it follows that the freedom of teachers has to be of secondary concern.

Effectiveness research is, as I mentioned in the introduction, basically empiricist and sceptical. The underlying premise is to look empirically at what works in achieving certain outcomes. I believe this is a particularly important perspective in education, where this view may sometimes be absent. Education professionals and governments are often seekers, looking for new wonder drugs and easily susceptible to gurus who appear to offer them ready-made solutions to some of the problems inherent in the complex undertaking that is educating the young. Furthermore, ideology frequently colours discussion to the exclusion of an empirical base. This has in many cases lead to the pursuit of novel ideas with scant empirical base, especially where it comes to equity considerations (Muijs, 2006).

HOW DOES EFFECTIVENESS RESEARCH NEED TO CHANGE?

While the above clearly shows the contribution effectiveness research can make to addressing equity issues, it has to be acknowledged that the contribution of effectiveness research to work on improving the education of the most disadvantaged groups in society is at this point in time nevertheless somewhat limited. This is due not only to a reluctance to engage on the part of different individuals working in different disciplines, but to inherent limitations in the effectiveness approach. These limitations take on a number of forms.

Firstly, effectiveness research, like most other educational research, is too strongly focussed on the short-term. Most studies are not longitudinal, or, when they are, define longitudinal as a three-year period. This is far too short to measure accurately the effect of education or schools, not least precisely due to equity issues over the longer term. The key issue for education is surely how they can affect students life chances over time—i.e., can we actually make a difference to children's futures rather than just their test scores? Many would say that the distinction is in some ways academic, as improving pupils' educational test outcomes in middle and upper school presents them with greater future possibilities in terms, for example, of access to higher education and employment opportunities. While this is certainly true, it is here that the impact of inequity once again rears its ugly head, in the form of class-based regression to the mean in performance among students and schools. Many studies in effectiveness look at outliers, both in terms of schools that perform better than you would expect based on their intake, and when looking at equity in terms of pupils from low SES backgrounds doing well or better than expected on exams. The problem with both is that long-term studies suggest that pupils from low SES backgrounds who do well in tests may regress back to lower performance over time, while pupils from high SES backgrounds who do poorly tend to see their performance increase over time. An example of this is taken from a recent study on the identification of giftedness by Lohman (2006), which demonstrated that of disadvantaged pupils identified as gifted in grade 3 (defined as being in the top 5 percent), only 50 percent still scored this high in grade 6. Conversely, the scores of low-achieving middle class kids had improved significantly. In some ways this is not surprising, as high SES students can draw on the social and cultural capital at their disposal to overcome poor performance, while the additional effort it takes for disadvantaged students to overcome their barriers may be harder to sustain. A similar problem exists with schools. Typically, while schools serving disadvantaged communities can improve performance and become positive outliers in terms of effectiveness for a while, they find it hard to sustain this level of performance. The school improvement maxim that schools facing challenging circumstances have to work harder to maintain performance certainly applies, but it is also certainly true that many schools fail to keep up high levels of performance over time as they are slowly overwhelmed by circumstances. Therefore, we need to do more longitudinal work to see how pupils' and schools' trajectories change over time, and what interventions can help to actually improve life chances rather than short term test performance which may well not be sustained at either the individual or the school level.

Likewise, a strict adherence to the school as the unit of research is becoming increasingly problematic as education changes. More flexible arrangements, which in due course may in some cases no longer include schools as we now know them, are emerging in many countries and contexts. Examples include Federations where a students' education takes place in a variety of schools, or arrangements where education in part takes place online. The growth of home schooling is another too often overlooked factor (Muijs, 2006). This does not mean that effectiveness research becomes any less important. The basic principle, finding out what works and what does not in reaching desired outcomes remains every bit as important. However, we need to look at educational effectiveness in a broad sense rather than narrowly focussing on schools, with an open mind as to what configurations of educational experiences may be best suited for education in the coming century, and in particular as to how these new configurations affect equity. A concern here is that where individual learning and online learning are promoted they may draw more strongly than more established forms of learning on social, cultural, and indeed financial capital.

This need to look at the community basis of equity and effectiveness forces us to reconsider our methodology as well. The most common statistical model used in the field, multilevel modelling, for all its many strengths reinforces a dichotomisation of school, classroom, and pupil factors, by partitioning the variance between these different levels. This has led us to think too strongly in terms of variables at these levels, and not strongly enough about interactions and correlations between school, community, pupil, and classroom, which may be highlighted more clearly by using other methods such as structural equation modelling. Similarly, the separate evolution of school improvement and reform through qualitative studies of the school as an organisation can also often lose sight of broader contexts and communities, and needs to develop more cross-disciplinary approaches.

Overall, then, it is clear that effectiveness and the fight against the crippling impact of poverty in education are not unproblematic partners, but need to be partners nevertheless. It is hard to see how genuinely equitable outcomes are to be achieved without stringently researching the effectiveness of the approaches adopted. This offers a greater opportunity to move beyond the pattern of intervention, followed by self-report suggesting enthusiasm and impact, followed several years later by the confirmation that in fact nothing has really changed and the educational outcomes and life chances of the majority of disadvantaged youngsters in the area remain unaffected. This situation is unacceptable. However, if effectiveness research is genuinely to inform moves towards greater equity, researchers in the field will need to adapt. They will need to go beyond the school and look towards effectiveness in terms of community and environment. Researchers will also need to be clear about what is meant by equity, poverty, and effectiveness and how they are operationalising this in their studies. This is by no means an impossible task, but it is one that researchers need to engage with as a matter of urgency. A more multidisciplinary approach is needed that moves us beyond school effectiveness and towards concepts of educational effectiveness more generally, that can then be brought to bear in dialogue with researchers working on equity issues to provide the push that is needed to turn the applied field of education into one that genuinely impacts on practice.

7 High Hopes in a Changing World
Social Disadvantage, Educational Expectations, and Occupational Attainment in Three British Cohort Studies

Ingrid Schoon

INTRODUCTION

In the era of growing knowledge economies, increasing numbers of young people aspire to participate in further education beyond the compulsory schooling age and are postponing the step into full-time employment in favour of lengthened education. It has been argued that motivation for maximising school achievement results from beliefs that more education improves chances for attaining better jobs, higher wages, and social status. In this chapter the premise that extended education leads to success or improved social mobility will be assessed, comparing transition experiences of young people growing up in relatively disadvantaged families and those from more privileged backgrounds. The study provides a contribution to the discussion of education and poverty by assessing the functionalist value of educational expectations in times of social change. Educational expectations expressed by young people can be considered as a functional explanation for understanding the link between poverty and education, as it has been argued that the supposed benefits associated with raised expectations often do not materialise in the case of individuals from poorer backgrounds (Raffo et al., 2007). Furthermore, the choices and desires expressed by young people, which are supposed to be linked to adult socio-economic attainments, are themselves already constrained by structural forces and socio-economic family resources (Schoon & Parsons, 2002).

Reviewing evidence from previous studies, this paper adopts an integrative life course perspective by comparing transition experiences in three British age cohort studies born in 1958, 1970, and in 1989/90 respectively, and discussing the role of multiple interlinked influences shaping development over the life course. Changes in educational expectations as well as in long-term outcomes, such as education participation and occupational attainment, are assessed in their relation to socio-economic family background, gender, and the wider socio-historical context. The findings presented here contribute to a better understanding of how experiences occurring on the macro level affect individual functioning on the micro level and how they are mediated via experiences in the family environment, i.e., the meso level. Although the study is based on data collected in the UK and England, the findings will have relevance in other Western countries, given the persistence of social inequalities in the developed world (OECD, 2008b).

Despite generally raised ambitions in the more contemporary cohorts, the evidence suggests persisting gender and social inequalities in young people's expectations and attainment. Young people from relatively disadvantaged backgrounds have generally lower expectations than their more privileged peers, even after controlling for academic ability, although the gap appears to be narrowing for participants in the most contemporary cohort. Linking teenage expectations to long-term outcomes and social status in the early thirties, the findings suggest that those with high expectations are achieving higher social status than their less ambitious peers, yet in both the 1958 and the 1970 cohort academically able children with high expectations from poor families are not achieving to the same level as their more privileged peers. Findings are discussed in terms of contextualized capabilities, differentiating between functional capabilities and actual life chances and opportunities that underlie variations in transition strategies, their antecedents, and outcomes.

THE DATA SOURCES

The findings reported here are based on three British age cohort studies: the 1958 National Child Development Study (NCDS), the 1970 British Cohort Study (BCS70), and the Longitudinal Study of Young People in England (LSYPE) born in 1989/90. NCDS and BCS70 both comprise data collected from large nationally representative samples of over 16,000 individuals born in single weeks in 1958 and 1970 who have been followed from birth to adulthood, using personal interviews and self-completion questionnaires (for more details see http://www.cls.ioe.ac.uk). Data for cohort members in NCDS were collected at birth and at ages 7, 11, 16, 23, 33, 42, 46, and 50 years. For BCS70 data collection sweeps have taken place at birth and when the cohort members were aged 5, 10, 16, 26, 30, 34, and 38 years. The sampling strategy for LSYPE was different than that for NCDS and BCS70. LSYPE is a panel study of just over 21,000 young people born between September 2, 1989 and August 31, 1990. Sample members were all young people in year 9 or equivalent in all schools in England in February 2004. Annual face-to-face interviews were conducted with young people and their parents since 2004, and linkage is available to other administrative data, such as those held on the National Pupil Database (for more information see: http://www.esds.ac.uk/longitudinal/access/lsype/l5545.asp).

EDUCATIONAL EXPECTATIONS IN
TIMES OF SOCIAL CHANGE

Educational expectations of young people can be understood as a reflection of their subjective assessment of how far in the education system they anticipate to go. Data on educational expectations of 16-year-olds in the three age cohorts suggest that there has been a general increase in educational expectations (see Table 7.1), and more young people in the later born cohorts want to continue in further education beyond compulsory schooling age. While the majority of young people born in 1958 wanted to leave school at age 16, about three-fifths of young men and women born in 1970 wanted to continue with further education after compulsory school leaving age. This has increased to nearly 86 percent in the Longitudinal Study of Young People born in 1989/90. In interpreting this dramatic increase in expectations, it has to be kept in mind though, that in 1973 the compulsory school leaving age was raised from 15 to 16 years, making the 1958 cohort the first to stay on in education until age 16, while in 2007 proposals have been made to increase compulsory school leaving age first to age 17 and then to 18 years by 2015 in order to increase the UK skill base in a globally competitive market.

The data underline the association between individual expectations and a changing social context. During the second half of the twentieth century education and employment opportunities in most Western countries have changed dramatically, following the introduction of new technologies and the disappearance of manual jobs. Between 1951 and 1991 the United Kingdom witnessed a fundamental transformation of the occupational structure as employment in manual jobs declined dramatically, while employment in clerical occupations has increased, and work in professional and managerial professions has tripled (Gallie, 2000). At the same time there had been an increasing participation of women in the labour market. Furthermore, between 1979 and 1987 the UK experienced the sharpest rise in unemployment since World War II. Compared to the early 1970s, when most of the 1958 cohort completed their compulsory schooling, during the 1980s unemployment rates in almost all developed countries have dramatically risen (Müller & Gangl, 2003; ILO, 2008). Young people have been hit particularly hard by the economic downturn, as unemployment and flexible employment among the young is generally higher than average (O'Higgins, 2004; Blossfeld, Klijzing, Mills, & Kurz, 2005). Following an economic recovery during the beginning of the second Millennium, young people making their way into the labour market now are again facing increasing uncertainty regarding their employment prospects amidst a major credit crunch and economic downturn which started in the autumn of 2008.

It has been argued that in a flourishing economy young people tend to enter the labour market early, to gain early financial independence and to form an adult identity (Furlong & Cartmel, 1997; Bynner, 2001). In recession

Table 7.1   Teenagers' Expectations to Stay in Full-time Education Beyond Age 16 by Family Social Background (in %)

	N	All %	Professional/ Managerial	Skilled RGSC IIIn/IIIm	Semi/ Unskilled
			RGSC I or II		RGSC IV/ V
1958 NCDS	11175	36.6			
Boys	5700	35.9	57.7%	30.3%	17.3%
Girls	5475	37.4	60.8%	30.0%	20.5%
1970 BCS70	5168	61.0			
Boys	2185	58.5	74.0%	50.3%	34.7%
Girls	2983	62.8	78.3%	55.5%	42.4%
1989 LSYPE	10536	85.7			
Boys	5300	79.3	86.6	74.6	66.1
Girls	5236	92.3	95.9	89.8	86.2

Note: Family social background is identified on the basis of mothers' and fathers' occupational status measured by the Registrar General Social Classification (RGSC). It is identified by the current or last held job of the father or the mother, using whichever is the occupation of higher status. Class I and II represent the highest level of prestige or skill (professional or managerial position), and class IV and V the lowest (semi or unskilled jobs). RGCS IIIn and IIIm indicate skilled nonmanual and manual occupations (Leete & Fox, 1977).

economies and times of rapid structural change, however, young people tend to postpone labour market entry and continue in further education (Reitzle, Vondracek, & Silbereisen, 1998). Since the 1980s there has been a continuous rise of young people participating in further education and training, and the average length of schooling continues to increase as a growing number of young people participates in higher education, once the preserve of a privileged minority (Bynner & Parsons, 1997; McVicar & Rice, 2001). Across all industrialised countries young people are now under increasing pressure to continue full-time education beyond the age of 16 years, and to acquire formal qualifications in response to changing labour market opportunities and increasing unemployment (Blossfeld et al., 2005; Bynner, 2006). Most young people born in 1958 who left school in 1974 could expect to obtain employment regardless of their educational credentials, whereas for young people born in 1970 school attainment became a key prerequisite for employment (Bynner & Parsons, 2002; Schoon & Parsons, 2002).

One explanation for the rapid expansion of participation in further education has been the impact of rising youth unemployment, especially following changes in benefit regulations in 1988 which effectively ended payments to unemployed young people below the age of 18 years. The low probability of finding employment made it more attractive for young people to remain in full-time education beyond age 16 (McVicar & Rice, 2001). An alternative explanation refers to changing education policies aiming to modify attitudes to further education and training. The introduction of a national curriculum and a unified system of secondary school qualifications in England during the 1980s, and the introduction of more vocational qualification and foundation courses have been associated with improvements in average attainment levels among those completing compulsory schooling and changing perceptions of further education which is no longer perceived as only an option reserved for an academic elite (Ashford, Gray, & Tranmer, 1993; Gray, Jesson, & Tranmer, 1993). In a move to create a workforce with relevant skills and qualifications to compete in a global economy the UK Government is currently pursuing a programme to widen participation in higher education to 50 percent of 18–30-year-olds by the year 2010. Historically, rates of participation in further education and training following compulsory school leaving age in Great Britain are lagging behind those in other OECD economies, resulting in a workforce with fewer skills and qualifications compared to other developed countries. Enrolment rates for 15–19-year-olds in the UK are currently well below the OECD average (69.7 percent in the UK versus 81.5 percent OECD average) and a comparatively large share of 25–34-year-olds have not completed upper secondary education (OECD, 2008b).

To achieve the target of 'widening participation' in the UK more students from previously under-represented groups, in particular from those from less privileged backgrounds, have to be recruited. The 'Aimhigher' programme (initially established as the Excellence Challenge programme in 2001) has been introduced with the intention to widen participation of young people from underrepresented groups in higher education by raising their aspirations and educational expectations. First evaluations of the programme suggest that there has been an increase in positive attitudes towards higher education among disadvantaged young people (Morris & Golden, 2005; Ireland, Golden, & Morris, 2006). To what extent these attitudes will be translated into education participation still has to be seen.

EDUCATIONAL EXPECTATIONS AND SOCIO-ECONOMIC DISADVANTAGE

Socio-economic family background is associated with educational expectations of young people, as well as their educational and occupational attainment, and it has been shown that the pattern of social inequality has been much the same across most industrialised countries (Shavit & Müller, 1998). It has been argued that the education system reproduces and reinforces class inequalities, especially in higher education which by definition is exclusive and noncompulsory (Bourdieu & Passeron, 1977; Archer, Hutchings, & Ross, 2003; Ball, 2008). Furthermore, socialisation experiences and socio-economic resources available to young people and their parents have been linked to differences in educational expectations and attainment. Young people growing up in more privileged circumstances have more educational opportunities, greater access to financial and material resources, role models, occupational knowledge and informal networks, and support systems (Erikson & Jonsson, 1996; Marshall, Swift, & Roberts, 1997; Schoon & Parsons, 2002).

As can be seen in Table 7.1, there are systematic differences in educational expectations by social background. Young people from relatively disadvantaged backgrounds generally have lower expectations than their more privileged peers, although it appears that the gap in expectations has reduced for the later born LSYPE cohort. Among young people born in 1958 about a fifth from the most disadvantaged background wanted to stay on in school beyond age 16 compared to nearly 60 percent of the most advantaged young people. This has increased to 66.1 percent of boys and 86.2 percent of girls in LSYPE from the most disadvantaged groups stating that they want to stay in school beyond compulsory school age. It has to be kept in mind though, that the question only taps into further, not higher, education. Gender differences were less pronounced regarding plans of young people to do A-levels, and about 65 percent of the most disadvantaged boys and girls (RGSC IV or V) expressed their intention to do A-levels, compared to nearly 90 percent of the most privileged young people (RGSC I and II).

Regarding ethnic differences in educational aspirations, the 1958 and 1970 British cohort data has only limited information available as the studies contain only about 3–4 percent ethnic minority members. In LSYPE about 30 percent of cohort members are from ethnic minority groups. Research on educational aspirations and expectations in LSYPE shows that Indian, Black Caribbean and African, Pakistani, and Bangladeshi pupils all had higher educational expectations than White British pupils (Strand, 2007). Gender differences were minimal for Indian, Pakistani, and Bangladeshi groups, as well as for Black African. Among Black Caribbeans, girls were more ambitious than boys. It is interesting to note that in both the US and the UK Asian students have been found to show higher aspirations for educational and occupational achievement than all other minority groups as well as whites (Kao & Tienda, 1998).

While it is encouraging that the majority of young people aspire to go to university, many might not be able to realise their ambition, especially those from relatively disadvantaged families. Young people are now expected, and they also express their intention, to pursue further and higher education—yet at the same time, state support for them has been gradually reduced. UK tertiary education institutions charge among the highest levels of tuition fees in the EU-19 area, and the share of private sources of funding for higher educational participation is above average (OECD, 2008b). Furthermore the youth labour market has eroded, leaving the major burden of supporting extended education participation to the parents. There are new expectations that parents will accept extended financial responsibility for their children, and support their education participation, even though many of them never had themselves personal experience of further or higher education and training (Jones, 2009).

Table 7.2   Parental Expectations for Their Sons and Daughters to Stay in Full-time Education Beyond Age 16 by Family Social Background (in %)

	N	All %	Professional/ Managerial	Skilled RGSC IIIn/IIIm	Semi/ Unskilled
			RGSC I or II		RGSC IV/ V
1958 NCDS	10338	46.6			
Boys	5310	43.5	67%	36.3%	25.4%
Girls	5028	50.7	75.4%	42.9%	31.3%
1970 BCS70	5708	60.0			
Boys	2743	55.2	74.1%	45%	32.4%
Girls	2965	64.8	80.7%	56.7%	45.9%
1989 LSYPE	11015	81.4			
Boys	5606	74.0	82.0	68.2	62.5
Girls	5409	89.0	92.7	86.4	83.1

Note: Family social background is identified on the basis of mothers and fathers occupational status measured by the Registrar General Social Classification (RGSC). It is identified by the current or last held job of the father or the mother, using whichever is the occupation of higher status. Class I and II represent the highest level of prestige or skill (professional or managerial position), and class IV and V the lowest (semi or unskilled jobs). RGCS IIIn and IIIm indicate skilled non manual and manual occupations (Leete & Fox, 1977).

THE ROLE OF PARENTAL EXPECTATIONS

As can be seen in Table 7.2, parental educational expectations for their children have generally increased, with over four-fifths of parents of LSYPE cohort members supporting further education, compared to about 47 percent of parents of NCDS cohort members born in 1958. There are however persisting differences in expectations by family social background. Parents employed in semi or unskilled occupations are less likely to support further education for their children beyond compulsory schooling compared to parents in professional or managerial occupations, although the gap in parental expectations has decreased for the LSYPE cohort. Expectations regarding further education are generally higher for daughters than for sons, especially among relatively less privileged families. This might suggest persisting templates for male careers in traditional manual occupations, or persisting perceptions of boys being less suited than girls for participation in further or higher education. It is also interesting to note that in the 1958 cohort parental expectations for further education appear to be higher than those of the young people themselves, while in the LSYPE study the young people appear to have higher expectations than their parents.

It has been suggested that the effects of social disadvantage and poverty on educational expectations and attainment of young people is mediated through parental expectations for their children. Parents in a relatively privileged social position, i.e. parents in professional or managerial jobs, generally have higher expectations for their children than less privileged parents (Sewell & Shah, 1968; Schoon, 2006). High status parents are also likely to provide the necessary financial resources and encouragement as well as the knowledge about how to navigate institutional practices in further and higher education (Reay, David, & Ball, 2005). Parental expectations for their children are often taken as markers of cultural influences operating at the family level (Roberts, 1980). On the other hand, it has been argued that one can separate out the effects of 'family culture' from those of poverty, and that a culture that encourages expectations will enable children to flourish, even when living in poverty (Esping-Andersen, 2004). A number of studies have confirmed that parents play an important role in providing support and encouragement to their children, socialising them the best they can (Osborn, 1990; Desforges & Abouchaar, 2003; Scott, 2004; Schoon et al., 2007). There is evidence in LSYPE that among ethnic minority groups parental expectations for their children were particularly high (higher than those of white parents), despite the often limited educational experience and qualifications among that groups (Strand, 2007). High levels of parental expectations are positively related with the child's expectation and achievement, independent from social class factors (Zellmann & Waterman, 1998; Sacker, Schoon, & Bartley, 2002; Schoon & Parsons, 2002). In their consideration of which careers are acceptable, young people orient themselves to social class reference groups, and are influenced by their parent's material resources as well as their expectations for them (Gottfredson, 1981; Schoon & Parsons, 2002; Schoon, Martin, & Ross, 2007).

Young people need the support of their parents if they are to achieve in education and employment. If more young people and parents are to follow the policy agendas for extended education and training, they need evidence that their investment will be worthwhile, which in turn becomes more difficult in a climate of over-credentialism (Jones, in press). Findings on global trends among OECD countries suggest that the earning advantage of completing tertiary education over persons with an upper secondary qualification remains high in the UK, and above the OECD average (OECD, 2008b). Recent research, however, suggests that many young people investing in their education now may struggle to attain the comfortable careers they aspire to, and that the UK might have to settle for a high-skilled and low-waged economy in order to remain competitive in a global market (Brown, 2008). Furthermore, appeals to economic rationality, i.e. expecting individuals to invest in their education with the prospect of future returns, might not be sufficient to increase participation from relatively disadvantaged young people, as they do not take into account the constraints and restrictions regarding resources and opportunities, nor do they consider family practices and underlying belief systems (Jones, in press), or the meaning young people and their parents ascribe to higher education (Reay et al., 2005). Aspirations and expectations of young people for the future, as well as those of their parents, have to be understood and explained in terms of the context in which they arise.

EXPECTATIONS AND ATTAINMENT

Teenage aspirations and expectations in combination with academic attainment are an important predictor of adult social status. There is now continued evidence that teenage aspirations are linked to subsequent educational attainment, career choices, and future earnings (Elder, 1968; Clausen, 1993; Mello, 2008). Comparing the role of teenage expectations in shaping adult outcomes in the 1958 and 1970 cohort, Schoon and colleagues could show that young people with high expectations, including those from less privileged backgrounds, are more likely to participate in further education, and to achieve prestigious occupations and educational credentials than their less ambitious peers (Schoon & Parsons, 2002; Schoon, Martin, & Ross, 2007). However young people from less privileged backgrounds with high ability and motivation do not necessarily achieve to the same level as their more privileged peers (Schoon, 2006). Furthermore, compared to cohort members born in 1958, those born in 1970 or later are encountering that the stakes have been raised against them, as more young people continue with further education, gaining degree-level qualifications. Degree-level qualifications are increasingly becoming a requirement for high status employment (Bynner & Parsons, 2002; Bynner, 2006; Schoon, Martin, & Ross, 2007). A number of studies suggested that the predictive power of educational credentials for occupational attainment has increased over the last decades, yet that the effects of social origin on the final transition patterns have tended to strengthen as well (Blossfeld & Shavit, 1993; Erikson & Jonsson, 1996; Müller, 1996; Blanden & Machin, 2007). There is also evidence of a decline in the partial relationship between education and class destination (Breen & Goldthorpe, 2001), and an indication that the not-so-able individuals from privileged backgrounds have benefited most from the educational expansion (Schoon, McCulloch, Joshi, Wiggins, & Bynner, 2001; Machin, 2003).

There have been heated debates about the role of merit (defined in terms of individual ability and effort) versus social structural factors (such as parental social class) in shaping adult social status attainment. While some studies suggest that the UK has to a large extent become a meritocratic society (Bond & Saunders, 1999; Saunders, 1997, 2002), others disagree (Breen & Goldthorpe, 1999, 2001, 2002; Galindo-Rueda & Vignoles, 2002; Galindo-Rueda & Vignoles, 2005). Using data collected for the 1958 and the 1970 British Birth Cohort, Saunders found that class background only has a small influence on occupational attainment, while individual ability and motivation play by far a greater role (Saunders, 2002). Breen and Goldthorpe (2002), on the other hand, using the same data, found that there is still a substantial effect of social class of origin on own adult social status after controlling for general cognitive ability and academic motivation. Furthermore, they found that qualifications are clearly more important than ability and motivation in mediating class effects of origin on adult outcomes. Differences in findings were attributed to differences in method and approach (Breen & Goldthorpe, 2002).

Other studies, also using the cohort data, suggest that time spent in full-time education is by far the most important determinant of social status attainment, independent of motivation, cognitive ability, and family social status (Schoon, 2008). Participation in further education, in turn, is more strongly influenced by social background than through ability, suggesting persistent inequalities in educational opportunities (Bynner & Joshi, 2002; Schoon, 2008). Young men and women from relatively disadvantaged backgrounds are more likely to leave school early than their more privileged peers, even those with good abilities and high expectations. Early school leaving, in turn, is associated with lower social status in adulthood. There is evidence to suggest that parental income has become a more important determinant of whether a young person continues into higher education or not (Blanden & Machin, 2003; Machin & Vignoles, 2004), although it has also been argued that much of the impact of social inequality on higher education participation occurs at earlier stages of the education system, i.e. well before entry into further education (Galindo-Rueda, Gutierrez, &

Vignoles, 2008). It may be that students may anticipate barriers to their participation in further education and are thus less engaged in schooling.

CONCLUSION: PERSISTING BARRIERS TO PARTICIPATION IN POST-COMPULSORY EDUCATION

The majority of 16-year-olds today expect to continue in further education beyond compulsory schooling. Social class differences in expectations are reducing, and more young people from relatively disadvantaged backgrounds are expecting to make their way into higher education. Girls have generally higher educational expectations than boys, especially girls from disadvantaged backgrounds. Teenage expectations, in turn, are associated with occupational attainment in adulthood, and young people with high expectations are more likely to achieve high status positions than their less ambitious peers. However, young people from relatively disadvantaged backgrounds with high ability and high motivation are not achieving to the same level as their more privileged peers, and are more likely to leave education earlier. Persisting differences in patterns of participation in post-compulsory education and differences in employment opportunities between social groups require an integrated and holistic intervention approach, simultaneously addressing multiple interlinked factors instead of piecemeal and unconnected interventions (Schoon, 2006). What is needed is the removal of multiple barriers on the macro, meso, and micro levels, including: a) dispositional barriers, b) lack of resources available to the young person, and c) institutional barriers (see also Gorard et al., 2006 and Raffo et al., 2007).

Dispositions and Information: Young people have to be engaged in the education system, and be convinced that their efforts will be worthwhile. Ambitions of young people play an essential role in shaping their successful transition to adulthood, and currently measures and programmes are in place aiming to raise the expectation and aspirations of young people. There has also been a considerable change in the UK higher education sector over the last decade, with an increasing number of entrants into higher education, which in turn might have a significant 'role model' effect across successive cohorts, with increasing value being placed on the benefits of education beyond compulsory schooling (Feinstein & Symons, 1999; McVicar & Rice, 2001). As more people go to university, a degree will become a passport to a good job. Moreover, the wage premium for a tertiary degree compared with an upper secondary degree for male workers in the UK was 65 percent in the year 2001—the third highest among 17 OECD countries (Strauss & de la Maisonneuve, 2007). These might be incentives to increase young people's expectations and change their perceptions regarding higher education—although the current situation of high returns for education might change in the future (Brown, 2008). It also has to be considered that raising expectations is not enough to equip young people to navigate unchartered territories. It is also necessary to provide information about the mechanisms about how to realize one's ambitions. In the US, for example, most young people have high educational expectations, but many fail to convert their ambitions into success (Schneider & Stevenson, 1999). Nearly 70 percent of high school students will begin a postsecondary experience, yet only a third of postsecondary students will complete a degree in a seven-year period (NCES, 2007). It is thus vital to provide information about the knowledge and skills necessary to succeed in education—but also about how to obtain a job and the steps for securing stable employment.

Rational choice theories (Breen & Goldthorpe, 1997), which are still dominant in current conceptualization of educational choice, emphasizes rational decision making and do not fully account for the cultural context in which decisions are made, or differences in belief systems. One has, however, to take into consideration that there might be different cultural values and interpretations of social reality, and different definitions of success. While for some young people staying on in higher education is associated with personal development, for others it might the attainment of early financial independence. There is also evidence to suggest that increasingly young people with good academic competences, including those from privileged and less privileged backgrounds, are becoming disengaged from school, and are not motivated to pursue an academic career (Steedman & Stoney, 2004; Schoon, 2008). Not all young people are able or willing to prolong their childhood dependence until their mid or late twenties, and there is need for flexible measures acknowledging differences in pacing and timing of education participation. Some young people with high ability and high expectations are leaving school early in order to make a living, although they might return to education at a later stage in their lives (Schoon, 2006; Schoon, Ross, & Martin, in press). It is thus vital to create opportunities for second or third changes, enabling reentry into education following early school leaving. Moreover there is a need to instill a learning habitus, a motivation for learning that will last for a lifetime, and not just the schooling period. Early school leavers will have to upgrade their skills as new technologies are likely to be incorporated into lower-skilled jobs, making it necessary to provide opportunities to learn new skills throughout one's working life (Moynagh & Worsley, 2005). Thus, education and training systems have to provide opportunities for lifelong learning, whether through formal or informal training programs offered by employers or through education and training institutions in the public or private sector—and they have to increase efforts in engaging young people into a love for learning and discovery.

Resources: The prolonged participation in further education involves both financial and emotional costs. State support for young people has been withdrawn and parents are expected to support their children, who in turn have to accept the prolongation of their dependence. This leads to a "paradox of support" (Jones, in press), as the extended period of dependent youth goes against the role of parents enabling their child's transition to independence, and for young people seeking it. Current policies are based on the assumption that there is a consensus between parents and their children about how best to navigate the transition to independent living. The evidence presented in this paper suggests that this is not necessarily the case. Parents might be less in support of further education than their children and vice versa. It is thus necessary to put support structures into place facilitating the successful renegotiation of family beliefs and practices, especially at a time when young people's relationships with their parents may be at a low point.

Family finances are another stumbling block. Many families will not be able to raise the necessary financial resources to support their children through higher education, and the prospect of student debt has been shown to prevent students from entering university (Davies, Slack, Hughes, Mangan, & Vigurs, 2008). Students from less privileged families are much more likely than their more affluent peers to be working long hours to pay for their studies, travel, accommodation, and course materials. Long working hours, in turn, impact on the time available for study and can undermine the possibility of attaining good grades (Payne, 2003; Reay et al., 2005). Furthermore students from less privileged backgrounds have little knowledge of the grants and bursaries available to them and are in need of advice and guidance about how to navigate the system of higher education.

Institutional barriers: There is a need to rethink the basic institutional structures currently in place to provide and support education and training, and creating bridges from school to work. Recent research evidence suggests that in most EU countries schools are organized in such a way that eagerness for learning is stifled in the course of their schooling career (Evans, 2003; Silberman, 2007), and that most students find school boring and uninspiring (Diepstraten, du Bois-Reymond, & Vinken, 2006). In the British cohorts there is also evidence to suggest increasing levels of school disengagement and lack of school motivation among bright young men and women (Steedman, 2004; Schoon, 2008). Engaging young people in the school context and making the school context relevant to their life planning might be one of the mechanisms to increase the realization of individual potential and to decrease social inequalities. Measures should not only be in place shortly before school leaving, but as early as in primary school, building up young people's competences and their love for learning and discovery.

Furthermore, one has to rethink existing templates regarding the timing and sequencing of education participation. The assumption of a single training period before entry into the labour market will be no longer sufficient, and future workers have to be prepared for continuous learning as well as up- and reskilling throughout their working life. Current policies of withdrawing funding for those pursuing lower or equivalent qualifications are not encouraging this process of reskilling and lifelong learning, and should be reconsidered. Policies should be able to respond adequately to changes in labour market opportunities and should adopt a broader and longer-term view. It is vital to offer a more flexible and permeable structure of education participation, enabling young people to return to education after a problematic or delayed start, and to provide the necessary resources and scaffolding enabling lifelong learning. To build up sustainable support structures and to improve the effectiveness of intervention programmes it is recommended that schools form coalitions with parents, employers, and the wider community building up a support network and facilitating exposure to multiple positive influences from different sources (see also Schoon & Silbereisen, in press).

Another aspect to be considered is persisting gender inequalities in expectation and attainment. Despite the fact that girls are more motivated to achieve and more likely to receive crucial support from their parents, in the long run they are less likely than men to enter the most prestigious occupations (Schoon et al., 2007). Women benefit less than men from a degree in terms of labour market participation and earnings (Purcell, 2002). Although women make up almost half of the labour force, proportionately fewer women than men rise to the top of their professions (Farmer, 1997; Crompton, 2006). There continue to be barriers and obstacles to female career development, as reflected in gender role stereotypes, gender discrimination, and occupational sex segregation (Scott, Dex, Joshi, Purcell, & Elias, 2008). Although women are doing well in building up their academic credentials, there is no guarantee that these convert into economic and social privilege. Social change, gender change, and educational change are interlinked with implications for education and employment opportunities as well as family relations. We have to recognise the continued reproduction of gendered and classed inequalities in education and employment and strive towards more equal opportunities for all, especially when educational attainment and income inequalities are seen to be divorced from meritocratic achievement.

ACKNOWLEDGMENTS

The analysis and writing of this article were supported by grants from the UK Economic and Social Research Council (ESRC): RES-225-25-2001 and RES-594-28-0001. Data from the Cohort Studies were supplied by the ESRC Data Archive. Those who carried out the original collection of the data bear no responsibility for its further analysis and interpretation.

8 Area-Based Initiatives in English Education

What Place for Place and Space?

Ruth Lupton

INTRODUCTION

In this chapter, I discuss a particular type of meso-level educational intervention to address the relationships between poverty and education: the area-based initiative (ABI).

In England, compulsory state education is funded by the central government and delivered mainly by local education authorities. It is an implicit principle of policy, though a poorly implemented one, that delivery should be place-blind—in other words that children should get the same standard of education, no matter where they live. To this end, the government's financial settlement with local authorities, and theirs in turn with schools, has been used redistributively, albeit to different degrees, with extra allowances to take account of area conditions and additional needs. This strategy has had limited success in evening out educational opportunities (Lupton, 2005) and from time to time, central government has also made use of additional ABIs: special programmes offering extra inputs in particular targeted areas to compensate for poverty and disadvantage. While I focus explicitly here on the English experience, it is worth noting that ABIs are not an exclusively English phenomenon, perhaps the closest parallel being the Zones d'Éducation Prioritaires, a long standing ABI in France (Bénabou et al., 2005).

ABIs are an interesting phenomenon in relation to education and poverty. They suggest, at least, an understanding that educational disadvantage and educational outcomes are spatially patterned, and that the central state has a responsibility to correct this. Their use may also indicate a belief that something about the nature of places, as well as or together with poverty, plays a role in structuring educational disadvantage or in shaping the way that educational institutions deal with poverty. ABIs ostensibly suggest that spatial processes are relevant in the link between poverty and education, and that interventions in particular places can mediate that link.

My aim in this chapter is to explore these links between poverty, space and place, education, and policy a little further, in line with the premise of this book that a more explicit awareness of the ways in which we conceptualise poverty and education should provide the basis for more reflexive policy-making. I start by drawing briefly on a growing body of work on spatial theory in education to examine the different ways in which poverty, space, place, and education might be connected. I then look at a range of education ABIs to assess the extent to which these concepts are operationalised in area-based policies in England, as a particular example. Like Green & Letts (2007:5), I start to ask "what would result from according spatial relations and dynamics and more deliberate, focused attention, with space taken seriously as a matter of interest and concern. . . . What happens when space is thought differently, and *other* places are drawn into calculation?"

PLACE AND SPACE, EDUCATION, AND POVERTY

To hold this account together, I need to start where I end, with a contention that within the context of England's centrally-directed, locally-delivered education system, education policy simultaneously (a) draws attention to particular places and the uneven spatial distribution of educational outcomes by income, wealth, and social class; and (b) denies that spatial processes and spatial relations have an active role in educational relationships and the construction of knowledge.

This situation has been made visible by the recent 'spatial turn' in educational theory and research (Gulson & Symes, 2007), which has drawn chiefly on the work of Henri Lefebvre, Doreen Massey, and Edward Soja. Lefebvre's work (1991) has perhaps been the most influential, embedding the understanding that space cannot be thought of as fixed or absolute, but as socially produced: a social construct not a physical entity. Space cannot exist independently of human activity, since its meaning is produced by the social relations of people within and outside it, through the ways that they use it and imagine it. Space also produces particular forms of activity and sets of relations by configuring the identities and understandings of people who occupy it. In this sense, particular places cannot be thought of only in physical and locational terms as a backdrop to human activity. Nor can they only be thought of as containers in which people are gathered and in which they interact. They are actively implicated in and made sense of by human activity and are thus also dynamic and relational.

Massey extends Lefebvre's view of space with the idea that because space is created out of social relations "it is by its very nature full of power and symbolism, a complex web of relations of domination and subordination, of solidarity and co-operation . . . a kind of power-geometry" (1994:265). Multiple and overlapping arrangements of power mean that the identities of places are always "unfixed, contested and multiple" (ibid: 5). Moreover space cannot be separated from time—we should always try to think of space-time. Thus any given place is a particular moment in the interaction of multiple 'nets' of social relations, some contained within the place, others stretching beyond. This more subjective and dynamic idea has been taken up within cultural geography illuminating the discursive construction of places for political purposes. Soja (1996) articulates a trialectic of spatiality in which space can be observable and measurable (firstspace), or understood only through thought (secondspace), or, embracing both of these concepts, a more complex and dynamic 'thirdspace'—a space which is neither entirely material nor entirely subjective. Echoes of this work are found in Gulson's (2007) claim that absolute space can also be discursively produced, as policy-makers use statistics and geographical techniques to position places, ostensibly factually, in particular ways to suit the neoliberal project of urban revitalisation or gentrification (see also Gulson, 2008; Lipman, 2008)

My aim here is not to review this work in toto, but to draw out some implications for understandings of education and poverty. If neither education nor poverty is to be thought of taking place in neutral or abstract space, how do we think about the relationships between them and the ways in which economic, educational, or spatial policy can have an impact?

A first implication is that space must play a part in structuring both the meaning of poverty and the meaning and value of learning. What it means to be poor[1], what constitutes valid and useful knowledge, and how institutions of learning appear to either alleviate or reinforce poverty are all understandings that are constructed in and through space. In many ways these are well-established 'truths.' Paul Willis' seminal book *Learning to Labour* (1977) gives an early account of working class 'lads' building and using subcultural capital to control school space-time through codes of masculinity that were validated by local tradition, and in resistance to the disciplinary power of school. School and the formal curriculum were middle class institutions physically located within, but culturally without, local and historical space. Anoop Nayak (2003) and Gillian Evans (2006) relate more contemporary experiences of young working class men positioning themselves in relation to local expectations of masculinity and school 'success.' Comparing neighbourhoods Anne Green and Richard White (2007) have recently examined the importance both of location (physical space) and 'place attachment' (social space) in establishing actual and potential territorial boundaries for work and further and higher education.

A key feature of many of these studies is the complexity of their accounts. Youth identities and positions towards education and schooling are not shaped by local cultures alone nor by entrenched class positions that exist outside particular spatial contexts. Nor are they the product of global forces of change alone or in isolation, but as Dillabough et al. put it:

> The relational negotiations achieved by youth, along with their associated phenomenologies of meaning, are rendered possible precisely through their daily exposure to complex cultural, spatial and historical

milieus operating at the local, national and local levels. (Dillabough et al., 2007:134)

For young men and women in Dillabough et al.'s study, the local context is a de-industrialised inner urban neighbourhood characterised, as a result of zoning policies, by low-income housing, but adjacent to gentrified central areas. As the central city regenerates, and neoliberal education policies create a market for schooling, inner urban youth become, as the authors put it, 'warehoused' in 'demonised' schools abandoned by more advantaged families. These global and local political and economic forces are internalised as school and neighbourhood become sites for intra-class and racial conflict in young people's attempts to reclaim meaningful symbolic territory. Complex modes of representation occur as girls (in this example) take on working-class resistance to school norms, while also resisting the traditional 'good girl' norms of their local communities, through a paradoxical conformity to established definitions of femininity and heterosexuality. Thus spatial processes at various levels help to structure what it means to be a young woman at school in this context.

This account takes me to the second implication of relative and historicised spatialised accounts of education for understandings of poverty and education: that these interactions of place, poverty, and education are likely to occur simultaneously and at different and overlapping spatial scales. Dillabough et al. demonstrate how the meaning of local neighbourhood is constructed by, and in relation to global economic, political, and cultural realities. Similarly Thomson (2002) talks both about the ways in which different neighbourhoods create particular contexts for different disadvantaged schools, through neighbourhood issues, neighbourhood narratives, and neighbourhood resources, and the ways in which such schools are:

> permeated by national and global events, saturated with flows of information and images, and tangled in complex networks of social relations. The changes for better and worse in neighbourhoods as well as in the far-reaching networks of associations and institutions that are commonly lumped together as 'globalisation' and 'restructuring,' are also *in* the disadvantaged schools as children, parents and teachers, as spatially distributed material and cultural resources and as possibilities for action. (Thomson, 2002:17)

Thus the global is in the local and the neighbourhood is in the school. While the framework for this book identifies relationships between education and poverty at different levels, it seems clear that contemporary accounts of space tend to integrate accounts in which macro, meso, and micro levels are indelibly intertwined and indeed meso levels incorporate multiple inter-related geographies: school, block, neighbourhood, city, and region. In Massey's (1994) terms, we need to recognise "the open and porous" (ibid:5) boundaries of places as well as the myriad interlinkages and interdependencies among them.

A third implication, once space is seen as relative and contingent, is that the importance of a school or neighbourhood might not be defined by its absolute characteristics but by its position relative to others. In her recent book on London, Massey (2007) notes the prevalence of a political discourse that positions the existence of poor neighbourhoods in London as almost coincidental—London has pockets of poverty *despite* its wealth. On the contrary, she argues, London's success and its poverty are "intimately related . . . the combined outcome of the politico-economic strategy of neo-liberalisation" (Massey, 2007:55). London's particular experience of advanced global capitalism—and Massey argues that it *is* particular—creates a new spatial order within the city, and new spatial behaviours, in which the rich try to separate themselves from the poor by the privatisation of space: gated communities, and the increasing withdrawal to private education or health, or to state institutions which are sufficiently colonised by the middle class to create a feeling of security (Thrift, 1996; Butler & Robson, 2001). The spatial distribution of educational resources, which Armstrong (2007) reminds us are presented as a more technical and rational matter in more neutral accounts of space, can also clearly be seen to be a function of political and educational power, reinforced by policies of parental choice in schooling, and the promotion of owner occupation of housing, allowing privileged access to residential space and school catchment areas. Armstrong (ibid) also shows us how educational spaces take on social meanings (the special school as the confirmation of abnormality) and reinforce them (through particular spatialised discourses, curricula, and therapies).

In summary, spatial theorists, and scholars who have applied their work to education, suggest multiple roles for space in the understanding of education-poverty relationships. Space structures the experience of poverty, and of education. The characteristics of particular places are shaped by spatial processes at local, regional, national, and global levels. What people experience in one place can only be understood in relation to what is happening in other places: one place is poor because another is rich; one school 'fails' because another 'succeeds' as global economic forces are translated through the mechanism of marketised education policies, into local 'choice-based' hierarchies of schooling. With this in mind, I now want to turn to policy, and to examine the extent to which different concepts of place, poverty, and education feature in policies which are ostensibly about exactly that.

AREA-BASED EDUCATION INITIATIVES, RATIONALES, AND CRITIQUES

My analysis here focuses on area-based initiatives specific to education, which have been initiated under two Labour governments since the Second

World War. First, the Wilson government of the late 1960s established Educational Priority Areas (EPAs), on the recommendation of the Plowden Committee (Central Advisory Council for Education, 1967). Following a long gap, Tony Blair and Education Secretary David Blunkett resurrected the theme in 1997 with Education Action Zones (EAZs), followed by Excellence in Cities (EiC) and City Challenge. Both in the late 1960s and late 1990s–2000s, these education ABIs formed part of a wider suite of ABIs to tackle growing socio-economic inequality between different areas and neighbourhoods. There is a long-running debate (often now forgotten in policy-making) about how space has been conceptualised in these broader place-based anti-poverty interventions, and about what can be expected of them (Massey, 1994). Here, I keep the focus on education, which is of particular interest because, of all public services, it has a unique combination of being locally-based and inherently social.

The scale and approaches of these initiatives have been somewhat different. In the case of EPAs, the Plowden Committee recommended that poor *places,* where "educational handicaps are reinforced by social handicaps" (Central Advisory Council for Education, 1967:para 153), should be targeted. Its intention was that the scheme should cover the 10 percent most disadvantaged areas. However what actually happened was that 572 primary *schools* were included in a programme to attract and retain good teachers by offering additional salary, and to improve school buildings. Additionally four areas in England and one in Scotland became the subject of a three-year action research programme to test out innovative approaches, including different types of home-school link and community school developments. The whole initiative had a clear objective to improve service delivery, first to equalise the quality of schooling between disadvantaged areas and others and then to make them better so as to compensate for educational disadvantages at home.

New Labour's first education ABI, EAZs, also worked with a geography defined by schools, although in this case groups of adjacent schools were targeted (usually two or three secondary schools and associated primaries), working in partnership with local authorities, business, and the community. Funds were allocated after a bidding process—in other words it was not necessarily the most needy areas that were supported, but those where there was both evidence of need and good plans to tackle it. Again there was a clear service delivery objective: to "modernise education in areas of social deprivation," so that "schools in our most difficult areas should provide as good an education as schools elsewhere" and "that young people in deprived areas get a fair educational start in life." Actual initiatives varied from zone to zone but included (as with EPAs) attempts to bolster the teaching workforce through flexible contracts and incentives and the employment of subject specialists working across several schools, as well as curriculum enrichment, additional in-class support, and mentoring. EAZs had priority access to other government funds for early excellence centres, family literacy schemes, and out-of-hours learning. Some also experimented with curriculum change, including more work-based learning.

New Labour's second programme was a broader one—Excellence in Cities. Launched in 1999, this aimed at all secondary schools in six large urban areas: Inner London, Birmingham, Manchester/Salford, Liverpool/Knowsley, Leeds/Bradford, and Sheffield/Rotherham. This time the programme had much greater central direction. There were two main strands. One focused on individuals, providing learning mentors, learning support units, out-of-school hours learning activities, and a new programme to identify and provide opportunities for 'gifted and talented' young people. The second strand focused on school improvement, again with recruitment and retention incentives, as well as a range of initiatives such as twinning poor schools with better-performing ones and tasking the National College for School Leadership with prioritising recruitment and training for city school leaders.

The third New Labour programme began as the 'London Challenge' in 2003 and was rolled out to two further areas, Greater Manchester and the Black Country, in 2008, as 'City Challenge.' This programme operates at a bigger geographical scale again, that of a group of local authorities or a whole city. The specific content of each programme is worked out at the local level. Some of the London Challenge features, supporting school improvement, were similar to those in Excellence in Cities: leadership training, consultant headteachers, and support to leadership teams in struggling schools (more positively named 'Keys to Success' schools). However, the programme also contained elements to address explicitly the links between the school system, learning, and the particular urban context. For example, London Challenge worked on the provision of 'key worker' housing for teachers, and instituted a 'London student pledge' to give all the capital's school students access to its unique cultural resources.

I am conscious of the danger of homogenising these policies, which were conceived in different political and intellectual climates, by trying to derive broad messages. Nevertheless, there are similarities in concept, and I want to try to bring these out, while trying not to lose sight of some of the important differences.

The first striking feature of these policies as a set is that they failed to make it clear whether it was really places that they were targeting, individuals, or schools (Smith, 1987; Smith et al., 2007). One could argue that these are genuinely only area-*based* initiatives; that is they take place in particular areas, rather than being motivated by any concern with spatial processes per se. Much ABI activity has been about schools. EPAs focussed on school buildings and staffing, EAZs on staffing, and EiC and City Challenge on staffing, management, and leadership. In fact, Plewis (1998) in an early critique of EAZs, argued that they were not really about deprivation but a top-up initiative to complement New Labour's broader attack on under-performing schools. Other aspects of ABIs have been about targeting individuals, particularly in the case of Excellence in Cities. That individuals were the target of EPAs was sufficiently evident at the time for the programme to come under fire for falling for the 'ecological fallacy'—that the characteristics of individuals can be determined from the characteristics of their neighbourhoods. Barnes and Lucas (1975) demonstrated that EPAs were an inefficient way of targeting help to individuals, since far more 'at risk' children lived outside EPA areas than within them, a criticism that has been frequently levied at ABIs ever since (Townsend, 1979; Tunstall & Lupton, 2003).

I have argued elsewhere (Lupton, 2003) that locating additional interventions in particular locations can be justified on grounds of efficiency, administrative practicality, or territorial justice (Pinch, 1979) and does not necessarily require an understanding of space as constructed by or producing social relations. Both in the 1960s and 1990s, these initiatives followed growing political awareness of widening spatial inequalities, driven by new research evidence. The Plowden Report cites the Milner Holland report on housing conditions as demonstrating how spatial disparities had widened in a time of unprecedented economic growth. New Labour's early ABIs appeared to be a direct response to a growing body of research on the spatial ordering of poverty (Goodman & Webb, 1994; Green, 1996; Noble & Smith, 1996; Social Exclusion Unit, 1998). In the latter case the government's analysis clearly pointed to a failure of public services in the poorest areas. This suggests that the ABIs were a response to uneven distribution of state resources, with space primarily conceived as a surface across which educational resources were unevenly distributed. Indeed the Plowden Report specifically calls for "a new distribution of educational resources" (Central Advisory Council for Education, 1967:para 146).

However, neither the ABI policy texts, nor the debates surrounding them, suggest that these initiatives should only be seen as redistributive of resources across space, with no active notion of the role of space in education. George Smith, who worked with A.H. Halsey, a member of the Plowden Committee, points out that Barnes and Lucas' criticism of the EPAs as a targeting mechanism missed the point—the Committee intended the EPAs to be an area initiative. Calls to action in policy texts from both periods are prefaced by descriptions of the educational problems of low-income neighbourhoods:

> . . . incessant traffic noise in narrow streets; parked vehicles hemming in the pavement; rubbish dumps on waste land nearby; . . . inadequate storage space with consequent restriction on teaching materials and therefore methods; . . . no privacy for parents waiting to see the head . . . (Central Advisory Council for Education, 1967:para 133)
>
> A whole variety of economic and social factors impinge on the work of schools in the most disadvantaged areas of our country. Unemployment, poverty of both expectation and income, poor health and a low

quality environment all make a difference. Poor housing, overcrowding and high family mobility conspire against success . . . Schools which take a large part of their population from deprived inner city areas struggle to meet all their pupils' needs. (DfEE, 1999:4)

However, *how* area contributes to educational disadvantage is weakly articulated in all of these policy texts and in the practical interventions which followed. The policy documents seem to acknowledge that learning is a social, historically, and spatially situated activity: where you live helps to shape what and how you learn. Yet, as indicated above, the initiatives themselves have focused not on areas, but on schools. Indeed EiC documents seem to clearly delineate the space outside the school (where problems are located) from the space within it (where problems can be overcome by the actions of school leaders and teachers). The document refers to external "barriers" that needed to be "broken down" (11) with a "can do" approach to overcome "a culture of fatalism" (5). Neighbourhood factors "may go some way towards explaining why standards in inner cities are low, they do not justify or excuse them" (DfEE, 1999: 11). The problem seems to be the need to bring the activities of some schools up to the level of others, as if these activities were abstract, uniform, and manageable, not configured by local social relations. It simultaneously promotes the importance of context while offering a largely decontextualised analysis and response (see also Thrupp & Willmott, 2003). As Plewis (1998:106) argued, the rationale for EAZs

appears to lie in the belief . . . that there are substantial differences between school performance. Moreover these differences are assumed to be attributable to the schools themselves, and to the teachers within them, rather than to the achievements and background of their pupils on intake.

Nor is there much evidence of a concept of overlapping spatial scales (always a problem for the practical administration of policy), or the interaction of different spaces and institutions within the 'meso' level. One could argue that ABIs have to some extent encouraged a bounded approach, making sharp distinctions between spaces that are included in the funding programme and those that are not, and focusing on specific institutions rather on than the wider political, economic, or institutional arrangements that impact upon them. A good example is provided by Tim Brighouse (2007), leader of the London Challenge programme. Brighouse describes how New Labour ministers made it clear from the outset that the issue of school admissions was strictly "off limits" (Brighouse, 2007:77), despite his own observation that

the way these secondary admissions operated in London . . . resembled . . . a hierarchy of private clubs ranging from the Carlton Club at one extreme and the East Cheam Working Men's club on the other. It

> seemed to me that in practice such an arrangement tempted heads to seek to make their schools attractive to ambitious middle class parents . . . conversely making the task of those schools at the wrong end of the league table more difficult. (loc cit)

The one exception to this focus on specific places, not the relations between them, is the acknowledgement, in the initiatives on recruitment and housing, that regional or urban housing economies and housing markets influence the localised pattern of educational resource distribution. In the main, however, these connections do not seem to have been made.

One reason for this bounded approach is that the ABI rationale *starts* at the level of the neighbourhood. New Labour's recent ABIs have been informed not only by new research on spatial inequality but on qualitative and quantitative accounts of 'neighbourhood effects' in areas of 'concentrated poverty.' Child development research from the US was particularly influential, indicating as it did the importance of neighbourhood context and triggering wider interest among quantitative social scientists in the question of whether neighbourhood has any measurable effect on life outcomes (Brooks-Gunn et al., 1993). Because of the difficulties of capturing the contingent and relative nature of neighbourhood in quantitative models, this has tended to shift the focus of debate on the effects of a concentration of low income individuals within the neighbourhood, and to their characteristics and interactions (Lupton, 2003). How these disparities between areas occurred in the first place is not the central focus. Little meaningful connection is made between meso and macro levels of explanation. In a telling analysis, Power and Gewirtz (2001) found that bids for Education Action Zones were often prefaced by accounts of the changing structure of employment opportunities more generally, but moved to more specific and localised accounts of problems of families as the reason for continued disadvantage. Because ABIs start with the problem of local spatial inequity, they tend to "embody an inadequate theorisation of the processes through which such disadvantage is generated" (Power et al., 2005:111).

The dangers of this situation are evident. In trying to draw attention to the needs for additional inputs, advocates of ABIs can easily fall into a form of social pathologising that discursively re-positions areas and their residents and thus risks compounding inequalities. Where concepts of area are articulated in policy texts, they tend to be expressed in relation to the education deficits of people within the area. Places tend to be seen either as containers of people with certain detrimental characteristics, or as sites for the negative effect of family or peer relations, but without any sense that these relations are influenced by spatial characteristics nor the product of wider power geometries. Thus for the Plowden Committee (Central Advisory Council for Education, 1967:para 134), poor areas contained a high proportion of children and families who have "learned only not to learn" with individual families not being willing or able to support their children's education, and perhaps, a neighbourhood effect, as children are socialised into a culture of low aspiration or negatively influenced by their peers. The EiC policy document suggests that:

> Children may not receive the parental guidance and support that they need. Poverty may sap their motivation or capacity to study. Lessons may be disrupted by a disaffected minority. Those who have special talent may be wary of showing it. The attitudes of the peer group can be very influential. (DfEE, 1999:11)

One result of this focus on individual and family deficits is that many ABI interventions have been designed to focus on how such deficits can be overcome, by better teaching, the provision of mentors, and so on. Curriculum and pedagogy, the areas in which schools might be expected to adopt tailored approaches to address the situated nature of learning, have been largely absent from these programmes.

CONCLUSION

What I have tried to do in this chapter is to explore a particular set of policy interventions on poverty and education through the lens of spatial theory. ABIs are not, of course, the only targeted policies in education. A great deal of spatial targeting goes on through mainstream funding, and there are other places, not least the day to day activities of schools, where space might appear in education policy or practice. Because of their explicit focus on place, ABIs make an interesting starting point for this enquiry. In this chapter, I have drawn on the English experience of ABIs as an empirical example.

I have argued that while particular places, as well as inequalities between places, have been to the fore in these policies, space as a concept in the education-poverty relationship is largely absent. When it is present, space tends to be seen as a surface over which educational resources are distributed—a container of people, or a site for social relations. I have tried to contrast, or at least juxtapose this, with accounts from educational research that use space in more social, historical, relative, contingent, and dynamic ways to examine the educational experiences of economically disadvantaged young people. Such accounts seem to demonstrate that both the meaning of poverty and the meaning of education are constructed in space, and that relations between places, as well as the characteristics of particular places, are instrumental in creating educational success for some groups of young people and educational failure for others.

What conclusions can be drawn from this example? The overriding one is that for place-based policy to be effective in addressing place-based disadvantage, it needs to come closer (a spatial metaphor) to young people's spatial meaning-making, as well as to recognise the porosity of schools and neighbourhoods and the wider power geometries that make them what they are as living and learning spaces. In other words, ABIs need to be founded on a closer understanding of the ways in which place shapes young peoples' understandings of what it means to be a person and what constitutes valid learning, and of how this matches (or not) the formal learning experiences of school. It follows that interventions in the everyday business of schools, their curriculum and pedagogies, must be included, not just add-on initiatives. It also follows that ABIs cannot just concentrate on 'fixing' specific areas: they must engage with the dynamic relations between schools and between neighbourhoods that drive some to the bottom of the hierarchy and others to the top.

However this broader view of ABIs may be a pipe dream, because it takes them beyond fixing problems with certain schools in certain neighbourhoods, and into the business of challenging who and what education is for. Except in revolutionary times, which we are not, government policy always takes a functionalist approach to education. In relation to place, this is likely to result, as Power et al. (2005) observe, in a conceptualisation of the problems of poor areas as being 'residual'—remaining pockets of disadvantage in an otherwise functioning system—and the purpose of education as being to re-fit residents in these areas for their place in the economy. For the Plowden Committee, the problem was that:

> In ... deprived areas ... too many children leave school as soon as they are allowed to with no desire to carry their education further and without the knowledge to fit them for a job more intellectually demanding than their father's or grandfather's. Yet they face a future in which they must expect during their working life to have to change jobs, to learn new skills, to adapt themselves to new economic conditions and to form new human relationships. They will suffer, and so will the economy. (Central Advisory Council for Education, 1967:para 133)

The problem with ABIs is thus not just a failure to integrate micro, meso, and macro level accounts but the nature of the connection that is being made. There is plenty of room for functionalist interventions which accord space an active role: for example changes to school admissions or different organisational designs and resources for schools in poor areas. However, from a socially critical perspective, education has to do more than this. It has to problematise and challenge the local spatial realities that globalisation produces. Space becomes implicated in what needs to be learnt, for what reason, and how. Whether education policy of the kind I have described will venture onto that territory seems a doubtful prospect at this space-time moment.

ACKNOWLEDGMENTS

I am grateful to the editors and to Alex Fenton and Felicity Armstrong for their perceptive and constructive comments on an earlier version of this chapter.

NOTES

1. Since the theme of this book is education and poverty, I use these terms. However, much of the material I draw on is concerned with the experience of being working class, not being poor per se. The relationship between poverty and class in education demands fuller exploration than can be devoted here.

9 A Critical Pedagogy of Global Place

Regeneration in and as Action

Pat Thomson

INTRODUCTION

Official writings about poverty and schooling often begin by stating the correlation of educational 'results' with socioeconomic statistics. Some discussions go further and translate the statistical snapshot into text, presenting descriptions of the kinds of 'contexts' in which schools find themselves and the impact on children and families. Some social scientists, seeking explanation for the connections between poverty and schooling, argue that 'context' cannot be simply dealt with as if it is a container within which schooling happens. Rather, poverty is embedded in the fabric of everyday lives, as well as in the historical practices of schooling which work to (re) produce not only the inequitable distribution of education but also the social relations we understand as class, race and ethnicity, and gender. There is also a body of work which addresses how to change the unjust practices of schooling for those designated by policy as 'the poor,' 'deprived,' 'the disadvantaged,' 'challenging,' and 'vulnerable.' The framework offered by the editors of this book suggests that this chapter may be positioned as a socially critical approach.

The chapter directly addresses the macro, meso, and micro levels of analysis as outlined by Raffo and colleagues (2007), not as a set of Russian dolls which sit inside each other (Swyngedouw, 1997), but as social relations and trajectories that operate at various scales and are tangled together in specific ways in specific locations. It relies particularly on a notion of 'place' which is "constructed out of a particular constellation of social relations, meeting and weaving together at a particular locus" (Massey, 1991:29). It mobilises a notion of 'glocalisation' (Robertson, 1992)—the ways in which globalised phenomena are enacted in local places—and 'vernacularisation' (Appadurai, 1996; 2001)—the ways in which local actors, institutions, narratives, truths, and traditions diffract global-national trajectories to make then distinctive and specific. The chapter is written out of a belief that the task of social scientists in these times must be not only to make comprehensible the ways in which various scales of globalised activities work together, but also to address their inequitable and toxic consequences.

I argue in this chapter that the social and economic situation-situatedness of schools serving poor communities creates obligations and opportunities to contribute to local regeneration. This is accomplished in part through curriculum and critical pedagogies that encourage students to understand their social and material place in the world and how it came to be the way that it is. Making this case necessarily involves some discussion of the purposes of schooling, critical pedagogy, and the official processes of regeneration. I begin at the outset with a brief discussion of globalisation and local 'place.'

NEIGHBOURHOODS MADE POOR: THE 'CONTEXT' FOR 'DISADVANTAGED SCHOOLS'

One obvious consequence of 'globalisation' in advanced Western nation states has been the sudden impoverishment of large numbers of people. A combination of factors—including the increasing use of high-tech machines, the escalating costs of farming, the movement of manufacturing industries to countries where labour is cheaper, and the collapse of resource-based industries such as coal mining—has left formerly working-class families, villages, and towns struggling to 'regenerate.' Historically low levels of wage substitute payments (generally known as welfare or benefits) compels many, who formerly had the security of continued employment, to grapple with their social identities and their present and future material prospects. Some do find new work, while others manage to piece together poorly paid contractual work and/or sponsored retraining with no guarantee of a job at the end. Some do not, and they join the group of 'long-term unemployed.' At the same time, mass media, influxes of new citizens, and new opportunities for travel have opened up these local and regional 'places' made newly poor to different ways of being, living, and speaking.

THE HOMOGENISATION OF CONTEXT

The postcolonial social scientist Arjun Appadurai (1996) argues that this poverty within affluence is a direct result of the loss of power and legitimacy of the nation-state. Now subservient to transnational forces, nation-states face the task of not only managing but also 'nationalising' global flows of: people (ethnoscapes); information and images (mediascapes); high speed technologies (technoscapes); investments and other financial transactions (financescapes); and policies, ideas, and ways of thinking and narrativising the world (ideoscapes) (27–37). Thus, he reasons, as a result, all nation-states must find new ways to imagine, represent, and re-make themselves. This is accomplished, he suggests, at the cost of local 'places.' The nation-state generates its 'self' and its legitimate sphere of action (its rationale and context) through appropriating and renarrativising the contexts of selected local places. Thus globalised scapes work both directly and indirectly through, and are mediated, nationally and locally; there are both national and local interpretations, variations, rewritings, and rejections of globalising trends. In this situation, many local places must struggle to maintain their distinctiveness or become largely 'context dependent' on the nation state.

Appadurai suggests that while globalisation is manifest and vernacularised in local places, each of these is becoming more and more alike. Local differences are now often contested, and sometimes obliterated. Corporate chains move into the high street and small local shops close down—one local high street begins to look like another. Small farms are taken over by larger agribusinesses. In many locations, distinctive local customs and dialects are maintained by aging populations, as young people leave to find work and take up the lifestyles constructed in mass consumerism and converged multimedia technologies. The heterogeneity of local places declines, but not disappears. Some local places, able to position themselves as tourist destinations and/or sites of national interest, flourish and maintain some of their uniqueness. Others survive as a result of conscious political action.

The trend to the reduction of local difference can also be seen in policy responses to the 'new' poverty. In response to de-industrialisation, the impoverishment of formerly productive neighbourhoods and regions, government sponsors regeneration schemes. These often combine upgrades of housing stock together with the attraction of a more economically mixed population (Cameron, 2003). Local community participation in regeneration is often highly constrained (Driver & Martell, 1997; Hughes & Mooney, 1998) and poorly supported (Duncan & Thomas, 2000), and young people are generally left out of consultations altogether (Matthews, 2003; Morrow, 2005). The construction of tracts of new houses often has a further homogenising effects on local places: networks of local associations are fractured, travel patterns to work are lengthened, and social amenities are standardised (Gough, Eisenschitz, & McCulloch, 2006). The visible signs of industrial production are literally redesigned: warehouses become apartments, mines are filled in and become parks, mills become designer outlets. The histories of working class lives are consigned to regional and national museums, many at a distance from the local places in which their substance originated. A national media and policy narrative of the cultural causes of poverty foregrounds families with low aspirations, parenting skills, literacy, and any kind of valued know-how, rather than the economic shifts and public policy decision which construct contemporary poverty (Fairclough, 2000; Meinhof & Richardson, 1994).

The homogenising trend that Appadurai discusses is also manifest in education. Like the local high street, local schools have also become very much alike in particular and important ways.

THE HOMOGENISATION OF SCHOOLING

Most nations, rich and poor, have shifted the way they approach attaining a more equitable distribution of educational 'goods' and have adopted some form of national benchmarking for student achievement via the use of indicators, tests, and/or standards which are applied to all schools and all children. Redressing inequity is seen to be achieved through removing differences—creating a degree of uniformity via a national curriculum, standards for school leadership and management, and reducing the variation in initial teacher education and teaching 'techniques." What counts as important sameness is what is measured on tests, exams, and audits: differences can exists outside this 'core'. Equity equates to the *distribution of outcome* of children from various social and population groups across this 'core,' framed in policy as a general commitment to both 'closing the gap' and 'raising the bottom' of achievement. This is the 'distributive' notion of curriculum.

In England, as in parts of the US, the most important outputs are measures of student performance. Key elements of the system that produces these outputs are isolated. Explicit standards and standardisations—of teaching, of school leadership, or school planning, evaluation, and performance management—have been developed and these are then combined with testing and target setting. Various pressures and points of measurement are instituted to ensure that the system works with as few failures as possible. Inspection processes and a firm approach to removing 'failures'—schools that do not literally measure up—are key means of diagnosing the 'weak performers.' The persistent nexus between poverty, levels of family education, and poor schooling outcomes are sheeted home to patchy teaching and to some inadequate, ineffective schools. Important questions of knowledge are neglected and pedagogy is translated as technique or method.

The kinds of pedagogies and curriculum espoused in the distributive and standardised approach to curriculum are predominantly transmission based. Even if the method is constructivist and 'creative,' the actual core of knowledge to be produced and tested is predetermined. The complex pedagogies necessary to support the acquisition and production of new and synthesised knowledge, critical questioning and evaluation, and the making of sophisticated meaning (see for example Newmann & Associates, 1996; Hayes, Mills, Christie, & Lingard, 2005) give way to audit requirements to set, grade, profile, and level: the resulting numbers are taken to equate to equitable learning. These are the pedagogies of poverty: they produce and reproduce existing hierarchies and differences rather than offer redress

(Haberman, 1991; Gillborn & Youdell, 2000; Apple & Buras, 2006). With such pedagogies and curriculum in operation, even if the mass level of education rises over time, the relative positioning of children and young people from wealthy and poor neighbourhoods remains much the same (Power et al., 2003).

In England, the problems created by homogenisation of schooling have been partially recognised by policymakers. Too much uniformity is seen as inhibiting all children achieving the mandated outcomes, and as preventing parents from making choices between schools. But stripping away local distinctiveness is dealt with as a procedural question—schools are exhorted to vary the ways in which they teach the national curriculum, to adopt creative approaches and to offer specialisations. But despite the increasing diversity of governance approaches, new curriculum options via new diplomas and the adoption of creative approaches to pedagogies the basic 'core' architecture of the standardised distributive curriculum remains.

A distributive approach to equity backgrounds the possibility that the very things which make the differences 'between' schools may also be implicated in making it difficult for individual schools to make *significant* improvements 'inside' school—even when they appear on simplistic measures to be 'like' each other. It sidelines the ways in which wider socioeconomic and cultural relations are embedded and enacted in schools, and consigns broader questions of redistribution to questions of welfare and counselling. It renders invisible the relational practices of schooling through which the very same things that make some students successful make many fail.

The current 'core plus creativity' approach to equity must be differentiated from that which espouses a public curriculum, an entitlement to common knowledge which:

- addresses common and collective issues, challenges, problems, achievements, histories, and cultural and scientific artefacts and processes
- critically evaluates difference—the different knowledges, narratives, heritages and teleologies of citizens, and
- produces knowledge which has explanatory and applied power that works in the interests of the public and works to further social justice.

This kind of equitable curriculum would put the question of difference and (in)equity at its heart. But this would mean shifting the national discourse of deficient, impoverished families with low aspirations and also making space in the curriculum for new pedagogies and family, local and community knowledges.

However, the current shift to loosening standardisation create opportunities for schools to engage in such renewed glocally-focused learnings. Because we all now live in a 'place' in which the global is not just 'out there' it is part of the character of 'in here' (Massey & Jess, 1995:226), the social and material production of place—and how much it is actually distinctively 'local'—requires the development of particular local circuits of relations and meaning, and the ongoing production and maintenance of metaphorical and sometimes literal boundaries (Pratt & Hanson, 1994). This is no certainty, but the possibility of constructing local meanings and local identities with and against national/global trends provides a 'space' for schools and teachers.

TOWARDS A CRITICAL PEDAGOGY OF GLOBAL PLACE

The chapter concludes by suggesting an approach to education for children and young people in new poor, de-industrialised places. The argument returns to the rationales made for particular school curriculum.

The Purposes of Schooling

Schools have multiple purposes and at different times policy makers put different emphases on them. At present, many nation-states anxious about financial matters emphasise the vocational—schools must educate all young people to take their place in an emerging knowledge economy. However reputation is also important, so performance on international tests of literacy and numeracy become significant for national claims about capacity in changed times. Within nation states, social pressures created by increasingly heterogeneous populations and the fallout from unemployment create pressures for schools to attend to citizenship, social order issues and to the health and welfare of the most vulnerable. In England, as in many other countries, this trip-partite kind of 'human capital' agenda dominates schooling at the expense of other important orientations (Henry, Lingard, Rizvi, & Taylor, 2001).

Robin Alexander (2008), one of the most trenchant critics of the English national curriculum, and Chair of the current, independent Primary Review (see http://www.theprimaryreview.org.uk), has consistently argued that England has opted for an impoverished view of a curriculum fit for a globalised age.

> There are two broad senses in which the architects of a national education system can think internationally. They can view the world as an essentially competitive arena of trade and influence and use education in order to maximise national advantage—economic, scientific, technological, ideological, military—over other countries. Alternatively, they can apply a more genuinely international outlook (international rather than contra-national) acknowledging that global interdependence carries moral obligations from which no country is immune; and that education can serve to unite rather than divide.

In the first category I place the kind of internationalism adopted by many of the world's advanced economies in response to globalisation . . . In such a climate the school curriculum concentrates on those subjects that are deemed to offer the greatest economic leverage, and students' attainments are not merely assessed, as they should be, but they are also translated into local, national, and international league tables of educational performance...This, I think, is also the force of all the talk in Anglophone countries of 'world class schools,' a 'world class curriculum,' 'world class skills' . . . if 'world class' here means anything (and it is now such a cliché that it may not) it means 'world beating.' (Alexander, 2008:123–24.)

Alexander goes on to argue that in a world where there are massive disparities in health and security, where the wealth of one country is dependent on the exploitation of people in others, and where ecological catastrophe knows no borders, policy makers need to look beyond their own national interests. What is required, he suggests, is an international curriculum which places such concerns at its head/heart. As he puts it

. . . if we contemplate the increasing fragility, inequality and instability of our world as a whole, and believe that these are not only unacceptable in themselves but are also, as a matter of fact, contrary to the national interest . . . then education will need to espouse very different priorities: moral no less than economic, holistic rather than fragmented, and collective rather than individualistic. (Alexander, 2008:127)

Alexander proposes that, in curriculum development, competing future scenarios need to be laid out for debate and discussion.

Schools might focus more strongly on their obligation to help young people to understand themselves as social beings who are able to act constructively, alone and together, in the public interest. Moving in this kind of direction requires a radical reconceptualisation of curriculum, and the generation of pedagogies that promote enquiry, debate, and knowledge production. Rather than delivery technologies suited only for the regurgitation of predetermined 'core' outputs and teaching techniques, schooling policy might instead promote the kinds of mutual endeavour that are necessary to tackle the broad global agenda. Rather than simply addressing the perceived needs of a global market they need to work on the kinds of ecological, moral, cultural, political, and economic issues that affect us all. This means more than understanding; it also means that young people ought also to know something about the ways in which such challenges can be collectively tackled.

Such an approach would redefine equity to include capabilities which allow all young people to leave school not only with knowledge and skills that allow them to make their way in the world, but also with hope and optimism, and with a sense of efficacy and agency. They would have acquired an ethical basis for living that allowed them to make wise use of the choices that they have (see Walker & Unterhalter, 2007), including the recognition of individual and social differences, and the importance of their 'place.'

Putting Differences Into Place(s)—(g)localism in Curriculum and Pedagogy

Gruenewald and Smith (2008) argue for a new (g)localism, which supports diverse 'acts of resistance' to globalisation and allows young people to stay in their home communities rather than leave them. This is an education, they say, which helps to materially, socially, and semiotically regenerate local communities (Sobel, 2004). Gruenewald and Smith (2008) call this a place-based curriculum. They suggest that this requires

> . . . a community-based effort to reconnect the process of education, enculturation, and human development to the well-being of community life. Place-based or place-conscious education introduces children and youth to the skills and dispositions needed to regenerate and sustain communities. It achieves this by drawing on local phenomena as the source of at least a share of children's learning experiences, helping them to understand the processes that underlie the health of natural and social systems essential to human welfare. (Gruenewald and Smith 2008:xvi)

A place-based curriculum forges new social bonds: it offers opportunities for schools to explicitly and critically foster identity work through events and tasks that allow students to encounter embedded social practices and agents that they would normally avoid. In doing so, it also avoids a narrow, insular, and potentially inequitable localism (Gruenewald, 2003); by connecting students with different peoples in their local neighbourhoods, teachers and students are imbricated in the trajectories of everyday lives which are not simply local, but are also 'stretched-out' relations, practices, and narratives (Massey, 1994; Childress, 2000; Davies, 2000). Place-based projects provide opportunities for situated identity work, as students engage with difference(s) and are assisted to produce texts in which they describe/inscribe themselves, those with whom they are in dialogue, and their mutual place in the world (Smith, 2002). Students are taught to critically question the relationship of people and nature and the histories of oppression of indigenous peoples (Bowers, 2005).

A place-based curriculum thus draws on different kinds of knowledges from that which is abstracted and distantiated in national curriculum. Foregrounding difference, and particularity, it sees community and place as both a relationship to be strengthened, and a text to be read (Sorenson, 2008).

While place-based education in the US is largely associated with rural communities, it has strong resonances with similar movements which work with economically impoverished communities.

Gonzales, Moll, and colleagues (Gonzales & Moll, 2002; Gonzales, Moll, & Amanti, 2005) have developed the notion of 'funds of knowledge' embedded in the labour, domestic, family, and community practices of itinerant agricultural border-crossing Mexican American families. These are routinely ignored and/or denigrated through schooling and the 'core' distributive curriculum. Gonzales, Moll, and colleagues support interventions, co-constructed with teachers who conduct respectful ethnographic studies of their students' homes, designed to make their experiences, understandings, and ways of making meaning a ' bridge' to the learnings that count as school success. The affirmation of home and community practices also builds positive social identities for students and sensitises their teachers to the myriad ways in which the mandated curriculum excludes some and privileges others. Central to this work is a rejection of the deficit views of a 'culture of poverty' in which communities and families are seen to have no worthwhile contribution to make to education.

A further related notion is that of the 'virtual school bags' (Thomson, 2002) of knowledges, experiences, and dispositions which all children bring to school. However, school only draws on the contents of some children's school bags, those whose resources match those required in the game of education. Children who already 'know' and can 'do' school are thus advantaged in the classroom right from the outset while those children who do not already have the required ways of speaking, acting, and knowing start at a disadvantage. Through the selective practices of pedagogy and schooling more generally, the gap grows between children whose lives are marred by poverty, and those who are born fortunate by virtue of their class, heritage, and gender. It is necessary but insufficient to open all virtual school bags in order to help students learn what is mandated—starting them where they are at as progressive education had/has it. Nor is it enough to have affirmative action so that those with subjugated knowledges can study them in addition to the mainstream. Rather the object is *also* to change what counts as important knowledge so that the dominant forms of knowledge are de-centered and more inclusive models of knowing—and being—are taught to all.

These three ideas—virtual school bags, funds of knowledge, and place-based education share important underpinning principles of alternative ways to 'do social justice.' However it is place-based curriculum which directly addresses the material relationships between everyday lives, localities, and school curriculum. Examples of place-based curriculum which teach important knowledge that reconnects students to place, identity, and their 'glocal community' while addressing the kinds of important international issues nominated by Alexander include:

- investigations into 'local' (Barton & Hamilton, 1998) and 'city' (Gregory & Williams, 2000) literacy practices invisible to the formal education system. Through collaborative work between adult educators and students, these can be used productively to assist 'officially illiterate' adults to acquire the formal spoken and written English practices that matter.
- recording of oral histories of apparently culturally backward and impoverished communities, e.g. the Foxfire project (Wigginton, 1986) which began in the Appalachian mountains now has partner projects all over the United States.
- engagement in critical community issues e.g. the closing of a mine (Romano & Glascock, 2002), the urban regeneration of a council housing estate (Comber, Thomson, & Wells, 2001), river pollution and regeneration (Comber, Nixon, & Reid, 2007), and the impact of degrading environments on working-class lives, neighbourhoods (Thomson, 2006) and schools (Thomson, McQuade, & Rochford, 2005).
- development of 'vernacular' language and literacy programmes in high poverty urban (Searle, 1998) and rural areas (Brooke, 2003)
- exploration of young people's material lifeworlds (Bloustien, 2003) and their digital engagements (Carrington & Robinson, 2009) (see also www.youngpeoplesgeographies.co.uk).

These kinds of projects are marked by active and experiential pedagogies which require the critical interrogation of official sources of information, the integration of multiple kinds of knowledge, collaboration and team-working, communication with a range of different kinds of people and organisations, and the reconnection of people and place. Through such approaches, children and young people in neighbourhoods made poor are positioned, together with their teachers, as active agents, able not simply to learn and obtain a necessary credential, but at the same time to also literally make a difference to their local communities and places.

IN SUM: REGENERATING LOCAL CURRICULUM

I have argued that in globalising times, neighbourhoods made poor are stripped of their local meanings, as well as their capacity to regenerate themselves. I have suggested that schools serving neighbourhoods made poor can make a positive contribution to keeping local difference live and countering negative representations by adopting a place-based approach to curriculum and pedagogies (see also Thomson & Hall, 2008). This is not at the expense of mandated learning, nor does it separate out the local from the large global issues that are of pressing concern.

Such curriculum and pedagogies must aspire to connect schools and communities, pair intellectual knowledge with life-world applications, assess the full impact of learning inside and outside the classroom and strengthen youth voice and youth-adult partnerships (adapted from the principles for assessment developed by the Rural Trust on http://www.ruraltrust.org). Developing such an approach is not easy, but schools and teachers might begin by opening a conversation with students and their families around some simple questions:

- Who am I? What does it mean to be me now—a particular class, gender, race, and ethnicity? How did I get to be like this?
- Where am I? Why is my/our world as it is? What will be my/our place in it? In whose interests does it work? Why is it like this? How can I change it if I/we think this is unfair or unjust? How can we live together?

Understood glocally, these questions may well provide the basis for an interdisciplinary curriculum which focuses on the individual/social and the local/national/global. It supports thinking about a curriculum which goes to the heart of local/global regeneration, pedagogies which support the learning of all children and young people, and runs counter to a system which continues to demonise children living in poverty. This is a curriculum approach which resists homogenisation, celebrates difference, and refuses the equation of poverty plus education equals failure.

10 Leaving School and Moving On
Poverty, Urban Youth, and Learning Identities

Meg Maguire

INTRODUCTION

In this chapter the intention is to examine the perspectives of some young people who live, study, and work in London. The aim is to explore the ways in which the experiences of poverty influence the learning identities used to navigate through the end of compulsory schooling and beyond. These identities are less recognised in policy attempts to overcome exclusion and lack of formal educational success. First, the chapter will briefly review what is involved in understanding the 'idea' of poverty and will explore the way in which it is currently being deployed in contemporary policy. The chapter will then consider the specificities of the urban setting in terms of social inequalities, education provision, and the labour market. The macro-level theme of poverty and the specificities of the meso-level urban setting, will provide a contextualisation through which to examine the micro-level life experiences and identities of some young people in order to provide scope to disturb some of the barriers to educational achievement arising out of poverty.

POVERTY: A MULTI-DIMENSIONAL MATTER

> The hurt of being poor comes from lacking what others enjoy as everyday necessities. (Toynbee & Walker, 2008:75).

Raffo, et al. (2007) argue that the relationship between poverty and education is frequently 'explained' in three ways—through a discourse that 'blames' or holds the individual as responsible; as deriving from the social context, such as 'poor' neighbourhoods or less than 'adequate' parenting; as emanating from social structures such as globalisation. They claim that functionalist approaches like these, frequently result in piecemeal policy interventions that assume that education is part of the solution, not perhaps part of the problem, and that individuals can be supported in overcoming difficulties. In contrast, they identify a socially-critical approach that suggests that:

> the failure of education to produce benefits for people living in poverty is not simply a glitch in an otherwise benevolent system, but is a result of the inequalities built into society and the education system alike. (Raffo, et al. 2007:5).

What the authors do is to present research from both functional and socially critical knowledge claims, and so they recognise that there is 'no single explanation' (xii) for why young people from poorer backgrounds do badly in terms of educational attainment. Thus, they call for an approach that takes account of this complexity and that intervenes at a micro, meso, and macro levels. They add that much education policy operates at the meso level and that in consequence, less attention is paid to structural features such as class. Simultaneously, attempts to engage with the so-called 'disadvantaged' and recognise their capabilities to be part of the solution through empowerment and community action is rarely undertaken, other than in a tokenistic manner.

Drawing on the theoretical framework of Raffo et al. (2007), I want to take a socially critical approach towards understanding poverty to ask what role poverty plays in society. I then want to explore in a limited way, the micro relationships between poverty and education, specifically concentrating on young people who are caught up in transitions beyond compulsory schooling.

THE MANAGEMENT OF POLICY—
A FUNCTIONALIST APPROACH?

Seymour (2008) believes that in the UK, "there is a widespread refusal to accept that so many people really are poor"; what Toynbee and Walker (2008:77) refer to as "social myopia." Although the reality of poverty has long been recognised by researchers, policy advisors, and anti-poverty activists, there is paradoxically, an alternative perspective that sidelines any in-depth engagement with poverty in the UK. One way in which this distancing is managed is through discourses of 'exclusion.' Another way is through the mass media's approach of portraying and 'explaining' poverty that sometimes contributes to a 'dangerous perpetuation of urban myths, such as the belief in some parts of the press . . . that people on benefits are well-off' (Pritchard, 2008:34). Indeed, there are even 'those who see poverty as useful, even desirable, for a society' (Spicker, 2007:99). This last point, about the function of poverty in society, has been analysed by Novak (1988) and Jones and Novak (1999).

Their basic premise is that poverty and inequality:

condemn vast numbers to intolerable conditions which are neither acceptable or necessary in a world which has the capacity to provide every single person with the means of a decent human existence. That this potential is not realised is not some inevitable mystery of nature, but rather a consequence of human nature. It need not be. (Jones & Novak, 1999:xi).

In his analysis of the way in which poverty has been tackled by the state over time, Novak (1988) illustrates how poverty is 'useful' to the state. It serves to valorise the need for self-sufficiency and hard work. Poverty becomes a spectre through which to instill fear and a need for conformity to authority. Even in a period where state welfare has been developed to a point where a wider range of social benefits have been made available, there has always been a moral agenda of support for the deserving poor and a short sharp shock for the less deserving citizen:

> By offering reasonable work at low wages we may secure the power of being very strict with the loafer and the confirmed pauper. (Joseph Chamberlain in a letter to Beatrice Webb (1886), cited in Jones & Novak, 1999:122)
>
> Welfare claimants had to believe that they faced a life without benefit entitlement in order to concentrate their minds and ensure they made sufficient efforts to leave welfare of their own volition ... to change and challenge aspects of a dependency culture, tough and frightening messages were believed to be necessary. (House of Commons Select Committee on Social Security, 1998:5 cited in Jones & Novak, 1999:194)

While state policies cannot be read off in a straightforward manner, and contradictions and moments of progressivism do occur, nevertheless, a number of powerful discursive formations have been sedimented down that are periodically revisited and reworked to generate a set of common-sense assumptions about poverty—that it is the 'fault' of the poor who choose not to work or who have 'low aspirations'; that the state should not assume financial responsibility for feckless and irresponsible people who can become a 'drain' on society; that the best way forward is for the state to ensure that the 'poor' are schooled and then shoehorned into work. The emotional and social consequences of these discourses are to stigmatise the poor and those caught up in the trap of poverty. Hills et al. (2002) have categorised policy responses to poverty as either active—that is, they encourage an escape from poverty or they are redistributive and support and protect those who are in extreme poverty. While these approaches inform the contemporary policy matrix (Alcock, 2006), Jones and Novak (1999:196) claim that New Labour is "obsessed by work" as an escape from poverty and that, in policy terms, "work is the best form of welfare". In consequence, at the meso level, New Labour have stressed the role of education and training in preparing young people for the needs of the labour market and education has "become narrowed to an economic function" (Tomlinson, 2005:216).

URBAN SCHOOLS AND EDUCATION POLICY

Turning now to the second contextualising theme—the specificities of the urban setting in terms of social inequalities, education provision, and the labour market. The relationship between poverty and education has been explored by many researchers in the UK and elsewhere (Jackson & Marsden, 1962; Kozol, 1991; Smith & Nobel, 1995; Mortimore & Whitty, 1997; Raffo et al., 2007). While there are studies that indicate that some families are able to develop forms of resilience that can protect against some of the injuries of poverty (Luthar & Zelazo, 2003), in high-risk settings, this is less easy to achieve. Cauce et al. (2003) illustrate the ways in which concentrations of poverty in urban US settings can work against the construction of resilience. For example, "the dangers they (urban neighbourhoods) pose and the sheer grind of daily living under the onslaught of poverty-related stress strongly militate against the development of parenting skills and other protective factors" (Raffo et al., 2007:28).

In terms of poverty indices, New Labour have 'mapped' out where the poorest housing estates are located, which are the poorest wards, and where the poorest families live on "an income 60 per cent below the median income level—an official definition of poverty" (Tomlinson, 2005:211). Most of those who are categorised as living in poverty are located in urban areas. One consequence of this has been the production of a raft of policies that have targeted urban areas and urban schools; for example, 'Excellence in Cities' and 'Education Action Zones.' However, constructing the urban in spatial terms rather than more broadly in terms of socio-economic processes may have displaced more critical and structural concerns of inequality and poverty. By concentrating on the place where poverty is being reproduced, rather than on the processes than contribute towards its production, targeted policies that are often short-term and underfunded, and thus more likely to fail, may simply lead to the further demonisation of those categorised as 'the poor' and the places where they live as places to avoid (Hanley, 2007). For example, Sure Start was set up in locations with high levels of deprivation and targeted families and their children at an early stage in their lives. As reported in Raffo et al., (2007:54) this intervention has been more successful for families in 'moderately disadvantaged' circumstances rather than those who are 'severely disadvantaged.' My point is that the production and circulation of negative discourses of the urban ignore and displace alternative perspectives (see Reay & Lucey, 2000). Put more strongly, urban space and place may do positive work as a support and as a source of community, as we shall see.

YOUNG PEOPLE'S URBAN TRANSITIONS

Drawing on two large-scale ethnographic studies of young people's urban transitions beyond compulsory schooling in London[1], the chapter will now consider the ways in which the experiences of poverty influence the learning identities that young people construct in order to navigate through their schooling experiences (Wexler, 1992). The original sample included one hundred and ten students drawn from one socially diverse inner London comprehensive school and two local pupil referral units (PRUs) selected in order to include young people who had already been excluded from mainstream schooling. From this, a sub-sample of fifty-nine students was constructed to take account of factors of race/ethnicity, class, and gender as well as routes from school to work and educational attainment. (For further details of the sample and the studies, see Ball et al., 2000). These fifty-nine young people were interviewed six times over the period of the studies.

> We wanted to avoid either portraying the young people as simply victims of their circumstances or pathologizing—othering—them. Our interpretations suggest a sense of struggle or creativity within the sample—sometimes 'making out', sometimes just 'getting by (McCrone, 1994) but not just giving in. (Ball et al., 2000:18).

However, somewhat contradictorily, we did identify a group of fifteen students who we categorised as socially, educationally, and economically excluded. Twelve of these fifteen young people were in direct and regular contact with a variety of state welfare professionals. There were others in the sample who could be described as coming from 'poorer backgrounds' although their home situations were relatively more stable.

Interviews from some of the students whom we had identified as being 'excluded' as well as interviews with others who had talked about the impact of a reduced family income have been recoded in terms of issues related to education and poverty—eighteen interview transcripts in all. From this, four key themes emerged. These were: learner identities, poverty and opportunity, the role of place, and work. It is only possible to draw on a fraction of this re-analysed data set and so, in what follows, data has been selected that illustrates these themes and that typifies the responses we received.

LEARNER IDENTITIES IN AN URBAN SCHOOL

Overall, from the full set of interview data what emerged was that those young people who were doing well had been recognised as 'good students' by their teachers and, even if they were not always successful in all of their subjects, they were able to construct a learner identity that was based on the expectation of doing well in the future (Wexler, 1992). What also became evident early on in the research was that many of the young people who were not achieving well had constructed identities that were "severely damaged by their experiences in compulsory education" (Ball et al., 2000:8). What was also apparent was the degree to which social class was tied up with the construction of these learning identities. Those students who were most ambivalent about themselves as learners were most likely to come from the least privileged backgrounds—although there were some anomalies.

Those young people who saw themselves as 'not good at school' and less likely to do well in their exams, tended to speak of school as 'boring' and 'stressful';

> Finding the work hard isn't enjoyable either, is it? And teachers that don't help you, don't make it enjoyable, do it? So, I don't get much out of this school, do I? (Debra).

They didn't enjoy classes that involved a great deal of writing, and they found it hard to sustain the capacity to listen for long periods of time. Repetitive work was boring and practicing for tests was not seen as useful by these students. In challenging urban schools, competing demands such as the need to do well in public examinations and league tables set against the demands of students in complex circumstances can sometimes prove impossible for the staff to resolve (Allen and Ainley, 2007). One way that young people managed in situations where they were likely to be devalued was to stop attending school, or at least those subjects where they felt less positively valued. Another strategy was to dismiss the relevance of schooling and concentrate on aspects of their identities that were emotionally affirming—their families and their friends outside school.

> Most people, you know, they have been in school so long they just want to get on with their lives now. They've had enough of sitting in classrooms . . . no more writing and learning things that nobody cares about. (Wayne).

Others suggested that teachers had mistreated them and reported being "fed up being told what to do by shouting teachers." One young woman claimed that teachers were not as caring as she thought they needed to be:

> I would feel better somewhere else, because so many things have happened here, not to me really, but there will be teachers there and they will see everything and they will swear blind that they didn't see nothing . . . but they don't want to get involved. (Kayleigh).

Another young person talked about having teachers that couldn't control the class; her challenging behaviour led to her exclusion from two mainstream schools. The extent to which she had constructed an identity as an 'unmanageable' student in preference to a 'failing' student is open to question:

> My math's teacher she just can't take me, every lesson she has to send me out. My city and guilds teacher. He just knows me man. 'Out' he says and out I go shouting to show him he can't have no last word. (Delisha).

What is less open to debate is the ways in which many of the more vulnerable students (from low income backgrounds) had quietly 'chosen' not to do school, not to participate in the educational competition, and to look elsewhere for personal validation and self-esteem. Some of these students had been almost set up to fail by a system that couldn't accommodate to their demands, their interests, and their educational needs. In a setting where all that is on offer is a damaged learner identity, it is counterintuitive to accept this version of oneself. Other more acceptable versions of self have to be constructed.

In terms of theorising these narratives of exclusion from and rejection of mainstream schooling in relation to the concerns of this chapter, what is evident is that meso education policies such as the standards agenda and its regimes of tests (Tomlinson, 2005) may exacerbate the difficulties that some young people face in compulsory education. There is a range of factors implicated in 'lack of achievement' and one of these may be the construction of damaging learner identities. It might be argued that I am falling back to individualistic or even pathologised 'explanations' of the sorts of learner identities that are constructed by students from poorer backgrounds. What I would argue is that the phenomenon of the damaged learner identity, has a relationship with structural conditions such as socio-economic status. In part, this identity is constructed out of and against experiences of poverty that limit opportunities on a micro level.

POVERTY AND OPPORTUNITY

None of the students ever described themselves as poor—instead they talked about 'not being rich'. Many of the students who were experiencing difficulties in school and beyond, talked of the ways in which financial problems limited their choices and dogged their lives on a daily level.

> Better off people with cash to spare easily forget how households on tight weekly budgets are plunged into debt by extras such as rising energy bills, school uniforms or new shoes. (Toynbee & Walker, 2008:77).

Of those students who talked about their family and financial situations (and many only did so in the fourth or fifth interview), there was recognition of the futility of being able to get around certain limitations. Replacing expensive items of clothing like coats and winter boots, paying travel costs, not being able to buy the latest mobile phones, teacher assumptions that everyone had access to the web at home—some limits could not be overcome. These limits restricted choice and access. "Where people do not have the things they need, they have to manage as best they can. People have to adapt; they have to compromise" (Spicker 207:98)

> Coz back then (when at school) it was quite a hard time, coz my Mum and Dad were both ill and money wasn't coming in. (John)

Some of the young people were dealing with complex situations where their parents were long-term ill. Sometimes parents were institutionalised because of mental health issues and some of the young people were 'looked after' or fostered for short periods. Some were the main carers for their families in situations of limited finances (Roker, 1998)

> I feel that I know what to do, if you understand, because I have brought them up from babies (her siblings) taken them to school, fed them, you know. My mother didn't really . . . (Gabrielle)
>
> My Mum didn't want me to leave sixth form but well they both needed taking care of. My Mum couldn't move, she couldn't get up the stairs or anything. My sisters didn't want me to leave college but I had to look after my Mum and Dad. (Kayeigh)

One meso-level UK policy with a redistributive approach is the means tested Educational Maintenance Allowance (EMA) that can allocate up to £40 a week to a person aged between 16–19 who comes from a lower income family and who is in full-time post-compulsory education and training. While this allowance has provided some support for young people who may otherwise have dropped out of post-compulsory provision (Middleton et al., 2005)—in terms of young people who could have benefitted from additional financial support at a much younger age, EMA might be seen to be almost too little too late.

At the same time, these young people were surrounded by a culture that privileges consumption. In a climate where not to have the 'right' trainers, or the 'right' clothes can expose you to being bullied and stigmatised, the desire to 'fit in' and have what others seem to have can be overpowering. A 'good' learning identity will not necessarily compensate for not having the right clothes or the 'desirable' commodities of dominant forms of youth identity.

> My Mum isn't a rich person, my Dad isn't a rich person and (mugging) that was the only way I could see of getting what I wanted. From a very

young age, I was buying myself things, or stealing myself things. Tucking it away somewhere. (Delisha)

Larger grants at a much earlier point and more financial support with travel costs to support post-compulsory participation in education and training could start to make a difference. However, policy interventions like EMA, that in practice are highly regulated, may merely reflect a meso-level intervention where one size fits all. In terms of a more critical and structural response to structural disadvantage (such as experienced in Kayleigh's home, for example), EMA's might simply not be enough.

THE ROLE OF PLACE

The young people in our study all lived in London. It might be suggested that living in a diverse, global city (rather than in an overspill estate on the edge of a city or in a rural locale) presents additional opportunities for employment, diversity, and excitement. It is likely that in large metropolitan settings, there will be an extended service sector, offering increased employment possibilities. However, while poverty, family disruptions, and the "immediacy of crisis and sickness" (Beck, 1992:89) are not unique to urban settings, it is in inner cities where the highest concentrations of the marginalised and dispossessed are to be found. Poverty, the "new hybrids between unemployment and employment" (Beck, 1992:89), family stress and disruption, and acute forms of social and economic polarisation distort and disrupt the lives and worlds of many young people in transition from youth to young adulthood. Yet, this may be disguised to a degree by the culture of individualism and the superficial homogeneity of youth patterns of consumerism.

What was strikingly evident right from the start of our in-depth interviews with all the young people in our study was the way in which social class was implicated in the 'use' of space. As Harvey (1973:82) has pointed out, those who are able to 'transcend space . . . command it as a resource. Those who lack such a skill are likely to be trapped by space." Kayleigh had to select a school, and later a post-compulsory college, in easy and cheap reach of where she lived. She wanted to go elsewhere but couldn't afford the travel costs. Some of the more affluent young people in the study talked of going to more prestigious post-compulsory institutions that involved costly travel. Those young people in our sample who had been brought up to calculate the cost of everything, in circumstances where making ends meet was a feature of every aspect of daily life, recognised their spatial limitations (Abrams, 2001). 'Staying local,' even if this meant second-best, was the only viable option.

For some of our sample, 'staying local' was positively constructed as staying in and around the immediate area where they lived with their families. For example, Fiona had dropped out of school as she "was bored going all the way to school. I didn't like it." Her social life revolved around friends and neighbours on the estate and she spent her evenings watching television with her family. What was also evident, for Fiona and for other young people in our sample in similar circumstances, was that these local networks were emotionally sustaining and were seen as potential levers into (local) work. Many of the young people in our study visited local shops and small businesses and sometimes picked up short-term, cash-in-hand work. Fiona frequently did paid baby-sitting and (unofficial) child-minding for young mothers on her estate.

For some of our cohort, generally the less well-qualified and less advantaged young people, "self-selected opportunities for work (were) set within these horizons and the immediate, local job market" (Ball et al., 2000:107). These localised identities could sustain a positive sense of self, particularly in offsetting any negative learner identities, simultaneously 'going and being local' could contribute to exclusion from better-paid work and other extended opportunities. Socially critical approaches that recognise these ambivalences may produce a more complex understanding of the role of place (in education, access, and opportunity) and displace some of the more essentialising discourses of 'poor neighbourhoods' that feature in many urban policy texts.

WORK

In the UK, the New Labour governments have pursued a policy of support and 'encouragement' for the unemployed to get into work as well as an attempt to raise wages so that work is seen as an attractive alternative to state benefits (Alcock, 2006). Young people have been 'encouraged' to stay in education and training through the removal of unemployment benefits. The UK government has developed its 'New Deal' whereby training and job placements are provided (for some benefit claimants) alongside the support of a personal advisor (Millar, 2000).

Youth unemployment has been a recurring problem in the UK—and there is not enough space in this chapter to do justice to its complexities and the range of schemes that have addressed this issue (Bash & Green, 1995; Dickens et al., 2003). In the main, many of the schemes that target young people lead to low-paid work as it is the less well-qualified school-leavers, particularly those who have not participated in post-compulsory education and training, who will tend to be unemployed. The intention is that these young people will take advantage of additional training and 'work their way up' the jobs ladder. This may well be the case for some young people, but for others, working in a low paid setting where they are 'going nowhere' may not match the work identities that they have constructed for themselves or that they see portrayed in the mass media as 'desirable.'

In our study, those young people in our sample who were less well-off financially and who were less pro-school had very firm ideas about work and pay. They were often scathing about poor money and jobs that didn't interest them as well as the prospect of lives stretching out before them where they did jobs that held no meaning for them in terms of the persons they wanted to be, their adult identities:

> What I wanna do? Photography. She say (my Mum) you dreaming, girl, you want to do something proper but I don't want no garbage job . . . don't want no £4.50 an hour, what that buy? . . . I don't really want to work nine to five for twenty years. You start to get that hunch back as well (hunched over a desk). (Delisha)

Kayleigh was focused on 'getting on' and 'getting out.' Money was extremely important to her. She had a determined outlook on life: "my mum and dad brought me up, do not depend upon anyone else, because most of the time you have to do things for yourself. Basically that is it." Although she was doing well academically, she had left college to take care of her parents. She had then decided that work was the best alternative for her to pursue—her learning identity had not transferred over to her working self.

> Even if I went to college, I don't even think after I left college there was a guarantee that I'd get a job anyway. Now I am working I pay my Mum and Dad rent and stuff, monthly. Everything's fine. I'm coping . . . It's like life is getting into order now, I know where I am going, I've got something to build on. I've got an aim. If I didn't get it (the job) I don't know where I'd be now. Probably be in bad trouble somewhere. (Kayleigh)

In our study, and in terms of the cohort of young people who had left school with few qualifications and a dislike of formal education and training, Kayleigh was something of an exception. Many of the young men, in similar economic circumstances to Kayleigh, found it hard to get organised and it was difficult for some of them to settle down and complete the courses that they had signed up for. The learning identities that had been constructed for them and by them at school now made it harder for them to move into work.

> I started with carpentry and did that for a couple of months... I preferred it when it was just the practical, the theory I just couldn't be bothered with that, do you know what I mean? . . . It was boring. I like the practical making things . . . (I) moved onto a painting and decorating course. That was all right. I liked the painting that was easy. I could do that but it had theory as well and I didn't like that, do you know what I mean? They were making me, pushing me to do it. (Darren)

Work and work-based schemes are sometimes seen as a universal panacea to the debilitating effects of poverty. However, research has demonstrated that while being in work has an impact, it does not necessarily move people out of poverty—particularly if the work is low paid (Kemp et al., 2004). There are also factors such as poor health or caring responsibilities within the family that are not amenable to being relieved by work. "Work cannot be a route out of poverty for all those who experience it" (Alcock, 2006:258). Functionalist perspectives that refuse to see the structural dimensions of (un)employment (and the way in which this is not always related to the possession of qualifications—but to the economic and labour market situation), and policies that fail to recognise that not all occupations are fulfilling or enriching, may simply not be dealing with the world as it is experienced by the sorts of young people whose narratives are contained in this chapter.

CONCLUSION

This chapter has briefly explored some of the ways in which various dimensions of poverty are implicated in the learning identities that young people make up to navigate through their schooling experiences and beyond. In consequence, the chapter suggests that the connections between education and poverty are not easily susceptible to policy attempts that largely focus on the meso level and that take a broadly functionalist approach (Raffo et al., 2007) In this final section, I want to briefly discuss some points that are raised by this work in terms of taking a more critically inflected approach towards relations between education and poverty.

First, I have tried to demonstrate the way in which a small number of young people from poorer backgrounds experience their schooling as a non-affirming, irrelevant, and emotionally damaging micro-level set of experiences. Policy currently calls on these young people to make 'choices' and 'decisions' in education (a functionalist and de-contextualised approach) that calls up discourses of individualisation and sidelines more complex discussions about power and participation. These young people are expected to be able to take responsibility for themselves and demonstrate a capacity to be resourceful, reflexive, and enterprising subjects (Rose, 1999); behaviours that may be compromised by structural and material factors and the construction of 'damaged learning identities.' Second, I have attempted to take seriously the need to address the connections between poverty and education in a multi-dimensional way that extends the meso-level of understanding. In this chapter, I have argued that a neighbourhood can simultaneously be a constraint and a powerful agent of support. Thus, to talk of disadvantaged neighbourhoods may be in some ways to miss the point. Third, I have tried to construct an articulation between work as a policy 'good' and work as it is more frequently understood by those who have limited choice and opportunities, and thus, illustrate the limits of a functionalist approach towards education policy and post-compulsory transitions as well as the need for a socially critical approach.

Through drawing on the experiences of a small group of young people, this chapter has illustrated some aspects of the interplay between education and poverty—not that these young people would describe their situation in this way. What their words reveal is the ways in which they negotiate the conditions in which their lives are situated as well as the complexities of tensions between education, poverty, and relative powerlessness. Making up a 'damaged learner identity' in school because of sets of lacks and losses produced by economic disadvantage will potentially have consequences for post-compulsory transitions to training and to work. What all this suggests is the 'need for extensive and complex policy interventions if the established relationship between poverty and poor educational outcomes is to be disturbed' (Raffo et al., 2007: xii).

NOTES

1. The Economic and Social Research Council (ESRC) funded the two studies upon which this chapter draws: 'Education Markets in the Post-16 Sector of One Urban Locale (L123251006) and 'Choice, Pathways and Transitions: 16–19 Education, Training and (Un)employment in One Urban Locale' (R00023726).

11 The Challenges of Poverty and Urban Education in Canada

Lessons from Two School Boards

Jane Gaskell and Ben Levin

INTRODUCTION

In Canada, the challenges of poverty in urban areas have grown over the past quarter century. Increasing wealth has been concentrated in the hands of those who were already relatively well off (Green & Kesselman, 2006; OECD, 2008b). The diversity of Canada's urban population has increased, and the resulting linguistic, cultural, and religious differences interact with economic inequality, leaving aboriginal, radicalised, and new immigrant populations at a greater disadvantage than they have ever been. In this context, the challenges of educating all children with the intellectual and social capacities they need to participate as citizens and make a living are of critical importance.

There is an increasing literature on the successes and mostly failures of urban areas in addressing the educational implications of poverty (Anyon, 1997; Henig et al., 1999; Stone et al., 2001; Cuban & Usdan, 2003; Hess, 2005). All these studies point out that politics drives, sustains, and/or defeats efforts to help the most disadvantaged. Each country and city has its own political dynamics, from which we can learn something about the challenges and the conditions necessary for successful reform. This chapter will draw from our study of two Canadian urban school boards, in Toronto and Winnipeg, over the past twenty-five years. It will examine their approaches to the education of students from poor families and draw out some of the political implications of their experience. Both boards demonstrated an interest in working to alleviate the effects of poverty on schooling. Their innovations were not always successful, but they illustrate the challenges and the possibilities of working on these issues through municipal politics.

In general, Canadian cities have avoided the worst of urban school failures observed elsewhere, but they have not managed to find any robust solutions to the problems poverty produces for families trying to educate their children. The Toronto School Board and the Winnipeg School Board were leaders in exploring new ways of approaching the education of poor children. Each board adopted some policies that were bold and controversial; they made systemic changes that gradually shifted the burden of responsibility for school success from families and students towards teachers and administrators. They were however unable to find any magic bullets for the problems they were addressing; the successes they achieved were fragile and contested. They did not decrease levels of poverty in their cities nor equalize the life chances of students from different backgrounds, for these outcomes depend on changes in economic and social conditions, not just in educational provision.

In the scheme of this book, we are concentrating on the meso level of analysis. Our work is premised on the assumption that macro-level changes— the economic, demographic, and cultural shifts of the larger society—do not automatically convert into educational change; they matter hugely, but they work their way into schooling through the actions of those who make and implement educational policies. At the same time, micro-level changes—the individual level efforts of students, parents, or teachers—will not have substantial effects on the persistent relationship between poverty and educational outcomes without changes at a systemic, structural level. As a result, we believe scholars can usefully focus more attention on the way political action brings about change in educational beliefs, policies, and experiences in particular historical and social contexts.

Our approach is both functional, in the sense of being descriptive and looking for implications for current policy, and critical, in the sense of questioning the parameters that are taken for granted by those in the system. Looking critically at the structures and actions that have perpetuated educational inequality, while developing a deep understanding of the context within which those actions take place, seems most likely to lead to the transformation we need. Learning from successful practice is as important as critiquing unsuccessful practice.

Every context has its unique aspects, making international comparisons both important and complex. Canada's education system is particularly decentralized. There is no Canadian ministry of education; jurisdiction is at the provincial level, reflecting the distinct status of Quebec, the historical belief that local communities should make choices for their children and the continued struggles for autonomy that all provincial jurisdictions have waged, even as arguments about the nation's interest in developing educated workers for global competitiveness have gained favour (De Broucker & Sweetman, 2002). Within provinces, the existence of elected school boards with governance responsibilities allows local neighbourhoods to allocate resources and make choices within a framework set in place by the province. Levin and Ungerleider (2007) have traced the decline of Canadian school boards over the past twenty years, and their powers can be stripped away by provincial governments. But they are still elected at the municipal level, with powers granted by legislation and a continuing commitment from electors. As an intermediate level of governance, they are closely connected to parents and communities, and an important focus for understanding political debates about education (Gaskell, 2001).

THE CONTEXT AND THE STUDY

The last twenty-five years of the twentieth century were a time when urban school boards were particularly influential in shaping educational provision for students in Canada. Before that time, boards were smaller and had more limited resources and power, while in the last ten or fifteen years, provinces have put more stringent funding and curriculum guidelines in place to restrain local school board action.

The two boards we studied were in different provinces, and in cities where the face of poverty and the politics of the community evolved in different ways. We interviewed key players, and examined archival documents in both cities. In this chapter, we cannot focus on all the changes that took place over 25 years in both boards, but we will focus on a few innovations we believe were both influential and important in trying out a new approach to issues of urban education and poverty. In each case, the board made a major and controversial effort to focus on changing schools to accommodate difference, rather than using difference to marginalize and fail students.

Toronto is Canada's largest city, with a current population of 2.5 million in its core, and over 5 million in the greater Toronto area. The city grew and diversified over the period from 1970 to 2000, as increasing immigration brought families from across the world to fill jobs in an expanding Canadian economy. In 1971, 5 percent of the Toronto area population was of non-European heritage; in 2000, that had grown to 40 percent (Ornstein, 2006). By 2001, 44 percent of the Toronto population was born outside Canada. Over this period, city neighbourhoods became more distinct and more unequal. The poorest and wealthiest neighbourhoods were both more numerous in 2000 than in 1970. Twenty percent of the city, located near the geographical centre, increased its average income more than 20 percent; middle income neighbourhoods became a minority, while half of the city's neighbourhoods became low-income (Hulchanski, 2007).

From 1970 to 1997, the Toronto School District elected 22 trustees, two from each of 11 wards. Trustees were not officially aligned with political parties. The district had 117 elementary schools and 41 secondary schools in 1984. Over this period, the Toronto Board of Education put in place a program of school reform directed at improving the education of the most disadvantaged. The provincial government was Conservative until the mid-eighties, but it left the board largely to its own devices. The board undertook a reform program, using research to identify the poorest neighbourhoods, and allocating additional resources to the schools located there. In some of these neighbourhoods, the board created 'project schools' with more staffing and more autonomy in order try out new approaches to literacy, community involvement, and teacher professional development. The board increasingly brought parents, community activists, and languages other than English into the school. These policies, and their implementation, were controversial, well funded, and ultimately ended when an amalgamation of the Toronto board with other area boards was forced by the provincial government in 1997.

Winnipeg is a smaller, prairie city of about 650,000 people. Immigration to Winnipeg peaked at the end of the nineteenth and early twentieth centuries. Over the period of our study, Winnipeg's growth primarily reflected the movement of the rural population, particularly the aboriginal population, to the city, while some immigration continued. Poverty in Winnipeg has long been concentrated in what is known as the 'inner city' around the 'north end.' Between 1970 and 2000, poverty became increasingly concentrated, increasingly Aboriginal and increasingly severe in this area. Inner city schools, which had been Ukrainian, Jewish, German, Portuguese, or Italian, became 80 percent or more Aboriginal. The number of children in the inner city did not fall as the total population of Winnipeg did, reflecting a relatively high birthrate in the area.

The Winnipeg School Division elects nine trustees, three from each of three geographical areas, called wards. Ward 3 includes most of the inner city. Winnipeg trustees are affiliated with political parties. The district as a whole includes about 80 schools, including 10 secondary schools. Over the period of our study, the provincial government alternated between the Conservative Party and the New Democratic Party. The latter, in office in the early 1970s, focused on poverty, and set up a planning and research unit in the Department of Education to introduce more innovation to the schools and more programs to address the problems of the inner city. However, the trustees of the school district were divided in their attention to inner city education due to both geography and political conviction. In the early 1970s, they started initiatives, with the support of the province, to revise curriculum, improve native education, and increase nutrition for children and parent involvement. Later these initiatives foundered as cooperation with the province faltered, funding was cut, and more conservative politicians were elected at both the provincial and board levels. Only in 1987 was a superintendent of inner city schools appointed by the board, and a deliberate effort to address inner city education issues in a distinctive way undertaken by an inner city schools department within the district. This unit focused on core practices in schools, including daily classroom instruction and family engagement. In the early 1990s, a heated public debate resulted in the designation of two 'Aboriginal focused' schools, one elementary and one secondary, that would reflect the traditions and languages of Aboriginal people.

FACTORS THAT MAKE A DIFFERENCE

In examining our cases, we are struck, as were Stone and his colleagues (2001) in studying US cities, by the difference that local politics makes.

Changes in schools took place through political discussion, not despite it or around it. Whatever educators and educational experts thought needed to be done, (and their interesting, important, and contested understandings did make a difference), they did not have the space for their work without support in the political process.

We focus here on three factors that were important in allowing these boards to bring about changes in their approach to poverty. First the boards were able to move forward when they found or created some agreement about the priority and meaning of addressing issues related to poverty. Secondly, they made a difference when they focused on changes in teaching and learning, developing new curriculum, and encouraging teachers' collective expertise. Finally, boards that paid attention to staffing and political organization were successful in turning the ideas and commitments they shared into programs that sustained the work over time. At some moments during the history of these boards, we could identify these conditions and see their impact on creating programs and teaching that benefitted the disadvantaged. At other times, we could see their absence.

Shared Ideas About Equal Educational Opportunity

Much of politics is about the defining of problems (Kingdon, 1994; Stone, 2002). Education is a complex and poorly defined intellectual space, and its relationship to poverty is especially contested. While there is wide agreement that education should be improved, and more people should be educated to higher levels, the specifics of what this entails are by no means agreed upon. Concerted efforts at educational change to improve the educational chances of the least advantaged depend on a broadly shared conception of what should be done, and why.

During the period of our study, ideas about education underwent a dramatic change in Canada, as they did in much of the western world. In the late 1960s, the civil rights movement, the feminist movement, President Kennedy's war on poverty, and community activism around urban renewal all inspired some rethinking about equality and education. Instead of assuming that students who did not do well in school were less intelligent than those who did well, and that the role of the school was to sort the more intelligent from the less intelligent, educational scholars and critics pointed out the ways in which socio-economic status shaped school performance, and schools created inequality (Coleman, 1966; Bowles & Gintis, 1976). These ideas crossed the usual educational borders separating the academic and high brow from the professional and popular. Some teachers, principals, politicians, and academics developed a powerful critique of the ways in which the status quo in schools became an engine of inequality.

One index of this remarkable and destabilizing ferment was a magazine, cleverly called This Magazine is About Schools, which began publishing in Toronto in 1966. A group of radical educators and journalists based at an alternative school called Everdale published it monthly, including in it articles from learned journals, poems written by students, cartoons and popular journalism. It was written and read by some of those trying to change the system in Toronto, Winnipeg, and around the world.

In Toronto, some of the editors and their colleagues were actively organizing downtown communities. In 1968, they were instrumental in creating a brief to the school board protesting the way teachers failed and streamed children from poor families into dead end classes. Their brief, from the 'Treffan Court mothers' stated:

> What we are increasingly led to think is that the school system—
> with Opportunity Class as its dead-end division—just isn't set up to
> be meaningful for our kids. It doesn't relate to the things they know
> about and care about. It doesn't touch the world as it's experienced by
> people who don't have much money, who are constantly threatened by
> unemployment, who are harassed by welfare officers or the police. It
> doesn't understand what it means to be a person with integrity under
> these circumstances, or where you find life and friendship. So the kids
> slide away, and turn their minds and their hearts off. And many of
> those who turn off the most end up in Opportunity Class. (Martell,
> 1974:41)

These parents articulated a powerful new view of the school's responsibility for equality of opportunity for their children. They blamed the school system for short-changing their children. They took issue with the idea that their children were not intelligent (titling their brief "Downtown kids aren't dumb") and argued that teachers' notions of academic and social success were far too limited, narrow and biased, undermining the confidence and enthusiasm their children brought to school. They wanted schools to recognize their childrens' existing skills and knowledge, not just to provide compensatory programs to lift them up or fit them in. This brief became one of the foundational texts for the movement for school reform in the city.

In 1969, a slate of candidates who shared these ideas, and in some cases wrote them, were elected to the Toronto school board. The new trustees were variously described as "young," "radical," "cerebral," "firebrands," "blue denim radicals," and "distrustful of the system." They had a bare majority on the board to begin with, but they organized energetically and kept a majority who shared many of their ideas until 1985. Although there were differences among trustees in their definitions of what needed to done and how much it should cost, giving priority to the issues of poor and immigrant children was accepted for virtually the entire period of our study. Many of the trustees rejected a 'compensatory' model based on the idea that children from poverty were deficient in their knowledge and abilities; instead they wanted the system to recognize and develop the diversity of backgrounds and capacities these children had.

In Winnipeg, this shift in the ideas and assumptions of the board was not as clearly marked. New trustees with very different ideas were elected. Some of these trustees in the early 1970s read the same books and developed the same educational philosophies as reformers in Toronto. There were conferences and meetings where ideas and experiences were shared across the country. However, in Winnipeg's three ward system, inner city trustees had no majority, and though NDP trustees regularly held a majority, they were not always agreed on an approach. Sometimes trustees from the southern, more affluent end of the district were often more committed to inner city issues than some of the other board members. For many years the board was split 5 to 4 on many critical issues.

Projects around nutrition, early childhood education, and parent involvement in Winnipeg were justified more by a compensatory model than by a radical vision of adapting the schools to inner city students. The projects that were started were funded for the short term as temporary extras. Issues of the 'fair' allocation of resources across the entire district were always contentious, with parents in more affluent areas often better organized to define the terms of the debate and ensure supports for their children and schools. The board did not adopt the view that schools in poorer neighbourhoods should routinely receive more resources than other schools.

The Winnipeg board was however confronted with a bold new set of ideas and issues around aboriginal education early in the 1990s. By this time, aboriginal communities in the city had grown and developed articulate leadership; across Canada, aboriginal politics had become more influential and aboriginal scholarship had developed a full blown critique of the colonization of aboriginal education (Native Indian Brotherhood, 1972; Kirkness & Bowman, 1992; Royal Commission on Aboriginal People, 1996). Failure rates for aboriginal students were appalling and the board was faced with a demand for aboriginal-focused schools, governed by the aboriginal community, to countermand the effect of decades of oppression.

This proposal led to a widely reported public debate about some fundamental educational beliefs, with heated disagreements in the media around accusations of segregation and lower standards. In order to establish the schools, trustees had to agree that different kinds of education were fair and appropriate for different kinds of students, that the Aboriginal community had a special status in Canada and that funding should respond to the needs of Aboriginal children. The board eventually agreed to two aboriginal focused schools—one elementary and one secondary—which would have staffing, curriculum, and social practices that reflected aboriginal cultures and worldviews but would be governed by the Division, not by a community group as originally proposed. As the 1996 policy adopted by the board states: "Whereas the Winnipeg School District recognizes that it serves a diverse population and is committed to making education meaningful to and inclusive of the cultural diversity that characterizes our society... and whereas the Aboriginal Community has made known the importance of the integration of aboriginal values, images, languages histories and cultures being promoted in all aspects of education," the board will support employment equity, aboriginal awareness programs, Aboriginal languages, and aboriginal schools (Winnipeg School Division Aboriginal Education Policy, 1996:1). The evolution of ideas was slow, but clear.

Teaching and Learning

Changing the processes of teaching and learning must be at the centre of any attempt to change schooling for the urban poor. New policies and ideas do not transform classrooms without making their way into teachers' practices and curriculum materials, which exist far from the boardroom and are loosely coupled to it (Lipsky, 1983). In both Winnipeg and Toronto, there were several moments when the board made a concerted effort to change the way teaching and learning were taking place for the most disadvantaged students. These can be most clearly seen in Toronto's "project schools" and its commitment to heritage languages and in Winnipeg's aboriginal-focused schools and inner city teaching and learning strategy. In each case, the school boards mandated continual, on-the-job professional development, new locally developed curriculum materials, and a responsive, community orientation.

In Toronto, student-centred literacy instruction was being advocated by staff by the mid-1960s. Reducing the importance of spelling tests, understanding language as a medium of learning across the curriculum, and introducing 'heritage' languages into the school day were important to central staff (Rutledge, 1988). The election of a reform board invigorated a lively ongoing debate about linguistics and curriculum and provided a much larger canvas on which new ideas about literacy could be tried out.

The board provided schools in poor areas with extra resources for staffing, curriculum development, and community liaison. They encouraged the use of curriculum which reflected the experience of children in Toronto, recognized that multiple forms of language could be a resource for learning, and supported school-based professional development for teachers. There were central initiatives, like a new elementary reader series based on the experience of inner city children and curriculum development projects around multiculturalism, anti-racism, and feminism, which were to be taken up across the system. But rather than insisting on a uniform approach, the board concentrated resources in schools where there was an appetite for change, and created personnel policies that hired and rewarded more a diverse and community oriented staff.

A few elementary schools, called 'inner city project schools' modelled ways of interacting with students. These were schools in areas of high need, whose staff applied to become both experiments and exemplars. They had to be committed to developing a distinctive curricular approach throughout the school and to ensuring a close connection between the school staff, the parents, and the community (Yau, 1996). These schools were exciting places to work, attracting some of the best teachers to the inner city. They had more autonomy than other schools and more staff. They were able to fund school-based professional development and select teachers who agreed on a basic philosophy of education. The principal of one project school described them as places where teachers "believed that inner city kids could do well at school . . . Believed that the connection with the community and the parents would make a big difference. And there was a big focus on literacy."

A multicultural report in 1976 encapsulated the debate about how the schools should approach cultural difference. A draft report developed a

> very comprehensive rationale for the inclusion of languages and culture maintenance programs as a segment of the school's regular program. The rationale is based on the recognition that such programs are necessary to the educational well-being of students from a cultural and linguistic heritage other than British or French. The necessity arises because schools very naturally reflect a dominant culture which is alien to these children. The draft report's position is that culture and language maintenance programs would function to help to dispel the negative impact of the dominant culture on the personal development of these children. (Toronto Board of Education, 1976:21)

This elision of the dominant culture and oppression was toned down before the report was passed. Trustees were not willing to agree that English instruction constituted a bias and assimilation was not a goal. But they supported the development of culturally diverse curriculum materials, and experimented with Italian, Greek, and Chinese bilingual programs. The School Community Relations Department was established as a result of this report, and it hired community liaison officers to build bridges to the new ethnic communities in the city

In Winnipeg, a concerted approach to teaching and learning grew more gradually and sporadically, reflecting changing political and economic trends beyond the city. In the early 1970s, inner city school projects involved bold changes in curriculum and teaching methods, often fuelled by young and idealistic educators who were prepared to devote extraordinary amounts of time and energy to this work. As in Toronto, new approaches to literacy teaching were developed and parent engagement was encouraged. 'Wrap-around' social services were put in place in a number of inner city schools, to a degree that has still not been replicated decades later. The first serious attention was given to the growing number of aboriginal students through eliminating biased books and other materials, and through efforts to train and hire more inner city and aboriginal teachers.

When the inner city department was established in 1987, the district began a concerted and focused emphasis on changing teaching, learning, and assessment practices in these schools. The district put a great deal of effort into developing new approaches that would be understood and shared by teachers, and so be deeply embedded in their daily practices. They spent considerable time developing a set of widely accepted principles for teaching and learning. The schools looked at ways of changing student assessment that would take more account of students' life experiences and would build greater student engagement. Much attention was also given to ways of engaging parents who would themselves have low levels of education and not necessarily trust the schools.

Around the same time the district created a Task Force on Race Relations, chaired by a trustee. The hearings of this group became a lightning rod for concerns about the treatment of aboriginal and immigrant children and families, and increased the willingness to change policies, practices, and staffing.

Staffing and Political Organization

New ideas, and new forms of teaching and learning, come and go. General concern and scattered activities do not sustain effective action for poor children. School boards can however create institutional legacies that live beyond the moment if they put in place the staff, the organizational structures, and the political traditions that sustain reform and insulate their schools from other pressures. We can see some ways in which both school boards achieved this, and ways in which they failed.

The reforming Toronto trustees worked systematically at building a new infrastructure, because they had been elected to oppose the status quo and had the resources to develop new programs. Toronto had a strong tax base, based on the corporate offices located in the city. The school board had the power to raise its own taxes, which it did, with very little resistance from the electorate. Although there were pressures to share the city's wealth with suburban boards, the staff were skilled at creating formulae and understandings that sustained the resources of the board. Anger at this fiscal imbalance became one reason for the province's amalgamation of Toronto with other boards in 1997.

The board used its resources to increase staff in the board office and in poor schools. It expanded the research department to more than 50 people. It hired equity advisors, responsible for gender equity, racism, multiculturalism, and homophobia. It created an inner city department, which developed curriculum, carried out professional development and made policy. Perhaps most remarkably, the board created a central School Community Relations department which hired community activists for each inner city neighbourhood in the city. The board was funding political work to ensure parents were involved in educational debates. This often meant support for new policies, but sometimes meant creating opposition, as parents and community activists filled board meetings and wrote briefs. The department remained in place for 10 years, and when it was disbanded, community liaison officers remained, although they reported locally.

The new staff were focused on the inner city and system change. They were hired to spread new ideas and practices through the system. As one director told us, "If you think George Bush is harsh in naming a judge, you should see the way we chose consultants." Workshops were another way of spreading new ideas to teachers and students. Tim McCaskell described the workshops he provided for students as "fundamentally different from other student leadership experiences. Not content with simply building skills or hoping that a shared experience would encourage diverse students to learn to like each other more, its goal was to forge a social analysis out of the collective sharing of experience" (2005:29).

And the Toronto trustees tended their political backyards. They earned enough money (up to $50,000), to treat their jobs as full time, although not all did. They were active in speaking about education, meeting their constituents, and keeping their networks intact. Several were allied to powerful social movements and political parties with substantial resources and expertise. Being a trustee was not an avocation to be taken lightly. Although in the 1985 election, the reform trustees lost their majority, this was for a short time. The effort to involve parents and increase the opportunities for disadvantaged children was so embedded in the organization and taken for granted by staff and even the opposition trustees, that few programs were discontinued. And soon reform trustees regained a majority.

Within the city, the school board was extremely effective at institutionalizing a program that focused reform efforts on inner city schools. But the voters in the rest of the province were less convinced. There was increasing criticism of the 'overpriced' and 'overstaffed' school board programs. A Conservative provincial government was elected in 1995 and, with the support of a majority outside the city, abolished the board by amalgamating it with others (Siemiatycki & Isin, 1997).

In Winnipeg, the focus on creating new institutions and structures was never as strong as in Toronto. While the Toronto board was largely independent of the province until 1997, in Winnipeg, inner city activity was driven to a significant degree by the provincial government, especially in the 1970s and 1980s when New Democratic Party cabinet ministers represented inner city Winnipeg constituencies. During the 11 years of Conservative government, from 1988 to 1999, the province was much less interested in inner city education and the board was more able to direct policy.

Winnipeg trustees were almost always part-time, and their salaries or honoraria were never high enough to support full-time trustee work. The nine-member board was fractious, with personal rivalries and differences in views trumping official political party allegiances. Reflecting this dissension, and exacerbating the lack of consistent direction, in the late 1970s and early 1980s the board hired and soon after fired several superintendents.

The board also reorganized its superintendent structure regularly, making continuity difficult.

Many of the early projects directed at inner city schools were designed as short-term interventions, not permanent reorganization. In the 1970s, the provincial government's inner city advisory committee funded community development in the schools of inner Winnipeg as short-term, compensatory projects. The board created the "Community Education Development Agency" (CEDA) in the 1970s as a more permanent structure to help support parental organizing in the inner city, especially among immigrant and Aboriginal parents. The CEDA played an important role, to the point where a later, more conservative board eliminated its funding from the Division. The lack of a shared ongoing commitment meant that jurisdictions competed for credit instead of working together on a jointly agreed agenda and created temporary, instead of lasting structures for inner city education. As funding dried up and politics became more conservative in the 1980s, many of these projects withered.

Still, there were ongoing efforts to address inner city issues throughout these years. A series of multi-year Core Area agreements in the 1980s and 1990s between the city, province, and federal governments provided funding for a range of education projects. An important program that did survive the entire period was the Winnipeg Education Centre, operated by The University of Manitoba (and more recently by the University of Winnipeg) to train inner city, largely Aboriginal people as teachers.

Winnipeg did not create an infrastructure for inner city education until the late 1980s. When the superintendency was reorganized so that the inner city had its own infrastructure, it had approximately the same resources as the other parts of the district. It had the ability to develop distinct policies, but had to manage its strategy without a great deal of external support. However, the patient and careful work done in the inner city superintendency over the years did have effects, including a much stronger shared focus on some core practices around teaching and learning, student assessment, and parent engagement.

Although the aboriginal population of Winnipeg has grown steadily, politics in the city have been more influenced by immigrant groups than by aboriginal politicians. The school board has almost always had at least one or two trustees from various ethnic groups. Aboriginal parents and organizations were quite active from time to time in board politics, but usually from the 'outside.' Only once has Winnipeg elected Aboriginal trustees, and they only served a single term in office. However, by the end of the 1990s, outside pressure was effective in creating the climate in which the board put in place two distinct aboriginal schools, and a policy on Aboriginal education. This provided an institutional base for the development of a wide range of policies and practices to enhance the success of Aboriginal students. The Aboriginal-focused schools are still in place and the beliefs that underlay their establishment have become much more widely shared.

They have been accepted as successful models for the rest of Canada, and are no longer contentious within the school district.

CONCLUSIONS

In both cities, we can see that committed trustees who agree to share power with and engage vulnerable communities can have a very powerful and positive effect on the educational opportunities of poor children. These effects are limited by the fiscal and political constraints of a democratic system and the understanding and collaboration of educators, but they are still important. This analysis suggests that the discussion of urban education and poverty needs to pay more attention to political factors, an area that is so far explored more by political scientists than by education scholars. In particular, the role of ideas in the political process, the centrality of teaching and learning to school reform, and the importance and difficulty of institutionalizing change deserve our careful study.

Part III

An Examination of Educational Policy

12 Policy and the Policy Process

*Helen Gunter, Carlo Raffo, Dave Hall,
Alan Dyson, Lisa Jones, and Afroditi
Kalambouka*

INTRODUCTION

The research and theorising presented in this collection of papers illuminates the complex relationship between poverty and educational experiences together with the problematic aspects of working for and securing appropriate change. This final section of the book will turn to the issues for policy and policymakers: first, this chapter will outline policy as a process and it will present an analytical framework for capturing and thinking through the possibilities for policy change; second, how policymakers have developed and implemented change strategies with an analysis of the consequences will be the focus of Chapter 13; third, given the challenges surrounding how policy has so far been implemented, Chapter 14 examines what is to be done by examining what policymakers might do to break the link between poverty and education. We do not intend to provide a recipe for action but we will generate some ideas and present some provocations as a means of thinking through possibilities.

We begin the section with this chapter where we draw on Raffo et al. (2007), and Ozga and Dale (1991) to examine, first, *sources* or where policy comes from; second, *scope,* what policy aims to achieve in ways that are systemic (macro), mid ranged (meso), and specific (micro); and third, *patterns* or the exercise of power through how strategy intervenes into existing policy practices and cultures. However, prior to engaging with this we would like to do some intellectual work that will enable this framework to be deployed in ways that will examine the research and analysis from the authors in this edited collection. The starting point has to be one of problem identification and developing from this one of agenda setting.

POLICY POSSIBILITIES AND STRATEGIES

Our approach to policy is based on the adoption of Ozga's (2000) conceptualisation of policy settings as a "contested terrain" as "places, processes and relationships where policy is made" (1). Hence while policy as text can mean official documents, we are interested in the processes by which the underlying philosophies, purposes, and positionings are developed and articulated (or silenced). This is a highly political process, and so defining and fixing a change strategy in education as represented in a text is, as Lingard and Ozga (2007) identify, usually a "compromise" because "policy texts are usually heteroglossic in character, discursively suturing together differing interests to achieve apparent consensus and legitimacy" (2). Therefore the productive possibilities of and for policy are located not just in a text, but are within social practices about that text where people invest in and stake claims for different positions. Like Bowe et al. (1992) and Ball (2008), we are interested in readings of and about policy, and the challenges within such readings, not least that "interpretation is a matter of struggle" (Bowe et al., 1992:22).

In examining the relationship between education policy and poverty our starting point needs to be with the fundamentals of the education project, where positions within and about policy can be traced back. Such projects have different things to say about the individual and the social, not least the ability of the person to exercise agency and how practice is shaped by social, economic, and political structures. When debates and solutions are presented in the here and now their archaeology is in the basic differences about the education project, and as such it is where the contested nature of the policy terrain has its origins. First, what we call the *Neo-liberal Project* is where education can be seen to be about the state's responsibilities for economic development. Philosophically this Project is located in the role of the individual to secure their readiness and capabilities for work, and hence education is about enabling this to happen in the family or the school. Here the emphasis is on skills, credentials, and what is known as human capital. Positions regarding the state are that it should connect public investment in education to market productivity, as well as act as guardian of moral values and of the security of money. For example, Mandelson and Liddle (1996), as architects of New Labour modernisation in England, have argued that "governments can best promote economic success by ensuring that their people are equipped with the skills necessary for the modern world" (89). The barriers in the way to doing this are vested interests in education who prepare "children from deprived backgrounds with an education fitted for the limited opportunities they expect their pupils to enjoy, rather than either concentrating on the achieving of adequate standards in the basic skills of reading and writing, science and mathematics or raising expectations of what some might attain" (91). A combination of universal and targeted reforms lead from such an argument, where basic skills necessary for a prescribed standard are for all children and additional support is provided to develop human capital in workless families and communities. The solution is investment in education in order that people from disadvantaged communities can do better in examinations and so be productive in the labour market. Private interests in the form of parents or philanthropists are enhanced whereas public sector interests (e.g. educational professionals) are marginalised.

A second approach that we call the *Civic Project* conceptualises education as directly linked to social democratic development. Philosophically this Project is also located in the role of the individual but through how work is a social process, not least through how agency works for social justice for the self and for others. This sees education as being central to enabling participation in decision-making that is both individual and social, and where the person develops autonomy within society and learns to listen, to negotiate, and to co-operate (Ranson, 1993). Positions regarding the state are that it should connect public investment in education to citizenship where work and other skills are progressed. Indeed what is argued is that democracy is not yet in existence in England and so it is to be worked for, where "the outstanding educational task is not to *defend* democracy by *reproducing* society, but to *create* democracy by *transforming* society" (Carr & Hartnett, 1996:199). The starting point lies with people and their lives, and what Sen (1999) identifies as giving attention "to the expansion of the 'capabilities' of persons to lead the kind of lives they value—and have reason to value" (18). Universal rights to education are seen as essential in order to build the public good and this interplays with developing opportunities for agency to be exercised. Consequently social justice is not primarily about the barriers to change, but is focused on how people and the control over their destinies is thought about and acted upon.

Such approaches, albeit characterised in a binary way, are a useful starting point for examining the emergence of political positionings in regard to the relationship between education and poverty. This is because the role of the state, markets, and the private domain of the person and family are central to how and why policy is framed in the way it is. The state is concerned with the development of citizenship, safety, and economic development, markets with trade, profit and a skilled labour force, and families with immediate needs along with aspirations for the next generation. The interplay between the state, markets, and the private domain are not necessarily antithetical but value positions do generate different readings and arguments about purposes, not least the deep issues about the "permanent agenda of problems for education systems in capitalist counties" (Ozga & Dale, 1991:9). The production of a workforce for and within an economy enables the state to guarantee, legitimise, and protect capital accumulation, not least through the safety of money and property (Harvey, 2007). As authors in this collection show the nature of the problem and the production of solutions has been and continues to be contested over time and in context. This is evident in the strategic fights over the establishment of public welfare and universal base provision free at the point of access with demand for markets and calls for the state to roll back and enable people to work for themselves and their families. The papers are mainly concerned with recent developments, not least the dominance of neo-liberal ideas that have generated state restructuring and reculturing around site-based delivery of public services combined with high stakes regulation and performance management. This enables Lipman to connect global interests with the realities of schools and schooling in Chicago that illustrates class and racial politics. For both Maguire and Smyth, beliefs about human beings in the simultaneous privileging and depriviledging of interests must be central to the analysis of education policy, not least Smyth's argument that people have to be thought about as more than failures in the market place.

Consequently, underpinning the chapters is a recognition that the possibilities of and for policy regarding the relationship between education and poverty is located in the handling of tensions between: first, workforce dependence on the needs of the economy to determine educational purposes and achievements with wider citizenship and aesthetic goals where education could be an end in itself; second, universalism of all having entitlements and access to education with targeted or group-based interventions that can differentiate the population through the operation of advantage and disadvantage; and third, expansion by looking for opportunities to develop and improve through public investment with retraction where public funding is cut in favour of self reliance, hard work, and family support. Such tensions are endemic, and while settlements may seem to be in place, not least post-war welfarism based on the Civic Project in England, there have been fractures with Neo-liberal Project challenges to the system of universal social security and education (Chubb & Moe, 1990; Bobbitt, 2002). Hence there is a need to examine agenda setting from which policies, legislation, and interventions are generated in such a way as to reveal the dispositions, discourses, and practices of those involved. There are value systems, attitudes to human nature, a complexity of experiences that shape and determine what is said and left unsaid, that makes understanding policy and its possibilities for generating change messy and complex. Indeed, whether poverty is a problem, and if so in what ways and who for, is central to the place of education within policy solutions.

SOURCES

Ozga and Dale (1991) argue that there are three sources of policies: the state or public institutions that is based on consent through e.g. electoral mandates; civil society or the working of democratic debates and activism, e.g. pressure groups; and, the economy or how there is demand for workforce numbers and skills, e.g. levels of literacy and numeracy. The complex interplay between the three with shifts in dominance is what is central to policy production, not least the workings of the global economy. Recognition is also needed about how, in Kingdon's (2003) terms, the ideas and strategies underpinning policy statements, legislation, and funding streams, are combined and recombined by policy entrepreneurs from government, research, private companies, and the voluntary sector.

The approach to claims about truths made within and about policy are fundamental to examining the relationship between policy and research, not least to ask questions about what is known, what is worth knowing and why, and where the silences are. This type of thinking is what is needed to underpin any analysis of the relationship between the state, public policy, and knowledge, and our approach in this book and being particularly addressed in this chapter is the identification of functional and socially critical approaches to policymaking and how research and researchers relate to this. For example, in the production of a policy intervention there is a need to examine what type(s) of knowledge is used to generate ideas, provide evidence, and legitimise what is to be done. We present three approaches to the knowledge claims within policy development in Table 12.1, where we outline the underlying conceptualisation together with the reasons offered within policy discourses and the narratives that are produced and articulated.

Our starting point is to recognise that there is knowledge and knowing based on experiential learning, trial and error, that we would call *traditional policy* approaches. Policy does not enter an empty terrain because there are always situated inherited ways of doing things with associated structures, cultures, and practices. The Neo-liberal Project may draw on notions of how the market has and might work better, whereas the Civic Project may make the case for social approaches to decision-making. Furthermore as policy waves hit the shores of peoples' lives this lays and overlays with how things have been done, and so impact is not a linear cause and effect process but a relationship between a potentially rational 'new' strategy with a messy ensemble of ongoing practices and beliefs. This can be underpinned by rationales based on competing demands for change as a matter of urgency or claims for noninterference based on how things are done as those who live their lives in a particular way should not be forced to adopt the approaches that others, namely politicians and researchers, deem appropriate. As Lipman shows this can operate simultaneously as city-wide interventions in Chicago are different from those taking place with and by the community.

Our research (Raffo et al., 2007), and the chapters in this collection, show that the underlying knowledge claims in the possibilities for and of current educational policy in most affluent countries, and particularly in England, are mainly *functional*. Functional approaches are located in models of policy science, notably which policymakers can measure the impact of inputs into a situation, processes that take place, and the outputs that are produced. While both the Neo-liberal and Civic Projects draw from this, it is the former which has developed and used functionalism in order to create and justify policy strategies in recent decades. Assumptions are made about the social world based on roles and structures where there is a sense of bounded unity (in a family, a school, or as Lupton identifies in the difference between place and space) so that variables can be controlled, manipulated, and outcomes predicted. This systems perspective can use and produce data that enables technical improvements to the types of interventions that secures delivery and impact. For example, Muijs examines school effectiveness as finding the best way to examine "what it is that organisations do to be optimally effective in reaching their goals." Seeking efficiencies and effectiveness is illustrative of Schoon's study of databases

Table 12.1   Policy Sources

	Situational	Functional	Socially Critical
Policy Model	Policy Tradition	Policy Science	Policy Scholarship
Conceptualisation	Knowledge and knowing is generated through practice, and it is people in families and schools who know about educational processes and outcomes. Policymakers and researchers may seek to demonstrate that they know through their experiences and through research findings, but knowing is through doing and living.	Knowledge and knowing is generated through positivist social science, where policymakers can be given access to evidence by practitioners, consultants, and researchers.	Knowledge and knowing is generated through positivist and interpretive social science, and through access to theories of power that challenge the established status quo. Policymakers can be given access to evidence and ideas by practitioners, consultants, and researchers. Not least through participating in project development and analysis.
Rationale	What works is what has been learned through practice. Utility is located in experience and personal ability to productively engage with situations as they arise. Funding should be based on recurrent need.	What works can be improved by access to positivist data and technical strategies. Utility is located in the efficient and effective delivery of evidence that can be transferred into practice. Funding should be based on proof of need	What works can be informed by an activist commitment to identifying social injustice and working for social justice. Utility is located in revealing ideas and evidence about social injustice and the exercise of power that can inform the development of practice. Funding should be based on recognition of rights-based needs.

Table 12.1   continued

	Situational	Functional	Socially Critical
Policy Model	Policy Tradition	Policy Science	Policy Scholarship
Narratives	Policy for and funding of research could be wasted if it does not begin with how people want to live their lives. People should be left alone to get on with their lives with help and support as required. Policy interventions and research are only relevant when there is something to say about real life concerns and provide techniques that make sense. The language is about commonsense needs and learning by trial and error.	Policy for and funding of research needs to be based on the production of evidence that will support interventions to improve practice. Policymakers as users of research evidence want to know that interventions informed by data will lead to measurable improvements. The language is about planning, monitoring, evaluating, and ensuring the effective, efficient, and economic delivery of the intervention.	Policy for and funding of research can produce evidence about social injustice and ideas about how the world can be different. Policymakers as users of research evidence want to know about the situation and also how complex and deeply embedded problems can be tackled. The language is about justice, activism, fairness, and opportunities, where interventions engage with the underlying issues of class and disadvantage.

where the focus is on an aspect of the system that is not working well, not least the relationship between economic circumstances with ability, aspirations, and achievement. The resolution to the problem is one of overcoming barriers within the person, income, and institutions. Notably, in functional studies the research evidence is mainly positivist with the use of statistical data to justify changes, with monitoring and evaluation to both prevent slippage between policy intention and outcome, and to discipline policy actors in regard to their practice.

Socially critical approaches are located in critical policy scholarship where policymakers, drawing on the Civic Project, can use evidence from both positivist and interpretive traditions. Underpinning this is an overt values-based commitment to change a situation based on social justice claims: to eradicate a wrong and/or to generate opportunities for improvements based on what is deemed right rather than what is technically needed. Lupton argues that contrary to the functionalist approach where the system is generally viewed as working okay but with an identifiable dysfunction that needs to be sorted, socially critical work challenges the assumptions underpinning the system. Indeed Maguire shows how poverty can be useful to the state and in revealing this there are issues about the amount, type, and sincerity of functional changes. Hence socially critical work can be based on universal interventions such as legal rights (e.g. suffrage) through to targeted projects in local areas to deal with a situation and/or pilot strategies. Lupton goes on to argue that functionalism conceptualises poverty as located in a place that can be identified as "residual" and so dealt with, whereas her socially critical analysis focuses on space as a way of understanding how people locate who they are and what meaning they bring to their lives.

A number of authors in this collection are concerned with the problematics of the thinking within the Neo-liberal Project and so are concerned to develop policy strategies from a perspective of fairness and human dignity. Hence while accounts are given about local and community activity in ways that respect the functioning of the law (though Lipman talks about radical action through hunger strikes), there is work reported where at a local level people can and do work against the grain. Smyth and Maguire both talk about educational experiences that are respectful of who the children are and what their experiences are; while Thomson shows that "place-based" approaches to curriculum and pedagogy can enable schools and communities to work together on regeneration. Gaskell and Levin identify and chart the politics of educational change within localities, not least the interplay between ideas and working for change. The emphasis in socially critical work is on building a commitment from people to challenge the status quo through activism that is pedagogic in intention: generating ideas through debate, developing strategies, and taking ownership of implementation. Here all are knowers, and can through their participation help to develop their own and other's knowledge.

SCOPE

Ozga and Dale (1991) argue that scope is "framed by conceptions of what is desirable and possible for education systems to achieve" (14). They note that what exists together with attitudes located in situated approaches can limit notions of desirability, and yet feasibility can be challenged by ideas and new imaginings for what is possible. Our research into the literatures on the relationship between poverty and education shows that policy does demonstrate assumptions about what can and should be done (Raffo et al., 2007). Policy can show a focus on system wide changes with major macro interventions (for example in this collection see the chapter by Schoon), meso- or mid-level interventions (for example, see Muijs and Lupton), and interventions focused on the individual, family, and community that have micro features (for example, see chapters by Maguire, Smyth, and Thomson). Functional approaches assume that problems with the system can be tackled by appropriate interventions whereas socially critical approaches argue that the system as a whole needs change and that can come from system wide through to localised gains which enable communities to make a difference. Functionalism assumes a clarity of difference that could separate the macro, meso, and micro as 'levels' with a system, where in Barber's (2007) terms it is possible to know who is responsible for what, and use targets and performance data to join the three levels up through a "delivery chain" from the policymaker at the centre to the child in a school. The majority of the chapters in this book would see the inter-relationship between different levels and locations of power in a system as realistically and appropriately more fluid, or even reconceptualise the focus of change as, in Bourdieu's (1990) terms, fields of practice where interventions that are systemic are always meso and micro.

Central to such analysis is thinking that sees the relationship between policy intention and experience as being located in the interplay between global and local economic and social capitals. A helpful conceptualisation is around "travelling" and "embedded" policy where:

> . . . travelling policy refers to supra-national and transnational agency activity, as well as to common agendas (for example for the reshaping of educational purposes to develop human capital for the information age). Embedded policy is to be found in 'local' spaces (which may be national, regional or local) where global policy agendas come up against existing priorities and practices. This perspective allows for recognition that, while policy choices may be narrowing, national and local assumptions and practices remain significant and mediate or translate global policy in distinctive ways. (Ozga, 2005:208–209)

The functionalist Neo-liberal Project has dominated the modernisation of public services and education in particular (Smyth & Gunter, 2009) in ways that seem to be a product of "homogenizing travelling policy" (Ozga & Jones, 2006:14), and so there is policy convergence in Western style education systems with site-based management, school effectiveness and improvement, and school leadership, and the global trading of reform packages to bring about rapid 'world class' systemic change (Barber, 2007). The authors in this book recognise the gains that can be made by universal and system wide changes, not least how post-World War II the concept of the public good was established as a rationale for how people want to live together. However, the embeddedness of the nation state, regions, and localities mean that "particular groups or societies can be encouraged to revisit and reconstruct the value basis of their organisation; and generate new energy in its production within social and cultural institutions" (Ozga & Jones, 2006:14). Policy is therefore open to localised Civic Projects with socio-critical possibilities, and so in the chapters there is a strong message about the existence and necessity for people as individuals, in neighbourhoods and in wider groups such as a city, to work on projects that can challenge neo-liberal assumptions about who they are and why they are in the situation they are in, and reveal the issues that functionalism can elide. Lipman identifies not only the operation of transnational capital in decisions about education in Chicago but shows the relationship with race and class. Similarly in London, Maguire shows that the discourse of stigmatising the poor fulfils a particular function in retaining the distinction between the deserving and undeserving poor as a useful lever to show people what happens when you don't work, and goes on to show the realities of what it means to grow up in that situation and how it stifles aspirations. There are examples within this edited collection of how embeddedness can be used to develop individual and localised responses to poverty, in ways that move away from an assumed deficit situation of disadvantage towards a recognition that people can do things differently, and in ways that are compatible with systemic shared interests.

PATTERNS

We have identified that functional knowledge claims are evident with multiple interventions in regard to what is targeted, how it is targeted, when it is targeted, and why it is targeted. This produces a complex process that can, as evidence in this book shows, generate tensions and contradictions. Hence a pertinent issue for any analysis about the productive possibilities of and for policy is in how to make interventions both differentiated in relation to need but also coherent, and so this requires an understanding of the model of change within the sources and scope of policy. For example, functionality assumes that change is based on a linear cause and effect relationship where a combination of vision and mission to communicate a future situation is outlined and targeted together with planning, monitoring, and evaluation is used to deliver. Socially critical approaches to change are based on the commitment to social justice and universal rights, and through localism the situation is described, understood, and a strategy for change worked out.

Ozga and Dale (1991) identify patterns as being shaped by: context, resources, and conditions (28). The politics of education is at the core of contextual matters, not least how discourses are related to the sources and scope of policy strategies and interventions. Analysis of the sources and scope of policy generated the understanding that there are divergent views on what public institutions can and should do, and what the market can and should do, and what the private person (as individual or in a family within civil society) can and should do. The re-emergence of the market from the 1980s onwards with neo-liberal ideas about how we are to live together has generated functional responses to crises that erupt over issues of poverty (e.g. street begging, crime, disease) so that the market is protected. Concessions are made to further capital accumulation through the private delivery of public services such as through the focus on schools as effective and improving organisations for private profit-making (e.g. Academies programme). While the chapters in this book reveal this situation across a range of nation states, they also show the problematics. While functionalism is assumed to be rational, in reality much policy is not fully thought through, and there are problems that Smyth identifies as a scatter-gun approach. Functionalism can create the illusion that a silver bullet can be made to resolve all the dysfunctions, where for example the use of targets to bring about reforms in England by New Labour has been shown to have some gains but also to generate problems (Chapman & Gunter, 2009). Whereas socially critical approaches not only show the delusionary and damaging nature of systemic change through targets (e.g. the consequences of high stakes testing and performance regimes on people) but also that the alternatives are more complex but worth working for.

Consequently, the operation of political interests in the policy process is an important feature. An important way in which interests can be detected within how policy and practice are related to each other is through the construction and operation of discourses. For example, while New Labour has made important interventions in regard to the relationship between education and poverty in England, this has been based on a "discourse of derision" (Ball, 1990) towards the research community. Indeed, Miliband (the then Head of the Policy Unit at No 10) said that "there is a big role for academics if they choose to . . . become engaged in debate beyond the confines of academic journals" (Lloyd, 1999:13). Indeed educational research in the UK was put under the spotlight for its deficiencies (Hargreaves, 1996; Hillage et al., 1998; Tooley with Darby, 1998; Blunkett, 2000; Woodhead, 2000). In England the solution has been functional with a number of interventions: first, the setting up of the EPPI review processes, where medical models of research, the cumulative building of evidence and testing of knowledge has been encouraged but has also faced detailed critique (Anderson & Bennett, 2003); second, the establishment of the National Education Research Forum (NERF, n.d.) which was the subject of controversy; third, the inclusion of some academics within government to act as a bridge between policymakers and researchers, and while it is reported that Philip Cowley is to work in the Treasury "helping social science research feed into policymaking" (Research Intelligence, 2008:29) it is not on the scale of the Obama presidency where academics are called in to take up leading roles in the administration (Marcus, 2008); fourth, the control of research through government commissioning (Gunter & Thomson, 2006), where, for example, fields such as school leadership have seen research purposes, methodologies, projects, and dissemination dominated by government (Weindling, 2004; Gunter & Fitzgerald, 2008). Again such matters are evident in other countries, where in the US the "No Child Left Behind" intervention has sought to control knowledge production through funding and determining what types of evidence count.

Education and social science researchers have engaged with the criticisms and interventions through examining the case being made, critiquing the evidence base, and developing alternative agendas (Rudduck & McIntyre, 1998; Pring, 2000; Anderson & Bennett, 2003; Ribbins et al., 2003). The American Educational Research Association has taken seriously the relationship between research and the public interest with its annual conference focused on this issue (Ladson-Billings & Tate, 2006). Significantly, having faced major criticism, the field in the UK has been concerned to highlight when the productive way forward identified by the government for a sharper link between evidence and decision-making is not being delivered. Mortimore (2009) in reviewing the current government's approach to accepting the latest Trends in International Mathematics and Science Study (TIMSS) but sidelining the Programme for International Student Assessment (Pisa) and the 2008 Unicef Report Card on Early Childhood Services argues: " . . . that all data need to be treated with respect and that lauding some studies and denying others—depending on whether they suit policies—is politically naïve and dishonest" (4). Furthermore, Holligan (2008) has identified the serious failure of the government to subject commissioned research to peer review prior to acceptance and publication, and consequently the drive towards evidence informed practice has turned out to "belong with pre-scientific times where magical beliefs prevailed" (27).

What an analysis of these debates and interventions during the past decade illustrates is that the relationship between policy and research is not only about issues of quality and relevance but fundamental questions about underlying knowledge claims. Which knowledge is used to frame and support public policy is not necessarily based on the inherent truths produced by a scientifically verified methodology. Indeed, policymakers use and dismiss evidence and researchers for a range of reasons, and often gravitate to a trusted thinker who is depended on to produce the way forward. Gunter and Forrester (2008) have shown how models of leadership promoted by New Labour policies are directly linked to selected school improvement and effectiveness research that has been recombined through the activity of policy entrepreneurs. Consequently, whether research is of a high standard and is pertinent depends on what a person or a team sets out to do in the first place and how it is read and used by others. Furthermore the socially critical approaches as outlined in this edited collection would want to produce data to demonstrate impact and achievement but would also want to seek recognition for changes and developments that cannot be quantified.

ISSUES FOR POLICYMAKERS

Our analysis of the sources, scope, and patterns of policy has shown that the policy decisions and interventions into poverty through educational processes and institutions are highly complex and contested. If we take the example of New Labour in England there is a mixture of the Neo-liberal Project based on Thatcherite market solutions and private sector products combined with a Civic Project located in its historical commitment to a just society evidenced in targeted welfare reforms:

> Modernised governance thus seeks to create a new hybrid of public and private, a space to be occupied by a redesigned socially and individually responsible citizen, embedded in networks, allowed the freedom to achieve economic and social targets at work and home, and encouraged to accept responsibility for success or the consequences of failure. (Ozga, 2002:334)

There has been a permanent revolution of change in the provision of public services, described by Pollitt (2007) as "repetitive, large-scale organizational re-engineering" which has produced " . . . a rate of repetition—of constant, if not accelerating disruption—which does not seem to be equalled anywhere else in the developed world" (540–541). The consequences of such decision-making are threefold: first, "this rate of change makes it impossible to find out which organisational designs work well and which do not" (538); second, "rapid change inevitably brings transition costs" (538); and third, there is "a general loss of faith in stability and an accompanying diminution of willingness to fully commit oneself to a particular organisation" (539). Hence a key issue is not only to give recognition to the sources, scope, and patterns of policy, but also the overarching approach of government to change and its impact on people's lives, attitudes, and general well-being.

Where does this leave us? Certainly policymakers have been busy with strategies to both eradicate poverty and to improve educational provision, and we intend to show in Chapter 13 the ways in which successive governments, particularly in England, have devised and implemented a range of interventions. We argue that such investment of intellectual and economic resources have led to gains in regard to the quality of people's lives and achievements, but we note that there are possibilities for change that have not yet been engaged with. In Chapter 14 we embrace this by raising questions about what policy and policymakers can do about the relationship between education and poverty. At this stage we would want to say that it seems to us that our analysis so far shows that in Western-style democracies and capitalist economies there are ongoing and deeply entrenched debates over fundamental matters about the role of the state in civil society, and the relationship of the economy with the public good. We know from our analysis of the literatures and research projects that there are no silver bullets as a functional solution, but at the same time politicians in our current political culture require clear solutions that can impact quickly and find evidence to support mandate renewal. Consequently socially critical local and community approaches can take too much time and can be difficult to translate into one side of A4 paper with clear recommendations for scaling up and rolling out across the country. We would therefore suggest that policymakers need to give attention to all the matters we have presented in this chapter, and recognise the consequences of what Pollitt (2007) calls "New Labour's re-disorganisation" (529) based on endemic restructuring with new targets, roles, and personnel.

CONCLUSION

Our task in this chapter has been necessarily wide ranging and we are mindful that how policy operates in different countries needs to be taken into consideration. Even within the four home nations of the UK there are emerging policy strategies that take at least nuanced and possibly different approaches to the Neo-liberal and Civic Projects that we have identified are a useful starting point. There is sufficient evidence in the research presented in this book that the local is important but also, as identified by Lingard and Ozga (2007), that there are possibilities for education policy to challenge parochialism. Indeed our identification of the Neo-liberal and Civic Projects in play crosses national boundaries, and the framework of sources, scope, and patterns is sufficiently generic to be deployed with particular systems and generate robust comparative analyses.

To return to the beginning, there are particular projects in play and our analysis based on the research reported in this book shows that the Neo-liberal Project has dominated but the Civic Project, while marginalised, remains vibrant and meaningful. We have given recognition to the way that functionalism is delivering the Neo-liberal Project, and also the problems with this, and how social criticality not only is exposing such problems but also developing alternative approaches. Such approaches may be off the radar because functionalism cannot recognise such knowledge claims and as such tends to dismiss them as esoteric and ideological. This then is the starting point for asking how the relationship between education and poverty is being dealt with by governments, and this is the focus of the next chapter.

13 Poverty and Educational Policy Initiatives

A Review

Carlo Raffo, Alan Dyson, Helen Gunter,
Dave Hall, Lisa Jones, and Afroditi Kalambouka

INTRODUCTION

In this chapter we will use the mapping framework from Part I, the case studies in Part 2 and the discussion about productive policy possibilities documented in Chapter 12 to provide an examination of, and commentary on, English priority education policy initiatives. These will at times be supplemented by exemplar analysis of education policy from other affluent countries but it is beyond the scope of this chapter to examine all international initiatives in any detail. Instead we have selected a number of English and other international examples, we believe, are both important in their own right and are typical of the sorts of approaches currently favoured by policy-makers across affluent countries. Our aim is not to characterise the whole of international education—let alone wider public—policy in terms of these particular initiatives, but to use them as examples of the ways in which policy interventions embody the sorts of explanations that have been outlined in previous parts of the book.

Perhaps at the outset we need to remind readers what appears to be the dominant discourse for education in most affluent countries. The priority of much educational policy of late has been about meeting the challenges of economic globalisation through enhancing the acquisition of educational credentials (i.e. an expansion of human capital) for a greatest number of young people. In Chapter 12, Gunter et al. described this in some detail and labelled it the Neo-liberal Project. This Neo-liberal Project has, for different countries and in varying degrees, resulted in policy makers developing educational strategies whose stated goals are the improvement of educational outcomes for all and in particular for those educationally underachieving and seen as most at risk of social exclusion from the mainstream—that is, those most likely to be living in poverty. Based on this emphasis much educational policy seems to approach the issue of educational disadvantage and poverty in two interconnected and yet hierarchical and sequential ways. Firstly and most importantly it attempts to deal with educational disparities through a universal approach that focuses on mainstream funding arrangements and universal curricular and pedagogical systems often linked to standards, accountability, and inspection regimes—sometimes referred to as performance regimes. These funding formulae, curricular, and pedagogical systems and performance regimes are generally designed to enhance system and school performance, and so raise levels of all student achievement and perhaps, most importantly, those who might be viewed as disadvantaged and underperforming. They generally involve a powerful mix of target-setting, curriculum and pedagogical development, and high-stakes accountability measures rolled out across the system as a whole. If these universal policies appear to fail to resolve educational disparities then most affluent countries appear to then develop a second thrust of priority education policies that target additional resources and attention towards those parts of the system and those groups of students where performance and achievement lag behind the levels that are seen as appropriate. In England, and many other affluent countries, the focus of these priority education policies are on poor and disadvantaged learners who are seen as at risk of social exclusion by virtue of their poor achievements and/or their disengagement from education, and on the schools and other parts of the system serving those learners. In England, policies developed to meet the needs of these learners have been of many kinds, frequently emerging and disappearing within the space of a few years and it is impossible here to catalogue them all for each country. However, what we can articulate for the English context (and perhaps for other country contexts), are three main foci of these policies:

(a) Micro-level group focused interventions, i.e. at-risk groups often living in poverty;
(b) Meso-level, area-focused interventions that focus on:
  (i) initiatives targeted at schools in disadvantaged areas;
  (ii) initiatives coordinating policies in disadvantaged areas across education, health, and social welfare;
  (iii) initiatives in particular cities where poverty is heavily concentrated; and
  (iv) area regeneration initiatives that include an education component;
(c) Meso-level institution focused interventions.

This typology is far from perfect, and there is a good deal of overlap between these different foci. Nonetheless, it is a useful way of making sense of what otherwise might seem to be a chaotic policy scene.

MAINSTREAM FUNDING ARRANGEMENTS AND UNIVERSAL CURRICULAR, PEDAGOGICAL, AND ACCOUNTABILITY SYSTEMS

In terms of educational funding arrangements in England, schools in disadvantaged areas, through various complex weighting funding formulae, are generally, if differentially and inconsistently (Freedman & Horner, 2008), more generously resourced through mainstream funding (Dedicated Schools grant, Schools Standard grant, and the Standards Fund) than schools elsewhere, although this can in many respects depend on the nature of how funds from central government to local authorities is then allocated to schools in those authorities. Educational funding arrangements in other affluent countries do not hold to any particular model. For example, in the US, funds available for schools are based on tax revenues of the district. For disadvantaged districts this has the perverse effect of reducing funds to schools located in such districts, even though these schools are likely to have additional needs. Lipman in Chapter 4 clearly highlights how schools in the most disadvantaged parts of Chicago have been historically under-resourced and in some respects have been "set up for failure." In an attempt to ameliorate this position Title I ("Title One") of the Elementary and Secondary Education Act in the US attempts to distribute federal funding to schools and school districts with a high percentage of students from low-income families. To qualify as a Title I school, a school typically has around 40 percent or more of its students that come from families that qualify under the United States Census' definitions of low income. Schools receiving Title I funding are regulated by federal legislation, including the No Child Left Behind Act (see below). Title I funds may be used for children from preschool through high school, but most of the students served (65 percent) are in grades 1 through 6; another 12 percent are in preschool and kindergarten programs. In contrast in many Nordic countries the level of public funding for comprehensive education is above the EU mean and generally more fairly distributed (for example in Finland each school educates children at the same per pupil rate). Although these various funding mechanisms may say much about the historical developments of education in different countries what they all demonstrate is a commitment to the public funding of education for all to at least upper secondary level.

Although public funding is the bedrock to efficacious education systems, most countries have also developed national curricular, pedagogical, and accountability education policies that have attempted to drive up performance of schools generally and particularly those dealing with disadvantaged and poor students. In the UK, links between disadvantage and educational failure, and the subsequent policy activities, are relatively long established; however, in recent years—predominantly since the election of successive New Labour governments from 1997—the policy process can be considered as both intensified and wider in focus and outlook. This intensification can be seen in the tendency towards central intervention and is also evident in a results-driven focus—which has lead to an increase in target-setting and a need for educational providers to meet these targets—and the focus on delivering a 'quality'-driven educational system. In many respects this policy agenda parallel's the US's No Child Left Behind 2001 Act which reauthorized a number of federal programmes aiming to improve the performance of US primary and secondary schools by increasing the standards of accountability for states, school districts, and schools, as well as providing parents more flexibility in choosing which schools their children will attend.

Part of the drive to enhance quality education in many educational systems has been through curriculum reform. For example, in 1988 the Education Reform Act in England stipulated a national curriculum that all pupils in the primary (Key Stages 1 and 2) and secondary stages (Key Stages 3 and 4) of schooling should undertake. This was complemented by tests that were developed in the core areas of English, Maths, and Science, and that could be administered at different stages of the curriculum. Data from these tests would provide evidence of the level at which pupils were operating and also provide benchmark data for schools and teachers to examine how they might improve the educational attainments of underachieving students. The existence of a national curriculum in what all (or nearly all) students are expected to participate means that curriculum plays a different role in priority policies in England than in some other countries. In principle, there is no separate curriculum track for low attaining or disadvantaged students. They follow the same curriculum as everyone else. The emphasis, therefore, is on exploiting such flexibility as exists in the common curriculum framework (and this has been increasing) and developing strategies and interventions to enable disadvantaged students to participate in that curriculum.

In principle, the English system enables the needs of different groups to be met without creating curriculum 'ghettoes' into which students are segregated. The reality, however, is somewhat different from this. In practice, low attaining students are likely to spend a greater amount of time than their peers on the basic skills of literacy and numeracy. They will receive additional tuition outside English and Maths lessons, sacrificing other parts of the curriculum, and/or they will receive interventions during those lessons, focusing on the basics while their peers explore the subjects more fully. They are also likely to be selected for other forms of intervention which may be delivered in ordinary lesson time. As they reach the final years of secondary education, they are likely to take more vocational options, so that their curriculum will begin to look very different from that of their higher attaining peers. Not surprisingly, this pattern is echoed in provision outside the statutory schools years, with low attaining and disadvantaged young people more likely to experience targeted intervention in the early years and to enter low-level vocational provision after leaving school.

Although many Nordic countries have moved to certain aspects of educational systems exemplified by the US and England, particularly in relation to freedom of school choice and decentralisation, there are still however, major differences in the educational philosophies, policies, and practices that underpin the systems (see Hargreaves, 2008 with regards to Finland) and the nature of the population being educated. One of the most important differences is that most Nordic countries have few relatively poor or wealthy schools. Most schools, whether part of the national education system or publicly funded 'independent schools' (Sweden), educate children at a similar per pupil rate and in addition teachers in most Nordic countries (in particular Finland) encounter few students who do not speak the national language. Where Nordic countries do have significant minority ethnic groups or refugees often located in particular parts of the country (e.g. the Sami minority in Sweden) then multi-language development is generally seen as a priority, with expensive initial mother tongue teaching running parallel with national language development at the outset (Moreno Herrara, 2008). This situation can be contrasted to the heterogeneous situation in the US where one in every twelve students is learning English as an additional language.

PRIORITY EDUCATION POLICIES

As was suggested at the outset of this chapter, targeted priority education policies seem most pronounced where there are stresses and strains in the universal educational system and where heterogeneity and entrenched inequality between pupils and schools are most pronounced—the example of England being a good case in point. And as we will show in the rest of this chapter it is in countries like England that priority education policies are seen as central to improving educational performance. Most of these policies are grouped and organised at either the micro or meso level.

Micro Level Group-focused Interventions

These types of interventions are targeted at groups of learners who are or might be at risk of underachievement, and hence of social exclusion. Most of the policy examples provided here emanate from England. A report on *Evaluating Educational Inclusion* by Ofsted (Ofsted, 2000) (the schools inspectorate in England) identified a wide range of such groups. These included boys; minority ethnic and faith groups; Travelers; asylum seekers and refugees; pupils who need support to learn English as an additional language (EAL); pupils with special educational needs; 'at risk' children; and any other pupils with the potential for disaffection and exclusion.

At various points in recent years there have been initiatives in England targeted at all of these groups. Perhaps most importantly most of these groups reflect aspects of disadvantage, poverty, and the potential for social exclusion. Some of these initiatives have simply taken the form of funding streams directed towards schools or local authorities (for instance, the Vulnerable Children Grant [VCG]). Others are structured national 'strategies' in which a series of activities have been set up to stimulate provision for particular groups (for example work with learners regarded as having special educational needs catalyzed through the Raising Barriers to Achievement

Programme). Perhaps one of the most concerted efforts in England of supporting at-risk students make progression through secondary school and a successful transition into post-compulsory education, training, or work was the setting up of the *Connexions* service. The *Connexions* service was developed to focus clearly on providing both individual support and careers advice to young people via Personal Advisors. Here the focus is very much on choices and paths with the recognition that transition from schooling and adolescence to adulthood and work for young people is now more complex, particularly with regards to accessing the more highly paid sections of changing labour markets. There is a recognition that young people who are most vulnerable or at risk require detailed and on-going support from a Personal Advisor (PA) who not only advises, but acts as a trusted advocate for the young person. One can see close parallels between this advocacy role and the importance that the risk and resilience literature in Chapter 1 places on supportive and aware adult relationships for young people.

Other examples in England of support targeted at individuals at the micro level include financial support provided to young people who might otherwise struggle to access education. For example, financial support for transition into post-compulsory education for disadvantaged students in England is provided through the Educational Maintenance allowance. This is available to 16–19 year olds from lower income families who remain in full-time education after the end of compulsory education. Its purpose is to enhance the educational progression, retention, and success of young people living in relative poverty.

Meso-level Area-focused Interventions

(i) Schools in targeted areas:

Certain interventions have targeted areas where learners at risk of under-achievement and social exclusion are held to be concentrated. Typically, these are urban areas marked by poverty and low educational achievement. The Excellence in Cities (EiC) programme in England is an example of area-focused interventions and was launched in September 1999 to raise standards and promote inclusion in disadvantaged inner cities and other urban areas. It focused on leadership, behaviour, teaching, and learning. Initially just based on secondary schools, the programme quickly expanded to include primary schools. The programme tackled underachievement in schools through specific strands targeted at underachieving or disadvantaged groups. Learning Mentors worked with underachieving students in schools, Learning Support Units were established to provide for students at risk of exclusion from school for disciplinary reasons, a Gifted and Talented pupils programme was developed (see above), and City Learning Centres were established to enhance adult learning opportunities (particularly through information technology) for local people.

Area targeted approaches have not only been important to English priority education policies but have also be central to both France and Portugal. France's Zones d'Education Prioritaires (ZEPs) were established in 1982 in order to support the work of schools serving areas of disadvantage through (a) the targeting of additional resources into schools in those areas; (b) the development of local initiatives and new educational methods; and (c) an attempt to strengthen local involvement in educational decision-making and practice. The development of area approaches in Portugal was developed in 1995 and termed Territórios Educativos de Intervenção Prioritária (TEIPs—Priority Intervention Education Areas in English). They took the form of a central designation of disadvantaged areas in which educational interventions were called for in order to enhance learning conditions for students in disadvantaged areas, and so combat social inequality. TEIPs shared some features in common with ZEPs. In particular, each TEIP was expected to develop a 'project,' the precise nature of which was defined locally, but which was expected to take into account a series of priorities:

- creating conditions to promote pupil achievement;
- defining the training needs of teachers and other staff members, as well as the needs of the community;
- promoting a close articulation with the local community;
- operating integrated resource management; and
- developing educational, cultural, sports, and free-time activities.

(ii) Coordinating initiatives across education, health, and social welfare:

There are a number of parallel and similar examples of coordinating policies that emerge from England, Australia, and the US. *Sure Start* was set up in England to enhance the functioning of children and families living in disadvantaged areas by improving services provided in local programme areas. In many respects Sure Start reflects the research of early child development studies highlighted in Chapter 1 of the book and of programmes such as Head Start in the US which was established under the Economic Opportunity Act of 1964. Both programmes were aimed at disadvantaged preschool children with the purpose of delivering programs and services that would prepare preschool children for elementary school. Typically such services included parenting support, access to health provision and child care, and educational facilities for young parents. Both Head Start and Sure Start were strategically situated in areas identified as having high levels of deprivation and were seen as interventions to enhance the life prospects of young children in disadvantaged families and communities. Programmes are area based, and with Sure Start all children under four and their families living in a prescribed area serve as the targets of intervention. This means that services within a Sure Start area are universally available, thus limiting any stigma that may accrue from individuals being targeted. By virtue of their local autonomy, Sure Start areas do not have a prescribed curriculum or set of services. Instead, each Sure Start area has extensive local autonomy concerning how it fulfils its mission to improve and create services as needed, without specification of how services are to be changed.

Community-oriented schools under the guise of *Full Service Extended Schools* (FSES) in England, the US, Australia, and other countries constitute focal points at which strategies for raising educational standards overall are supported by strategies for targeting support to schools serving disadvantaged populations, and strategies for tackling neighbourhood and family problems. In England the detailed guidance from the Department of Children schools and Families on FSES proposes no fewer than 23 possible outcomes from community-oriented schools, ranging from improved access to childcare and ICT, through reductions in health inequalities and the number of unemployed people, to better school security and improvements in students' behaviour (DfES, 2003a). In other words, FSES are expected to intervene in the multiple problems which beset children, families, and communities living in disadvantage. However, at the heart of these interventions is a commitment to education as the pathway to achievement and hence to employment and social inclusion—and to raised expectations as a necessary precondition of raised achievement. Although clearly orientated within a functionalist perspective one can detect elements with the FSES initiative that mirror a more integrating explanation of the link between education and poverty and that focus on both micro issues associated with holistic child development needs and meso-level development through enhanced family and community engagement via parenting classes, crèches, and skills development programmes. In addition there is a recognition of the need for a more integrated approach to delivering certain core public services via a multi-agency strategy located in the school that links into meso level multi-agency working documented in Part I of the book.

(iii) City Initiatives:

Whereas many of the initiatives highlighted above have been available to targeted areas across a particular country, the London Challenge is an example in England that recognises the distinctive difficulties facing schools in the capital—in terms, for instance, of low levels of achievement, high levels of disadvantage, the problems and benefits of a multi-ethnic population, and the balkanisation of governance of London education, which is divided between a large number of local authorities. The Challenge deploys a range of functionalist strategies at both the meso and micro level to address these issues, including targeted intervention with low-performing schools, programmes aimed at increasing teacher recruitment and retention, a gifted and talented programme, and support to local authorities in managing their education systems (see, http://www.dfes.gov.uk/londonchallenge/). Similar programmes are now being set up in other major cities.

(iv) Regeneration initiatives:

In England the concern with area-focused interventions is repeated across many aspects of government social policy. Schools and early years centres in disadvantaged areas also participate in interventions that are developed by government departments and agencies other that the Department for Education and Skills (DfES). For instance, the early experiments with extended schools arose out of the cross-departmental National Strategy for Neighbourhood Renewal (Social Exclusion Unit, 1998); see also http://www.neighbourhood.gov.uk/page.asp?id=908). Likewise, the Single Regeneration Budget (http://www.communities.gov.uk/index.asp?id=1128087), and New Deal for Communities (http://www.neighbourhood.gov.uk/page.asp?id=617) managed by the Department for Communities and Local Government has had dedicated education strands and has often been a source of funding for schools and early years centres. This type of approach can also be exemplified in Australia by the State of Victoria's 'A Fairer Victoria: creating opportunity and addressing disadvantage' programme that attempts to integrate strategies of renewal for the state that include the development of universal services and educational strands that focus on pre-school and targeted activities at key transition points including improving access to services, housing and justice for communities, and the building of stronger communities (http://www.dpc.vic.gov.au/CA256D800027B102/Lookup/SocialPolicyActionPlan/$file/fairer%20vic.pdf).

Meso-level, Institution-Focused Interventions

In England much recent mainstream education policy has been concerned with driving up standards of achievement by improving the performance of schools and other educational institutions. Governments have tended to operate with a 'carrot and stick' approach, offering incentives and rewards for improvement on the one hand, but punishing poor performance on the other. In effect, this results in a targeted approach, with institutions regarded as under-performing being singled out for special attention on the grounds that their ineffectiveness threatens the educational and life chances of their students. Most of these schools are in socio-economically disadvantaged poor areas. Although most schools identified as causing concern rapidly move out of that category in response to intensive intervention, some do not, and may find themselves being closed down and replaced by a new school (albeit, usually in the same buildings). There are two school renewal programmes of this kind—Fresh Start and the Academies Programme. The assumption in both cases is that interventions to improve the existing school have failed repeatedly, and that fundamental changes are needed in facilities, staffing (usually including the head teacher) and governance arrangements. In the US under the guise of No Child Left Behind, similar sanctions are available to schools that are deemed to be failing to meet to the targets and challenges posed.

EVIDENCE OF IMPACT

There seems little doubt that both universal and priority educational policies of the sort described above have been effective in raising attainment generally and in focusing attention on particular groups, areas, and institutions, and in stimulating activity in relation to them. For example in England additional mainstream funding has provided opportunities for schools to resource a whole variety of additional teaching support for students most 'at risk,' many to good effect, although there is also a real recognition that perhaps these funds are insufficient and at times misdirected to meet the additional needs that these schools encounter (Thrupp, 1999; Lupton, 2004; Freedman & Horner, 2008). In addition, school-focused research shows how schools in the most challenging circumstances through various management, leadership, pedagogical, and accountability polices targeted at raising achievement can make a difference in educational outcomes for some of those young people most disadvantaged (Muijs et al., 2004). Likewise priority education policies such as the Vulnerable Children Grant (Kendall et al., 2004) and strategies to raise the achievement of boys (Younger et al., 2005) and of students from minority ethnic backgrounds (Cunningham et al., 2004) have each been successful in directing attention to groups that might easily have slipped beneath the radar if government had concentrated solely on whole system reform. Research by Hoggart and Smith (2004) suggest that *Connexions* is achieving some positive impact, of different types, with different groups of young people, including those at risk. The findings from the EMA evaluation by Middleton et al. (2005) suggest that EMA has the strongest impact upon the destinations of specific target groups who tended to be under-represented in post-16 education; namely young men, young people from lower income families, and those who were not high achievers at year 11.

Similarly, area-focused initiatives in England, such as Excellence in Cities (Kendall et al., 2005), full service extended schools (Cummings et al., 2005), and Sure Start seem to have acted as catalysts for considerable activity on the ground. These policies have generated some of the improved outcomes at which they were targeted. For instance, the rate of increase in GCSE (national examination) performance for EiC areas has been around twice that of non EiC schools for a number of years in succession (Kendall et al., 2005). This means there has been a narrowing of the achievement gap between EiC and non-EiC areas from 12.4 percent in 2001 to 6.9 percent in 2005. Moreover, there have been improvements for targeted groups of young people. Melhuish et al. (2005) in their review of Sure Start suggests that there were benefits to the programme; however, it produced greater benefits for the moderately disadvantaged than for the more severely disadvantaged which resonated with other evaluations of such interventions (e.g. Early Head Start, Love et al., 2002) and points to some of the issues highlighted in Chapter 1 about how particular groups are better placed to make use of current resources and can acquire further resources of support through their engagement with networks. And with FSES there was anecdotal evidence of positive outcomes with regards to raised attainment, increased pupil engagement with learning and a growing trust and support between home and school. There was also multi-agency working that brought some benefits to children and their families (Cummings et al., 2005). The authors also suggest that these initial data provide some evidence for a way of intervening to break the cycle of disadvantage in some of the areas that they serve.

However it is also evident that given the various investments in both universal approaches and the plethora of targeted priority educational initiatives, the basic premise still holds in most affluent countries that the more disadvantaged an individual's background the less well he or she will achieve in education (Chitty, 2002) and the more that social hierarchies are reproduced through generations (Blanden & Machin, 2007), particularly in those countries where social disparities are clearly more evident. In the next section we attempt to make sense of why this might be case, utilising explanations developed in the earlier part of the book.

POLICY INTERVENTIONS AND EXPLANATIONS

As we have briefly indicated above, the various policy interventions described imply one or more of the explanations set out in Parts I and II of the book about the nature of the relationship between poverty and poor educational outcomes. Universal mainstream funding approaches and various curricular, pedagogical, and organisational features of schooling are generally couched in meso-level explanations linked to schools improvement and effectiveness literature. Targeted priority educational policies demonstrate a diversity of potential explanations. For example explanations for the Sure Start and Head Start initiatives are couched in terms, amongst other things, of family processes and early child development issues. The Excellence in Cities initiative implies an explanation predominantly in terms of school improvement that focuses on resilience-building activities and enriched environments. Although these examples of universal and targeted interventions demonstrate diversity of explanation and intervention, what they also demonstrate is the acceptance of a particular perspective about the nature and purpose of education and also a specific level at which explanations and interventions are explored separately to improve education in areas of poverty. First the sources, scope, and patterns of policy development are suggestive of a neo-liberal project that is essentially functionalist in its orientation towards defining the problem and developing solutions for educational disadvantage and poverty. Both universal educational systems linked to organisational, curricular, and pedagogical developments and targeted initiatives such as *Connexions*, Sure Start, Excellence in Cities, Full Service extended schools, and so on are all about functionalist interventions to enable young people to improve how they engage with education as it is currently constituted, to improve their educational outcomes as they are currently constituted, and hence improve their labour market position through improved levels of narrowly focused human capital development. Secondly there is an implicit and perhaps at times an incoherent theory of change in the way such varied educational policy and practice is seen as ameliorating the problems of poverty and poor educational outcomes.

This incoherence is reflected in the disparate micro- and meso-level explanations and interventions that focus separately on (a) improving the universal educational processes in schools and (b) providing the appropriate targeted support for young people and families in order that they might be able to maximise these opportunities within school and that underemphasises the extent to which disparate meso-level functionalist interventions can resolve the problem of education and poverty. This may be particularly the case given that the educational problem may have at its root social disparities that reflect particular macro-level, socio-economic developments that have created conditions of poverty for many young people and families and generated a deprivation of capability to engage successfully with education and life more generally. This may suggest the need to not only examine universal and targeted educational strategies but also the way young people have been disadvantaged by social, cultural, and economic inequalities and power relations that predicate their engagement with education, and what Lupton refers to in her chapter as the "local spatial realities that globalisation produces" (Lupton, 2008: 122).

In contrast to this potentially narrow and limited theory of change, Parts I and II of the book suggests that the linkage between education and poverty, whether from a functionalist or socially critically perspective, is one that is a complex, interacting, and hierarchical system with little indication that one single explanation or disparate set of explanations can hope to account for the essential reason for the linkage. Hence there is every reason to believe that no single universal or disparate set of interventions can resolve the problem. So for example, one might argue that universal school-focused approaches will always be doomed to failure in dealing with the problem of educational inequality because they have focused almost exclusively at one level—the meso level—from one perspective—the functionalist perspective—and located within one site of the school with specific neo-liberal pedagogical and curricular educational processes linked to that site. Of course improvements have been made but in the most optimistic of analyses these have only been marginal for those young people most disadvantaged. One might suggest that there are two reasons for this. Firstly, and reflecting critiques outlined in Parts I and II of the book, many universal school systems do not take into account in a detailed, considered, or integrated way other meso-level functionalist factors. As Muijs argues in Chapter 6, too much attention on improving a school's effectiveness has perhaps resulted in schools becoming too inward looking for solutions to their problems— solutions that perhaps fail to fully recognise numerous factors external to the school that include:

- risk factors linked to communities experiencing poverty, exemplified by Schoon's chapter that focuses on how young people from relatively poor socio-economic backgrounds have generally lower educational and life aspirations than their more privileged peers,
- the importance of parents in preparing and supporting young people through education,
- the need for education to work with other public sector services to effectively meet a more holistic set of family and community needs generated by the experience of being socially excluded.

In addition in many universal school-based approaches also fail to respond to meso-level socially critical perspectives such as those outlined in chapters by Lupton, Thomson, Smyth, Lipman, and Maguire in Part II of the book who separately point to the need to:

- authentically include student voice, in particular "to young people's spatial meaning-making" (Lupton, 2008: 122) in the development of schools,
- to implement critical pedagogies that reflect the lived experiences of young people and their families,
- develop more democratic school governance mechanisms that might empower schools to reflect the needs of its communities,
- provide significant and strongly weighted additional funding for schools serving disadvantaged students and the communities within which they live.

In a sense much universal educational provision is located within a dominant neo-liberal agenda that provides few opportunities or openings for different sources and patterns of curricular and pedagogic policy development associated with the civic project for social democratic development.

The second reason is that universal school-focused developments generally do not recognise factors at work at other levels of analysis. They rarely appreciate how the forces of globalisation are impacting on certain communities and creating social disparities, nor do they see what Smyth documents in Chapter 5 of how schools and education might take part in the re-developments of those communities through various regeneration initiatives and democratically engaged activity. Schools generally do not see themselves as an embedded part of social and economic policy but merely there to uncritically contribute to it. In addition, and as Maguire notes in Chapter 10, school-focused research and policy rarely recognises how poverty and the spatial context within which it manifests itself generates constrained levels of decision-making and choice in the changing transition experiences of young people living in poverty.

But what of priority educational policy initiatives that are arguably more closely targeted at those young people, communities, and schools most disadvantaged? The FSES initiative, in its various guises, is arguably one of the most ambitious priority educational policies. Its most general aim, pertinent to various international examples of the genre, is not only to deal with at-risk young people in challenging schools, but to also intervene and support families and communities within which these young people are located, recognising how multiple barriers can impact on educational achievement. FSES are expected to intervene in the multiple problems which beset children, families, and communities living in disadvantage. Above all, FSES focus heavily on meso-level factors that are proximal to children's educational achievements. In an evaluation of the FSES initiative in England undertaken by Cummings et al. (2005), a number of themes became apparent. At one level these schools, within the overall 'crusade for standards,' focused on the classroom and institutional processes which impacted most directly on children's learning. At another level, however, they intervened in family functioning in terms of the health and social needs of families, but also in terms of family expectations and attitudes towards learning. In addition they intervened in neighbourhoods by creating focal points for communities, increasing the skills levels and employability of local people, and changing expectations. Perhaps most importantly the evaluation study of FSES generated anecdotal examples of improvements in the lives of disadvantaged families and young people. At the same time, however, almost totally absent from FSES policy development and implementation was a discussion of macro-level factors which might be thought to underpin and explain these meso factors. For instance, much is made of the potential impact of FSES on the expectations, achievements, and employability of young people and adults. FSES in all countries are intended to contribute to the (much contested) system-wide drive to create a high-skills economy by driving up standards of educational achievement. In England they also have a reduction in adult unemployment as one of their targets. However, the emphasis is very much on preparing and enabling local people to be more competitive in the existing local labour market rather than on more direct and radical interventions to change and improve the nature of that market. And given the focus on labour market preparation, one might again argue that the FSES educational project reflects functionalist neo-liberal agendas and narratives often based on deficit thinking about young people and communities in relation to those markets.

Similarly, although it seems that FSES are expected to make a contribution to overcoming the multiple problems of disadvantaged areas, it was much less clear what they should or could do to prevent those concentrations of disadvantage from appearing in the first place. From reviewing FSES in England, US, and Australia there appears little sense in government guidance that schools should be linked to local housing, community development, or regeneration strategies aimed at dispersing concentrations of disadvantage and reducing the incidence of disadvantage overall—much less that they should contribute to subregional or regional strategies in these fields. On the contrary, their emergence in areas of disadvantage seem to indicate an acceptance that such areas must inevitably exist, and that the only strategy available is to concentrate service provision to match the concentration of disadvantage. Perhaps in part because of this apparent lack of concern with macro-level factors, it was debatable how far there is any theoretical coherence in the rationale for FSES. Certainly, at the level of the activities which schools were expected to undertake, there is a distinct sense of multiple, disconnected responses to multiple problems. The focus on educational expectations and achievements offers a degree of coherence but there is no further exploration of how worklessness arises; how workless people come to be concentrated in particular neighbourhoods; how far 'low expectations' account for differential achievements between different social groups; how worklessness, low expectations, and low achievements relate to poor health outcomes and high levels of street crime; or a host of other questions that arise in respect to disadvantaged people and areas. Repeated statements to the effect that problems are multiple and connected take the place of any deeper explanation of process. In a sense this critique reflects Lupton's thoughts in Chapter 8 which point to the way that area-based policies such as FSES have articulated some notion of context but only in surface ways that do not fully explore the social, historical, relative, contingent, and dynamic nature of context as space.

Our review based on Parts I and II of the book points to the fact that education policy in affluent countries needs to simultaneously reflect on a whole series of factors and at different levels if it is to have any meaningful impact. In other words it needs to have an overarching vision of how various interventions fit together, ensuring, as Gunter et al. in Chapter 12 remind us, that it recognises which knowledge and narratives about education and poverty it privileges and why. Table 13.1 summarises the various explanations and interventions that perhaps need to be incorporated into those reflections.

At present much targeted educational policy in affluent countries is piecemeal and largely focuses on those issues at the functionalist meso/micro level that are easiest to examine, most susceptible to short term interventions, and that reflect a neo-liberal agenda that some might argue make them perhaps less socially and politically destabilising. This has resulted in a plethora of initiatives at the school, family, and, to a lesser extent, the neighbourhood level. And as we have shown concurrently, significantly less attention has been paid to the spatial, social, and economic conditions created by aspects of globalisation and the associated class, gender, and ethnicity issues within which these initiatives are set.

Our examination of literatures associated with aspects of the socially critical perspective point to the way inequalities are inherent at the macro level and reproduced at all other levels. From this perspective, policy that attempts to 'improve' the meso level without examining the inherent inequalities associated with the macro level can only at their very best be described

Table 13.1   Education and Poverty—A Summary of Explanations and Interventions

Function-alists	Sites	Explanations—Factors Affecting Education	Interventions
Macro	National and local economy, social structures, 'the system'	Globalisation and changes in local and national economies Resultant social exclusion Tax and spending on public services Reductions in child poverty	Local and national economic development strategies
Meso	Neighbourhoods, peer groups, school systems	Work/unemployment Income and wealth Health Neighbourhoods and ethnicity Parenting Schools operating in challenging circumstances School improvement Multi-agency working	Support for parents and parenting skills Multi-agency working to support individuals, families, and communities Improved school effectiveness in areas of poverty and disadvantage
Micro	Individuals, the family	Providing choices and social capital to encourage and support education (e.g. mentoring) Inherited capability and intelligence	Recognition and development of positive and productive relationships
Integrating	Combinations of the above	Psychological development and interaction of genetics and environment Risk and resilience	

Table 13.1 continued

Socially Critical	Sites	Explanations— Factors Affecting Education	Interventions
Macro	National and local economy, social structures, 'the system'	Education reproducing inequality, social disadvantage, and poverty	Human rights, social justice, democracy
		Challenging politics of choice, standards, middle-class values, and the market	
		Ethnic disadvantage (Critical Race Theory)	
Meso	Neighbourhoods, peer groups, school systems	Curriculum	Community activism
		Teaching practices Leadership and engagement	
		Reinterpreting 'disadvantaged neighbourhoods'	
		Parenting and resilience	
Micro	The individual psyche	Identities are heavily shaped by external power relations which constrain or enhance the possibilities that individuals can achieve	Small scale changes in the location and exercise of power

as ameliorative. However the problem for the socially critical perspective is that it is policy makers who need to address these issues and policy makers by their very position are often viewed as part of the problem rather than as part of the solution. There is, however, some hope with regards to developments in pupil voice, critical pedagogy, and aspects of community engagement and/or control over education which reflect the civic project and which points to possibilities for change from below that would create a momentum with the potential to drive policy (Smyth et al., 2008). In addition, hope for radical, scaled up, and yet achievable policy objectives located within the Civic project is perhaps most clearly articulated in the

Toronto School Board case study that Gaskell and Levin document in their chapter in the book. What this case reminds us is that different sources of political activism can generate scope and patterns of policy development that do not necessarily have to reflect a dominant national/international neo-liberal agenda and that can be developed in both functionalist and socially critical ways.

We wish to conclude this chapter by recognising that policy development is complex and constrained by numerous factors. We also at this stage have provided only a general sense of what these issues might mean for policy. In the final chapter we intend to deal with both the complexities of policy development highlighted in Chapter 12 and the imagined possibilities of educational reform that might draw on issues of coherence, scope, power, and governance to bring about educational equity in areas of poverty. What this chapter does suggest is that although the challenges are great, there is scope for an educational politics and policy development that might make the difference. It is to this agenda that we now turn.

14 What Is to Be Done? Implications for Policy Makers

Alan Dyson, Helen Gunter, Dave Hall, Carlo Raffo, Lisa Jones, and Afroditi Kalambouka

THE LIMITS OF POLICY

The review of frameworks and interventions in the previous chapter makes it abundantly clear that policy makers in Western democracies have been highly active in attempting to break the link between poverty and education. England and the US may be extreme cases, but the rapid succession of initiatives and reform efforts in those countries demonstrate that policy makers have no difficulty in finding levers to pull. Indeed, common to both the 'Neo-liberal and 'Civic' projects, as we labelled them in Chapter 12, is the belief that breaking the poverty-education link is important, not simply because it is unjust that social background should determine educational outcomes, but because a 'good education' is seen as the way of creating a more just society. As a Secretary of State for Education in England once put it:

> . . . of all the areas that government can influence it is education and learning, which has perhaps the most potential to open up opportunity. Sure Start centres, nurseries, schools, colleges and universities are the cradles of aspiration and achievement that embody the hopes we all have for our children. That is why I see my department as the department for life chances. And that is why I see it as my job to boost social mobility. (Kelly, 2005)

Unfortunately, as the previous chapter documents, the level of policy activity is not matched by the effectiveness of interventions. Despite years—in some countries, generations—of initiatives and reforms, it remains the case that social background and educational outcomes are inextricably linked. This is not to say that policy interventions make no difference at all. However, their tendency to focus on what we call the micro and meso levels, and to overlook the structural inequalities embedded at the macro level, means that their effects will always be limited and precarious. The conclusion Rees et al. reach about the limitations of area based initiatives (ABIs) in the UK could, in fact be applied to all policy interventions:

> Once social and economic disadvantage is redefined as an aspect of the
> wider inequalities which are characteristic of British society, then these
> limitations become apparent. The state is not in a position to engage
> with issues of social inequality, structural shifts in the organization
> of economic activity and their consequences, except at the margins.
> The kinds of redistribution which would be necessary to do so simply
> do not appear on the policy agenda. ABIs and the conceptualizations
> of disadvantage on which they are based reflect this. They provide a
> means of presenting the promise of 'active government', but within the
> highly restricted policy repertoire which in reality is available. (Rees,
> Power, & Taylor, 2007:272)

Bearing in mind our own analysis in Chapter 12, we could reach an even
more pessimistic conclusion. The reason that policy makers' repertoire is
so 'limited' is that education policy in many Western democracies forms an
integral part of a 'Neo-liberal project' which protects the market and the
accumulation of capital, and draws on functionalist analyses to 'fix' the
social and educational problems which this project generates. Given that
neo-liberal ideology enjoys something like hegemonic status in those countries, there is no reason to suppose that the policy repertoire is likely to be
extended anytime soon.

As we seek to answer the question, 'what is to be done?' this pessimistic
analysis places us in something of a dilemma. It is relatively easy to say
what, in principle, *should* be done. The link between poverty and education could, presumably, be broken through a radical combination of economic, fiscal, and welfare reform measures to end poverty, accompanied
by equally radical equality-based educational reforms, all, perhaps, underpinned by an expansion of participatory democracy. We could, therefore,
use this chapter to articulate such a programme of radical change in detail
and exhort policy makers to adopt it. However, if Rees et al. are right, and
radical change is simply off the agenda, what would be the point in such
exhortation? Perhaps we would be better advised to focus on what is *likely*
to be done, setting out a programme of ameliorative actions that policy
makers might reasonably be expected to take. Such an approach would be
more likely to connect with policy makers' agendas, but it would have little
hope of having any significant impact on the relationship between poverty
and education.

The remainder of this chapter seeks to navigate a path within and
through this dilemma. Rather than focusing solely on what *should* be done
or on what is *likely* to be done, we focus on what *might* be done. Accepting
that we must start from current social and political realities, we ask questions about the room for manoeuvre that exists within the policy process,
and seek evidence about how things are done differently in different times
and places. In this way, we seek to remain critical of the status quo, but to
open up options both for those with formal positions in the policy process,

and for those who hold no such positions but are nonetheless key players in the 'formation' of policy. Throughout, we try to resist the temptation either to be naively optimistic or unduly pessimistic about the possibilities for change. Instead we adopt a stance of what Grace calls "complex hope"— "an optimism of the will that recognises the historical and structural difficulties which need to be overcome" (Grace, 1994:59).

With this in mind, in the next section, we ask what evidence there is that policy makers can in fact make any difference to the poverty-education relationship that is other than trivial. We move on to examine the kinds of difference they can make at each of the three levels—macro, meso, and micro—that we have used as an organising device throughout this volume. We conclude that there are many options for meaningful policy action, and ask how those options can be pulled together into something more than a disconnected array of interventions. Finally, we consider what the implications of our analysis are for our own position as researchers.

THE POSSIBILITIES OF POLICY

Our 'complex hope' stems from the conviction that meaningful policy action to tackle the poverty-education relationship is indeed possible. We derive this conviction from three conclusions which we draw from the contributions to this volume. First, as we noted in Chapter 1, *although poverty and education are linked, educational processes, experiences, and outcomes are not simply* determined *by poverty.* Work on longitudinal cohort studies, illustrated by Schoon's chapter in this volume, has traced meticulously the associations between background factors in children's lives and their outcomes as they pass through and beyond the education system. What emerges is something much more complex than a simple linear relationship between single background factors—poverty, for instance— and outcomes. Instead, it appears that background factors interact with each other and with a series of mediating factors to compound or moderate the impacts of adverse circumstances. In a recent analysis, Duckworth (2008), reflecting some of the ideas of Bronfenbrenner (1979) highlighted in Chapter 2, asks us to conceptualise these different factors as a series of interacting contexts—constituted by socio-demographic factors, parent-child relationships, the school, and the characteristics of the individual learner—such that it is this interaction of contexts which shapes outcomes rather than any single factor. Similarly, Schoon elsewhere (Schoon, 2006) asks us think not in terms of cause and effect, but of risk and resilience (see Chapter 2 for a more detailed development of these ideas). Adverse circumstances, she argues, should be seen not as 'causes of' but as 'risks for' poor outcomes, since other factors may serve to make children 'resilient'—that is, able to do well despite the presence of adversity.

This has important implications for policy. If the relationship between background and outcomes is not deterministic, and if there are multiple mediating and moderating factors, there are also multiple points at which policy can intervene. Even if, as Rees et al. (2007) argue, policy makers are unlikely to tackle fundamental social restructuring, they can strengthen protective factors in the family, school, and community and so impact on educational outcomes and subsequent life chances. There is, moreover, evidence that even quite modest interventions can have significant ameliorative effects in the long term—the High/Scope initiative in the US being perhaps the most obvious example (Schweinhart et al., 2005). The implication is that the sort of policy interventions noted in the previous chapter, or the school improvement efforts reported by Muijs, should not be dismissed out of hand simply because their immediate impacts are not transformative. However desirable wide ranging and radical policy approaches may be, there is also something that can be done through much more modest interventions.

The second conclusion we reach is that, although it may in general terms be true that policy in a country such as our own has been captured by the Neo-liberal project, *the policy process is never so coherent and linear that all alternatives and all dissident voices are ruled out.* As we saw in Chapter 12, policy is a 'contested terrain' in which the apparent coherence of policy texts conceals compromises and contradictions as different interests struggle to control the meaning of policy and are brought into (often uneasy) alignment. This may, of course, result in the illusion of 'active government' to which Rees et al. (2007) refer, through which social and political concerns about education and poverty are reduced to a limited repertoire of ineffective actions. However, it may also mean the opposite, that efforts to progress the dominant Neo-liberal project are not straightforward, that contests arise, dissident voices are heard, and interventions are formulated which tackle the issue of poverty and education more authentically. We note in particular that this inherent instability can sometimes produce quite dramatic policy reconfigurations. If, in our own country, the cumulative tensions and external shocks of the 1970s launched a Neo-liberal project which still remains dominant, it is also true that different tensions and shocks launched the welfare state in the aftermath of World War II, and that the current (2009) financial crisis might yet lead to significant change.

The account of policy in Chapter 12 also leads us to our third conclusion—*that policy is made not only by designated decision makers at the 'centre' of education systems, but by actors throughout those systems.* In most systems, of course, there is formal acknowledgement that local administrations, individual schools, and teachers enjoy some degree of discretion within the broad frameworks formulated at the centre. The area-based initiatives in England, France, and Portugal, described in the previous chapter, are obvious examples of where such discretion has been called upon as a means of generating innovative approaches to breaking the link between poverty and education. However, what our account makes clear is that, whether such discretion is 'allowed' formally or not, centrally-formulated policy will inevitably interact with what Chapter 12 calls "a messy ensemble of ongoing practices and beliefs" through which it will be interpreted and reinterpreted. Policy may be formulated at the centre by designated 'policy makers,' but it is 'formed' (Ozga, 2000) throughout the system by all who have to act upon, within—and often against—it.

Taken together, these three conclusions, we contend, define a space in which meaningful policy action is possible. Far from policy being power-less in the face of the poverty-education relationship, there are in fact mul-tiple points at which intervention is possible, and multiple possibilities for policy formation to escape what may sometimes appear to be the tyranny of dominant agendas. These possibilities become more apparent when we examine what can be done at each of the three 'levels'—macro, meso, and micro—that we have used as organising devices throughout this volume. These levels are, in reality, deeply interactive, so although we now deal with them separately, we will in due course return to a consideration of what a coherent approach *across* levels might look like.

THE MACRO LEVEL

Whatever the limitations of the capacity and willingness of national policy makers to tackle fundamental socio-structural issues, the reality is that countries with similar broadly democratic political systems, and with 'developed' economies, do in fact make choices about the extent to which they will allow inequalities to grow and will tolerate poverty. As the OECD regularly point out, countries with similar levels of aver-age income differ from each other considerably on measures of poverty (OECD, 2008b). On recent figures (see http://stats.oecd.org), for instance, the US had over 11 percent of its population living below a poverty thresh-old of 40 percent of median income; Italy, Germany, and Canada had 6–7 percent; Norway, the United Kingdom, and the Netherlands had 3.5–4 percent; while Demark and Sweden had less than 3 percent. OECD also provides figures on income inequality in the form of the Gini coefficient (a measure in which values closer to 1 and 0 represent greater and lesser inequality, respectively). This has come to seem increasingly important as work coming out of the medical epidemiology field suggests that the negative effects of poverty on outcomes may be part of a wider pattern in which (income) inequality per se is associated with unequal outcomes across a society (Wilkinson & Pickett, 2009). Using this measure, the US is amongst the more unequal countries, with a Gini coefficient of 0.38; the UK has a coefficient of 0.34, while Sweden and Denmark are amongst the more equal countries with coefficients of 0.24.

Moreover, although such differences may result from choices made cumulatively over extended periods of time, it is also clear that levels of poverty and inequality respond in the short and medium term to decisions taken by policy makers. This is the case even where policy changes take place within a broad political consensus and are relatively modest in scale. We can certainly see this in the case of our own country, the UK, where the replacement of a (broadly) left wing Labour government by (broadly) right wing Conservative administrations after 1979 led to increasing inequalities, a process that was partially halted by the advent of more centrist New Labour governments from 1997 onwards (Hills, Sefton, & Stewart, 2009). It may well be that poverty reduction alone is not an adequate mechanism for improving educational outcomes, and that there is a point beyond which marginal enhancements of family income have little educational impact (Plewis & Kallis, 2008). Nonetheless, it remains the case that poverty is not simply a fact of life to which education systems must respond.

How policy makers respond to the poverty-education relationship is likely to be embodied in wider 'narratives' (Roe, 1994) about how societies work, what the place of children is in those societies and what, therefore, is the role of education. Some of these narratives may be deeply rooted in national social and political cultures (Moss, Petrie, & Poland, 1999). Some, however, may be susceptible to change over time even within the same national culture. Gaskell and Levin, for instance, writing in this volume from a North American perspective, alludes to the 'war on poverty' in the 1960s and to the ways in which the social and political support for that war evaporated thereafter. It is not difficult to trace in the war on poverty particular narratives about how people become poor, how society should respond to poverty, and what the role of education is in this response. In particular, clear narratives are apparent about how social disadvantage produces cultural 'deprivation,' and how this in turn produces educational 'failure' (Bloom, 1965; Bloom, Davis, & Hess,1967). If we wish to see how far these narratives have shifted (and, indeed, what has stayed the same) in the North American context about which Lipman writes, we need only look at the very different narrative of the US "No Child Left Behind" policy under the Bush administration, where poor educational outcomes are attributed firmly to the inadequacy of schools, and where social disadvantage and cultural explanations scarcely warrant a mention (see, for instance, US Government Department of Education, 2005).

From our perspective, the point is that policy makers can play a part in leading or holding back narrative changes such as these. In our own UK context, perhaps the most famous intervention in recent history was Prime Minister Jim Callaghan's Ruskin College speech of 1976, where he wondered aloud about the purposes of education, its role in relation to inequality, and the adequacy of the education system of the time, and where he called for a 'national debate' on these matters (Callaghan, 1976). The speech is widely regarded as having marked the end of a postwar consensus on education, and having thereby opened up new policy possibilities. While the domination of the subsequent 'debate' (if such it was) by voices from the Right should alert us to the limited control exerted by individual politicians, the construction of narratives nonetheless remains an important form of action. Policy makers can, in however limited a sense, choose which narratives they help construct and which they seek to deconstruct. They are not bound inescapably to narratives which tolerate poverty or which sustain the role of education in reproducing disadvantage.

THE MESO LEVEL

If, as we argue, policy makers have some scope to influence macro-level characteristics of their countries, it is reasonable to suppose that they will have even greater capacity to impact on what we have called in this volume the meso level. The organisation of the education system and the characteristics of its institutions and institutional practices are, after all, central concerns of policy making. Nonetheless, within the context of a hegemonic Neo-liberal project, it is easy to assume that policy makers can do little but follow a narrow set of policies that 'travel' from country to country, as described in Chapter 12. The reality, however, is not quite so simple. Policy makers in different countries do, in fact, make different choices about how to structure their education systems and, more specifically, about how much educational inequality and failure they will tolerate.

Again, OECD is a useful source of evidence. Although the Organisation's emphasis on comparing system characteristics and performance might be regarded as a prime mover in the internationalization of education policy, it is also a means of showing how countries respond to international trends differently. For instance, OECD observes that different countries are more and less successful in reconciling the quest for improved 'standards' with a concern for equity:

> **The countries with high quality and high equity have embraced student heterogeneity and avoided premature and differentiated structures:** Evidence from PISA . . . and from countries which have introduced comprehensive schooling, suggests that early tracking is associated with reduced equity in outcomes and sometimes weakens results overall. In countries with early selection of students into highly differentiated education systems, differences among schools are large and the relationship between socio-economic background and student school performance stronger. (OECD, 2009:78)

If, therefore, we look at particular education systems, we can see points at which the decisions of policy makers about the characteristics of those systems have significant implications for the impact of poverty and education.

For instance, Lipman's chapter in this volume reinforces a widely held perception that the US' large urban school systems are deeply troubled as they struggle to respond to the disadvantages experienced by their students. Whilst this undoubtedly has much to do with macro-level factors—notably, the significant socio-economic inequalities we noted earlier—it is also clear that these factors are compounded by decisions about the characteristics of the education system. Foster (2007), following Weiner (2006), characterizes US urban schools in the following way:

> . . . urban schools are those marked by three factors. First, these schools are part of large school systems, with large impersonal bureaucracies that are removed from the communities they serve. Second, the schools are also poorly funded, overcrowded, and lack the necessary material, human and time resources required to do a competent job. Finally, these schools are responsible for educating a group of very diverse students from many ethnic, religious, and socioeconomic backgrounds. (Foster, 2007:774)

These three characteristics stem to a significant extent from policy decisions that are made differently in other countries. Taking our own country as an example, policy towards urban schools emphasizes increasing 'freedom' from the bureaucracies of local authorities, and sustains a funding system which directs resources towards rather than away from schools serving the poorest areas. Moreover, although English urban schools experience all the stresses and strains resulting from local concentrations of families facing poverty, and of population flows as people migrate into and around the country, there are at least some efforts to diversify neighbourhoods and create mixed populations that are more manageable by schools (Silverman, Lupton, & Fenton, 2005). It is also the case, as we saw in the previous chapter, that policy makers have generated a wide range of educational interventions targeted at schools serving poor areas and groups of learners facing poverty and other disadvantages. If the evidence suggests that those interventions are a long way from having broken the link between poverty and education, they have nonetheless mediated that link in such a way that some of the negative impacts of poverty have been moderated.

On the other hand, lest we present England as a policy heaven, it is equally possible to point to policy decisions that seem likely to have compounded the effect of poverty on education. So, for instance, policy makers in England have come out in favour of grouping children by attainment (HM Government, 2005) and maintaining a more-or-less separate form of special education (DfES, 2003b). Yet, in our work, we have seen how these forms of provision are disproportionately populated by children from socio-economically disadvantaged backgrounds (Dunne et al., 2007; Dyson & Gallannaugh, 2008; Dyson & Kozleski, 2008). Likewise, policy makers have resolutely refused to tackle the issue of the relatively small numbers of secondary schools which select by attainment, though it has long been known that such selection becomes a *de facto* form of selection by social background (Floud, Halsey, & Martin, 1956; Floud, 1961; Coe et al., 2008). Whilst the direction taken by policy makers in each of these cases is entirely consistent with the Neo-liberal project, none of them is central to that project and, as the OECD analysis shows, they may actually be antithetical to the aim of raising standards of educational attainment.

Drawing on its cross-country analyses, OECD offers a set of ten recommendations to policy makers keen to develop more equitable education systems:

Design
1. Limit early tracking and streaming and postpone academic selection.
2. Manage school choice so as to contain the risks to equity.
3. In upper secondary education, provide attractive alternatives, remove dead ends, and prevent dropout.
4. Offer second chances to gain from education.

Practices
5. Identify and provide systematic help to those who fall behind at school and reduce year repetition.
6. Strengthen the links between school and home to help disadvantaged parents help their children to learn.
7. Respond to diversity and provide for the successful inclusion of migrants and minorities within mainstream education.

Resourcing
8. Provide strong education for all, giving priority to early childhood provision and basic schooling.
9. Direct resources to the students with the greatest needs.
10. Set concrete targets for more equity, particularly related to low school attainment and dropouts. (OECD, 2008c:6)

Such a list may well be full of problems, paying no attention to context, and extrapolating policy directions from the simple association of system characteristics and outcomes. Nonetheless, what it makes clear is that different countries, with similar levels of wealth and broadly similar education systems, do things differently and get different results. The implication is that policy makers have options. If latching onto the latest policy to 'travel' from a high-status country is not necessarily a good idea, a rigorous interrogation of how the current characteristics of the education system exacerbate or ameliorate the impact of poverty might be a better one.

THE MICRO LEVEL

We referred earlier to the role that longitudinal studies have played in uncovering the complexity of the relationships between poverty and education. As a recent study of children moving through primary education in England has shown, educational outcomes depend not only on macro and meso level factors—on socio-economic status or the characteristics of the school system, say—but on how these interact with micro-level factors. So, the ways in which particular parents engage with their children, the child's experiences of pre-school provision, the practices of particular teachers, the organisation of particular classrooms—all have an impact separately and in interaction with one another (Sylva et al., 2008).

Micro-level factors of this kind are, of course, less susceptible to the direct control of national policy makers—and, to a lesser extent, of local policy makers—than are the characteristics of the national education or welfare systems. Although the report just cited finds that the quality of experiences on offer in schools makes a real difference to children, it also finds that the experiences on offer in schools serving disadvantaged populations remains stubbornly inferior to that elsewhere (Sylva et al., 2008:109)—and this despite decades of school 'reform' by policy makers aimed at ensuring high standards everywhere. At this level, it is the individuals who come into direct contact with learners who become important, and, amongst professional groups, this means their teachers, mentors, social care workers, youth workers, and others. We see this clearly in the initiatives taken by particular groups of teachers and their leaders as reported in this volume by Smyth and by Thomson. Regardless of the constraints imposed by the policy frameworks within which they work, committed professionals can develop interactions with learners which seek to mitigate or overcome the effects of poverty on their educational experiences and outcomes.

However, it is not necessary to see policy makers as simply impotent or negative at this level. Although they cannot control the nature of micro-level interactions, it is their decisions which shape the context in which those interactions occur. For instance, the experience of the English system is that vigorous efforts by policy makers to specify and enforce minimum standards of practice do make some difference. If learners from poorer backgrounds continue to do significantly worse than their peers, they also do significantly better now than they did some years ago, and there is even evidence of a small narrowing of the attainment gap (Schools Analysis and Research Division 2009:32–3). Moreover, as Muijs' chapter in this volume makes clear, there is a rich knowledge base relating to what makes schools and classrooms 'effective' for these learners. This knowledge base has undoubtedly been misused in the past, as Muijs acknowledges, and the assumptions on which it is based have long been questioned by critical scholars (see, for instance, Slee, Weiner, & Tomlinson, 1998). Nonetheless, more sophisticated use is possible, and as the knowledge base itself becomes more sophisticated, this offers a potentially powerful tool for policy makers to deploy.

Policy makers can also determine which kinds of professionals, trained in what kind of ways, will work in what kind of relationships and to what kinds of ends with children. Two examples will illustrate the point. The first is the development in a number of countries of what are variously known as school-linked services, full service schools, or, in our own context, 'extended' services (see, for instance, Dryfoos, 1994; Szirom et al., 2001; Whalen, 2002; Cummings et al., 2007; Dryfoos, Quinn, & Barkin, 2005; Forbes & Watson, 2009, amongst many others). In effect, these initiatives reconfigure existing services and/or create new kinds of professional roles in and around schools. This process opens up: 'new spaces of action' between traditional services and shapes 'new practices' (Edwards, in press). Our own evidence suggests that, at their most effective, these new spaces give learners—especially those from disadvantaged backgrounds—easier access to a range of supportive relationships (Cummings et al., 2007).

We also have evidence from a second initiative where policy frameworks opened up possibilities at the micro level in ways that, in this case, surprised us. Not long after the first New Labour government took office, one of us (Dyson) with colleagues spent some years working with groups of schools in England seeking to develop 'inclusive' educational provision (Ainscow, Booth, & Dyson, 2006a,b). Our expectation was that the closely-specified, centrally-directed policy frameworks of the time—aligned closely, of course, with the 'Neo-liberal project'—would either make it impossible for teachers to think deeply about their learners' experiences or distort their understandings until the learners were lost in the dominant policy agendas. In many ways, our expectations were not disappointed. However, we also saw how the policy focus on standards of attainment invited teachers to look again at those children who were not meeting the standards, how the policy emphasis on performance data gave teachers new tools for identifying children who were not flourishing in their schools, and how the high stakes nature of the accountability system for teachers spurred them to seek ways of taking action rather than allowing them to wash their hands of their most disadvantaged learners. What struck us, therefore, was the way in which national policy opened up new spaces for teachers, and how little it would take for policy makers to open those spaces wider.

PUTTING IT ALL TOGETHER

Reviewing this evidence, it seems to us that policy makers do have choices, and that they do in fact make decisions that have significant implications for the levels of poverty in a society and the extent to which poverty impacts on educational outcomes. The key question for us, therefore, is not whether policy makers can do anything at all—they clearly can. Rather, it is what kind of actions, configured in what kind of way, are likely to make most difference in the context of the social and political realities of affluent, democratic countries. An answer to this question involves, we suggest, considering three aspects of the actions policy makers might take—their scope, their coherence, and the ways in which they deal with power. It is to these that we now turn.

SCOPE

Writing specifically about poverty in urban contexts, the American scholar Jean Anyon argues for a reconceptualisation of what policy to tackle the poverty-education link might mean:

> Policies such as minimum wage statutes that yield poverty wages, affordable housing and transportation policies that segregate low-income workers of color in urban areas and industrial and other job development in far-flung suburbs where public transport does not reach, all maintain poverty in city neighborhoods and therefore the schools. In order to solve the systemic problems of urban education, then, we need not only school reform but the reform of these public policies. If, as I am suggesting, the macro-economy deeply affects the quality of urban education, then perhaps we should rethink what "counts" as educational policy. Rules and regulations regarding teaching, curriculum, and assessment certainly count; but, perhaps, policies that maintain high levels of urban poverty and segregation should be part of the educational policy panoply as well . . . (Anyon, 2005:2–3)

Although the details of Anyon's argument relate to the US urban context, the wider point she makes holds good in any situation where policy makers take seriously the need to tackle the poverty-education link. To be successful, policy interventions need to have a sufficiently wide *scope*. Specifically, while they need to address the response of the education system to the academic challenges posed by learners living in poverty, they also need to tackle what she calls the "macro-economy." This includes what we have characterised as meso-level mediating factors—housing, transportation, and 'area effects' for example—and could be expanded to include a wide range of other mediating factors, such as family functioning, peer groups, and local cultures.

The implication is that effective policy strategies are unlikely to be single strand, and the somewhat exclusive focus on education reform that has characterised many economically developed countries in recent years has to be seen as inadequate. In terms of political feasibility, this conclusion has mixed implications. Anyon titles her book *Radical Possibilities*, yet the very breadth of action that is needed opens up the possibility of more modest—and therefore more politically acceptable—interventions across a wide range of areas. In our own country, for instance, despite what is arguably an overall alignment of New Labour policy with the Neo-liberal project, we have seen a willingness to intervene not only in the education of learners from poor backgrounds, but also in child and family support, health, the labour market, welfare arrangements, housing, and area disadvantage. It is at least possible that such interventions, however modest in themselves, might have a significant cumulative effect as small improvements in one area build upon improvements in others.

COHERENCE

Undertaking wide ranging interventions of this kind brings its own problems. We have seen how, in many political contexts, generating initiatives is relatively easy and creates the illusion of action (Rees, Power, & Taylor, 2007). However, as the previous chapter pointed out, initiatives of this kind tend to be short-term and disconnected one from another. A scattergun approach is likely not only to reduce the cumulative effect of interventions but may also produce a situation in which different interventions work against one another, leaving those who have to make policy work on the ground confused and disenchanted. It follows that policy strategies for tackling the poverty-education link have to have not only scope, but also *coherence*. If there is to be a cumulative effect, policy interventions need to build upon one another and be sustained over time. Given what we saw of the 'contested terrain' of the policy process in Chapter 12, this is a significant challenge for policy makers who inevitably find themselves focused on their own area of responsibility (for instance, the remit of one or other ministry) and come under pressure to 'fix' problems in that area before damage is done to the administration's reputation—and, if they are elected politicians, certainly before the next election.

It seems to us, therefore, that policy makers need some sort of 'road map' that lays out the multiple fields in which interventions are necessary, shows the interconnections between them, and makes it possible to chart a sustained course of action. In this respect, policy making in education may have something to learn from international developments in the field of health inequalities. A recent report produced by a Commission, working under the aegis of the World Health Organisation, for instance, uses the concept of 'the social determinants of health' to map out how health inequalities arise and what governments might do about them. The overview it offers is worth quoting at length:

> The poor health of the poor, the social gradient in health within countries, and the marked health inequities between countries are caused by the unequal distribution of power, income, goods, and services, globally

and nationally, the consequent unfairness in the immediate, visible circumstances of people's lives—their access to health care, schools, and
education, their conditions of work and leisure, their homes, communities, towns, or cities—and their chances of leading a flourishing life.
This unequal distribution of health-damaging experiences is not in any
sense a 'natural' phenomenon but is the result of a toxic combination of
poor social policies and programmes, unfair economic arrangements,
and bad politics. Together, the structural determinants and conditions
of daily life constitute the social determinants of health and are responsible for a major part of health inequities between and within countries
. . . Traditionally, society has looked to the health sector to deal with its
concerns about health and disease . . . [But] action on the social determinants of health must involve the whole of government, civil society
and local communities, business, global fora, and international agencies. (Commission on the Social Determinants of Health, 2008:1)

If, in this passage, we substitute 'educational outcomes' for 'health,' we have
an analysis not very different from that we have proposed throughout this
volume—and, indeed, very close to Anyon's analysis quoted above. However,
instead of framing its analysis in terms of radical opposition to current policies and policy makers, the Commission goes on to propose a wide-ranging
programme based on three principles: improving daily living conditions;
tackling the inequitable distribution of power, money, and resources; and
measuring and understanding the problem and assessing the impact of action
(Commission on the Social Determinant's of Health, 2008:44). This in turn
leads onto proposals for specific actions—proposals that, at the time of writing, are being reformulated by governments in relation to their own contexts.
In other words, the Commission offers policy makers a road map to guide
their actions—one that is certainly challenging, but which offers some prospect of engaging with the constraints and possibilities policy makers face.

Crucial to road maps of this kind are the causal explanations they
embody. In the Commission's report, we see a clear line drawn from "poor
social policies, unfair economic arrangements, and bad politics" to health
inequalities. This removes such inequalities from the domain of 'natural
phenomena' and locates them squarely amongst the responsibilities of policy makers. Causal explanations of this kind, of course, form the basis of
the policy narratives to which we referred earlier—stories of how social
problems come about and, therefore, of how they can be tackled. Whilst
such narratives are inevitably infused with implicit assumptions, ambiguities, and contradictions, there is no reason why they cannot be made more
explicit and their inherent rationality (or otherwise) laid open to examination. Much of our own work, for instance, takes the form of engaging
with policy makers—usually at local level—to surface the theory of change
(Connell & Kubisch, 1998; Connell & Klem, 2000; W.K. Kellogg Foundation, 2004) on which their actions are based.

POWER

The Commission's observation that health inequalities are the product of social injustice rather than of natural forces reminds us that poverty and its consequences cannot properly be addressed without also addressing the unequal power relations which maintain unequal societies. This brings us face to face with a paradox which has underlain our consideration of what policy makers might do. Put bluntly, policy makers who have the power to change things are part of, and are likely to work on behalf of, a social and political elite who have the least interest in fundamental change.

This paradox leads some commentators to conclude that the only way to respond is to confront and resist policy elites. We see in this volume how Lipman aligns herself with activists resisting the Chicago 'reforms.' Similarly, Anyon is quite clear that the 'radical possibilities' of which she writes can be realised not through traditional politics, but through building a 'new social movement' around educational justice. As she puts it:

> Most of these [radical policies] would threaten America's corporate elites and the politicians dependent on their largesse, and may indeed appear impractical. . . . [Therefore] to obtain policies that could set the stage for economic and educational justice, we need to apply the pressure that a social movement can provide . . . (Anyon, 2005:151–52)

It may well be that in some situations, resistance of this kind is the only way to tackle the issue of power. Certainly the US, with its rampant inequalities, (sometimes) sharp racial divisions, tendency towards 'small government,' and history of civil rights struggle and community organising seems ripe for such an approach. However, political cultures are different in different times and places. Elsewhere, the complexities and ambiguities of the policy process may open up spaces in which power relations can be addressed through other means. In such situations, there may be two keys to avoiding 'poor policy' and 'bad politics'—consensus building and democratization of the policy process.

Consensus Building

Significantly, Gaskell and Levin's chapter in this volume, one of whose co-authors has also spent periods of time as a policy maker, identify building political support as a key issue in tackling the poverty and education link. The kind of wide-ranging strategies we are advocating cannot be carried through, even at local level, without the support and active involvement of a wide range of actors. At the national level, they cannot be carried through without a significant level of political support. In countries such as our own, where people living in poverty constitute a relatively power-less minority, generating such support inevitably means convincing people who are doing well to take action with and on behalf of their less advantaged compatriots. It is therefore necessary to build a consensus, which will embrace significant numbers of those who benefit from current arrangements, around the proposition that wide-ranging policies to change those arrangements are necessary.

As Gaskell and Levin's contribution to this volume demonstrates, such a progressive consensus is possible, even within the confines of 'normal' politics, but it is not at all easy to achieve. Our recent experience in the UK has been that the limited moves towards greater equity promoted by New Labour governments have been 'sold' to comfortably-off voters on the basis of enlightened self interest. 'Social exclusion,' for instance, has been presented as bringing costs not only to individuals who find themselves excluded, but also to 'wider society,' in the form of " . . . reduced social cohesion, higher crime and fear of crime, and higher levels of stress and reduced mobility." At the same time, society has had to bear a set of 'financial costs' in the form of:

> . . . paying for crime, school exclusions, drug misuse and unemployment, and in lost tax revenue. Business suffered too from a less skilled workforce, lost customers and markets, and—like the rest of the population—had to pay the tax bills for social failure.

The conclusion, not surprisingly, is that " . . . it would benefit everyone in society if social exclusion could be reduced and made less likely in future" (Social Exclusion Unit, 2001a:introduction, par. 7).

We can see a similar consensus-building move in the work of the WHO Commission cited above. Cleverly (from a political point of view) the Commission shifts attention away from the minority of people who do particularly badly, and onto the "social gradient of health inequalities." The 'poorest of the poor' do indeed have the worst health, it argues, but that is not all:

> . . . the relation between socioeconomic level and health is graded. People in the second highest quintile have higher mortality in their offspring than those in the highest quintile . . . [Moreover, t]he social gradient is not confined to poorer countries. (Commission on the Social Determinants of Health, 2008:31)

The implication is clear: it is in the interests of the vast majority of the population, even in rich countries, to tackle health inequality. The impact of poverty on health is thus positioned as a part of a fundamental social concern rather than simply as a concern for those on the fringes of society. Interestingly, Wilkinson and Pickett (2009), with their background in health inequalities, take this appeal to enlightened self interest a step further, arguing not only that there are gradients across a range of social outcomes (including education), but that everyone does better in societies where the gradients are shallower.

Insofar as such moves depend on a logical sleight of hand, or arguments constructed at particular times to support limited policy initiatives, they are unlikely to be sustainable. However, what these examples point to is the possibility of constructing powerful policy narratives capable of maintaining a progressive consensus over time. In particular, these examples begin to explore ways of escaping the "othering" (Lister, 2004) of the poor—that is, the creation of a binary in which the poor are constructed as different in kind and need from the 'mainstream' of society. The discourse of social in/exclusion does not go far in this exploration, with what Levitas calls its "dichotomous model of society, insiders and outsiders" (Levitas, 2004:7). However, there are other discourses upon which policy makers could draw. There has, for instance, been considerable interest in Amartya Sen's capability theory in relation to education—and particularly in relation to educational inequality (Madoka, 2003; Walker & Unterhalter [eds.], 2007; Terzi, 2005; Reindal, 2009). It is beyond the scope of this chapter to explore the strengths and limitations of this theory in any detail. What is clear, however, is that the development of capabilities is located within the kind of complex micro, meso, and macro level interactions with which we have been concerned in this volume, and that such development is the concern of everyone, not simply of a marginalized group of 'the poor.' It is not difficult to imagine a policy narrative being shaped out of these resources, emphasizing not the measurable outcomes from education (of which some individuals have more than others), but the capabilities which all need to make real choices, and the complex interactions which promote or inhibit those capabilities in individual cases. Indeed, in the UK, the Fabian Society—a centre-left political society numbering many national politicians amongst its members—has proposed a politics of equality based on the concept of 'life chances' (Fabian Society, 2006). Whilst this may be philosophically less rich than the capability approach, it embodies some of the same principles in a form that might be more accessible to policy makers.

Democratisation of the Policy Process

Democratisation in our use of the term implies loosening the control by elites over policy through the involvement of a wider range of stakeholders in policy formation. Such diversification implies, amongst other things, the multiplication of sites in the system that are enabled to generate policy. Individual teachers, schools, and local bodies (such as local authorities or municipalities) will, we know, take centrally-formulated policy and reconstruct it according to their own situations and understandings. As we see in the chapters by Smyth and by Thomson in this volume, this can be a creative process of generating new approaches rather than simply a means of undermining centrally-transmitted policy. It is, moreover, open to policy makers to foster and learn from this process rather than to seek to suppress it in the interests of compliance. In the previous chapter, for instance, we referred to the Educational Priority Areas which were promoted by governments in England during the 1960s and 1970s. Not only did these encourage local innovation, but they also sought to learn from that innovation through large action research projects (Halsey, 1972; Smith, 1987). It is arguable that the creation of such feedback loops has been all too rare, and that policy makers have failed to sustain or deepen the work done through area initiatives of this kind. Nonetheless, the potential for multi-site policy-making of this kind remains.

Democratisation also implies the multiplication of voices that are heard in the policy process. The stark reality is that policy-making about poverty is rarely undertaken by poor people. It is scarcely surprising, then, if the narratives that inform policy, however well-meaning they may be, are characterized by deficit thinking and a failure to engage with the structural inequalities of the status quo. The implication is that people living in poverty have to be brought into the policy process. The problem here is that those people who are most marginalized are also least likely to engage with policy making. To take an example, we recently, with colleagues, undertook a study of school governance in schools serving disadvantaged areas in England (Dean et al., 2007). State schools in England are required to have governing bodies giving stakeholders—including local people—a say in how the school is run. What we found, however, was that local people often lacked the inclination, resources, and confidence to engage with schools in this way. Frequently, they were reluctant to participate in governance, and unable or unwilling to challenge professionals when they did so. As a result, governance was exercised not by local people who were typical of those sending their children to the school, but by others with greater confidence and wider experience of managerial work who decided what it was that local people needed.

Widening the range of voices is thus difficult. It is not, however, impossible. We see in Smyth's chapter how student and community voices can be included in decision-making processes. In some countries, moreover, there are traditions of community activism, and community development work to build the capacity for activism, that are largely absent in countries like our own. Anyon's (2005) call for the development of a 'social movement,' which we earlier characterized as a form of resistance might equally be seen as an attempt to widen the range of those involved in the policy process. For this reason, in earlier work, she has advocated that educators within the system should bridge to others outside—tenants' associations, legal groups, coalitions for the homeless, voter registration organizations, and others who represent or work on behalf of marginalized urban residents (Anyon, 1997:168–69). Even amidst the depressing picture of school governance in our own country, it was possible to identify instances where professional decision-makers had been proactive in recruiting local people from disadvantaged backgrounds, and had provided the encouragement, support, and training to enable their involvement in policy to be real.

IN CONCLUSION

Throughout this chapter, we have tried to maintain our optimism about the prospects for policy approaches that will make a real difference to poverty and education. Yet, on the day we write this conclusion, the newspaper headline reads "Labour's record on poverty in tatters," above a story about how the UK government, formed from a traditionally left-wing party, has failed to hit its targets for poverty reduction, presided over widening inequalities, and now has apparently abandoned its flagship policy of halving child poverty by 2010 (Savage, 2009). This story reminds us sharply both of the resistance of poverty and its effects to ill-formulated policy interventions, and, more significantly, of the political difficulties of marshalling a sustained attack on poverty in inherently unequal societies.

With this in mind, it is worth reminding ourselves of the reasons for optimism: that there is scope for policy makers to take action; that policy formations are not fixed, but that they change and are open to contestation; that even limited policy interventions can make a difference; that we know in broad terms what an effective policy approach might look like (and no doubt could specify more detail in particular contexts); and that the policy process need not be—and in any case is not—restricted to those in designated policy making roles. There is, therefore, hope—even if, bearing in mind the structural inequalities of our societies, it is, as Grace (1994) reminds us, likely to be of a 'complex' kind.

This brings us to one final issue. Although this chapter is addressed to the concerns of policy makers, it is written by researchers. Our implicit assumption is that our voice as researchers will be heard in the policy process, and that what we have to say will in some way contribute to a more just society. However, the position of researchers in the policy process is highly problematic and takes us back to the dilemma which we outlined at the start of this chapter. On the one hand, researchers wish to place their work at the disposal of policy makers, helping them to find good solutions to social problems and to base their policy decisions on robust evidence. On the other hand, they are aware that the policy process itself is deeply implicated in structural inequalities and power asymmetries, and that policy makers may be part of the problem rather than part of the solution. Sometimes this situation is presented as a stark choice facing researchers—between 'policy science' and 'policy scholarship' (Grace, 1984); or, as we have expressed it here, between 'functionalist' and 'critical' research perspectives; or, in Cox's classic formulation, between 'problem solving theory' which:

> ... takes the world as it finds it, with the prevailing social and power relationships and the institutions into which they are organized, as the given framework for action and 'critical theory', which: ... stands apart from the prevailing order of the world and asks how that order came about. (Cox, 1981:128–29)

Presented in this way, it is not surprising that, as we suggested in Chapter 12, relations between researchers and policy makers can sometimes be troubled. Policy makers are hardly likely to find much common ground with researchers who see their role not as being to help them make good decisions, but as questioning the legitimacy of the decision making process itself. Moreover, 'critical' researchers are likely to be deeply suspicious of their 'problem-solving' colleagues who, in their view, are complicit in the maintenance of social injustice—a charge, as Muijs' chapter points out, that the school effectiveness movement has often had to face.

However, the analysis we have undertaken here leads us to suggest that the sharp dichotomies on which these characterizations of research rest may be more useful as heuristic devices than as accounts of the complexities of the practice of research. As the British educational sociologist Geoff Whitty, puts it:

> ... I have always argued that it is not an 'either/or' issue. Good policy scholarship should subsume some of the more positive features of policy science but also go beyond it ... Unless we constantly remind ourselves—and others—of both the possibilities and the limits of educational policy and practice, education researchers are liable to be misunderstood. (Whitty, 2002:14)

This view is, as we understand it, close to our own position. In a situation where poverty is a manifestation of deep structural inequalities and where the policy process is characterized by power asymmetries, education research must be capable of adopting a critical stance. It must expose what Whitty calls the limits of policy action, and the failure of policy makers to push sufficiently hard at those limits. To this extent, it must 'stand apart from the prevailing world order,' and if the price of this is a breakdown of trust between researchers and policy makers, then researchers may have to accept that in an asymmetrical power system, their role may be to resist those 'in power' and forge alliances with those who are 'power-less.' On the other hand, researchers have to recognize that the policy process is complex and offers spaces into which their work can be inserted, that policy-makers are not a homogeneous group and offer opportunities for alliances, that incremental change is not necessarily the enemy of transformational change, and that even a transformed world order will generate problems that require functional solutions.

Above all, this volume, we believe, demonstrates the diversity of research and of the research community that addresses issues of education and poverty. Whilst it may be illuminating to characterize research perspectives as 'functionalist' or 'critical,' the reality is that individual research studies and individual researchers commonly forge their own stances by combining these perspectives in response to the issues they choose to address. Perhaps more important, regardless of the stances taken by individual researchers, the corpus of available research knowledge as a whole, and the 'research community' that produces it, is multi-perspectival and multi-voiced. Our view is that this diversity are an essential element of any democratization of the policy process. Whilst individual researchers may or may not find themselves impelled to choose between 'problem-solving' or 'critical' stances, the contribution of research as a whole to the policy process lies precisely in the diverse perspectives and understandings it contributes to the democratic efforts to create an equitable society. As the Dewey scholar, Alison Kadlec puts it:

> . . . the point of reflective inquiry is not to generate final principles, but rather to improve our capacity for tapping into the critical potential of lived experience in a world defined by flux and change. The political, social, and economic challenges we face require that we arm ourselves not with fixed absolutes, but rather with a commitment to open-ended and flexible inquiry aimed not at final consensus about our aims, but rather at achieving a greater understanding of the consequences of our practices and policies. (Kadlec, 2006:541)

Contributors

Alan Dyson is Professor of Education and co-director of the Centre for Equity in Education at the University of Manchester. He has written widely on inclusive education, urban education, and the relationship between social and educational disadvantage. He is currently researching area-based strategies linking schools with community services and regeneration initiatives, and is evaluating the national programme of school-linked 'extended services' in England.

Dave Hall is Senior Lecturer in Education at the School of Education, University of Manchester. He is an education policy researcher who has worked on a range of projects including ones relating to schools in challenging circumstances, the relationship between education and poverty, and young peoples' transitions between educational sectors. Dave is currently Principal Investigator on an ESRC-funded project examining the social practices of school organisation.

Jane Gaskell is a Professor and Dean at the Ontario Institute for Studies in Education at the University of Toronto. She has written on exemplary secondary schools in Canada, educational policy, the impact of feminism on educational research and practice, and school-to-work linkages. She is currently working with Ben Levin on a book-length manuscript on educational approaches to poverty since 1965 in Canadian cities. She is also involved in research on teacher education in Canada and internationally.

Helen Gunter is Professor of Educational Policy, Leadership, and Management and Director of Research in the School of Education, University of Manchester. Her main research interest is in education policy with a particular focus on leadership. She has produced over seventy publications including books and papers on leadership theory and practice. She is particularly interested in the history of the field of leadership, with a focus on knowledge production.

Lisa Jones is a researcher for the Centre for Equity in Education, School of Education at the University of Manchester. Her research interests focus on aspects of education related to poverty, social disadvantage, and social class. Much of Lisa's work investigates new teachers drawing on notions of identity and her work also involves exploring extended services in schools.

Afroditi Kalambouka is a Research Associate at the School of Education, University of Manchester. She has been a lead researcher on a number of projects in the area of educational disadvantage, inclusion, and diversity. These include a systematic review of the impact of inclusion on attainment; studies for the UK government on post-school transition for students with disabilities and social and emotional literacy for primary school children; a study of inclusive practice with digital technologies; a project developing evaluation tools for Nurture Groups, and a study of financial literacy in post-school education. She has experience in a range of research approaches and lectures in quantitative methods.

Ben Levin is a Professor and Canada Research Chair in Educational Leadership and Policy at the Ontario Institute for Studies in Education at the University of Toronto. He has moved during his career between academia and government, including serving as deputy minister of education in Manitoba and Ontario. His research has focused on broad issues of educational reform, policy politics, and economics. His most recent book is *How to Change 5000 Schools* (Harvard Education Press, 2008).

Meg Maguire is Professor of Sociology of Education in the Centre for Public Policy Studies at King's College London and she is also Lead Editor for the *Journal of Education Policy*. Meg teaches and researches issues of policy and practice, schooling matters, and social justice concerns in urban contexts. She has published in the areas of urban primary schooling, post-compulsory transitions in urban settings, as well as the classed identities of the school teacher. Currently she is working on an ESRC-funded project with Stephen Ball and Annette Braun on 'Policy enactments in the secondary school: theory and practice.'

Daniel Muijs is Professor of Pedagogy and Teacher Development at the University of Manchester, School of Education. Previously he worked as Chair of School Leadership and Management at the University of Newcastle and as senior lecturer at Warwick Institute of Education. He is an acknowledged expert in the field of Educational and Teacher Effectiveness and is co-editor of the journal *School Effectiveness and School Improvement*. He has published widely in the areas of educational effectiveness, leadership, and research methods, and has conducted research for government agencies (DCSF, NCSL, QCA), Charitable Trusts (Gatsby), and Research Councils (ESRC).

Pauline Lipman is Professor of Educational Policy Studies at the University of Illinois-Chicago. Her research and publications focus on race and class inequality in schools, globalization, and the political economy and cultural politics of race in urban education, particularly the relationship of education and neo-liberal urban development. She is active in social movements and is a founder of Chicago *Teachers for Social Justice*.

Ruth Lupton is Senior Research Fellow at the Centre for Analysis of Social Exclusion, London School of Economics and Political Science, and is currently serving as a member of the National Equality Panel. She researches and writes about relationships between poverty, place, and education, particularly the ways in which urban, neighbourhood, and housing policies are related to educational policies and outcomes. She is currently working on the implications of 'mixed community' policies in urban regeneration and on the implications of school composition and context for day-to-day school processes and practices.

Carlo Raffo is Reader in Equity in Urban Education at the School of Education, University of Manchester. Carlo's main area of research is in the area of education and poverty and educational equity in urban contexts. He is grant holder for the Joseph Rowntree Foundation project: Education and Poverty—a critical review of theory, policy, and practice and has been involved in numerous other externally funded projects that focus on schools and education in areas of urban disadvantage. His publications have recently featured in the *Journal of Education Policy, British Journal of the Sociology of Education* and the *International Journal of Inclusive Education*.

Ingrid Schoon is Professor of Human Development and Social Policy at the Institute of Education, University of London. Her research interests focus on issues of human development across the life span course—in particular, the transition into adulthood in a changing socio-historical context; the study of risk and resilience; the realization of individual potential; social equalities in attainment, health, and well-being; and the intergenerational transmission of (dis)advantage. Ingrid is currently involved in two major UK interdisciplinary research networks funded by the Economic and Research Council (ESRC): the Priority Network on Gender Inequality and Production (GeNet), and the Centre for the Study of Learning and Life Chances in the Knowledge Economies (Llakes). She is also Director of PATHWAYS, an International Postdoctoral Fellowship Programme for the Comparative Study of Productive Youth Development, which is funded by The Jacobs Foundation. She has published widely, including her recent publications with Cambridge University Press *Risk and Resilience: Adaptations in Changing Times* (2006) and a forthcoming edited volume on *Transitions from School to Work*.

John Smyth is Research Professor of Education, School of Education, University of Ballarat, Australia where he is also the multi-disciplinary cross-university Research Theme Leader for *Addressing Disadvantage and Inequality in Education and Health*. His most recent books include: *Activist and Socially Critical School and Community Renewal: Social Justice in Exploitative Times* (co-authored with Angus, Down & McInerney, Sense Publishers, 2009); *Critically Engaged Learning; Connecting to Young Lives* (co-authored with Angus, Down & McInerney, Peter Lang, 2008); *Teachers in the Middle: Reclaiming the Wasteland of the Adolescent Years of Schooling* (co-authored with McInerney, Peter Lang, 2007); and *'Dropping Out', Drifting Off, Being Excluded: Becoming Somebody Without School* (co-authored with Hattam, Peter Lang, 2004). His research interests are in policy ethnographies of schooling, social justice, community renewal, and policy sociology of students' lives and teachers' work. He was the Simon Visiting Professor in the Faculty of Humanities, University of Manchester in 2008.

Pat Thomson is Professor of Education and Director of Research in the School of Education at The University of Nottingham; she holds adjunct positions at Deakin University, Australia and the University of South Australia. She also works as a consultant for the Arts Council England funded organisation Creativity, Culture and Education. Pat researches and writes about why and how education can be more equitable and just. Drawing on twenty years experience as a headteacher of schools serving neighbourhoods made poor and research in Australia and England, she brings together interests in policy, school change, and inclusive pedagogical practices. She is currently working on projects which look at: creativity, the arts, and school and community change; pupil mobility; and change leadership. Her most recent publications are *Doing Visual Research with Children and Young People* (Routledge, 2008) and *School leadership—Heads on the Block?* (Routledge, 2009).

References

Abrams, F. (2001) Below the breadline: Living on the minimum wage. London: Profile.

Acheson, D. (1998) Independent enquiry into inequality in health. London: The Stationary Office.

Ainscow, M., T. Booth, and A. Dyson. (2006a) Improving schools, developing inclusion. London: Routledge.

———. (2006b) Inclusion and the standards agenda: Negotiating policy pressures in England, *International Journal of Inclusive Education.* 10(4–5):295–308.

Ainscow, M., A. Dyson, S. Goldrick, and K. Kerr. (2008) Challenging inequities within education systems: Some lessons from a development and research project. Paper presented at the American Educational Research Association, New York.

Ainscow, M., M. West. (2006) Improving urban schools: Leadership and collaboration. Ballmoor, Bucks: Open University Press.

Alcock, P. (2006) Understanding poverty (3rd Ed.). Basingstoke: Palgrave Macmillan.

Alexander, R. (2001) Culture and pedagogy. International comparisons in primary education. London: Routledge.

———. (2008) Essays on pedagogy. London: Routledge.

Allen, M. and P. Ainley. (2007) Education make you fick, innit? What's gone wrong in England's schools, colleges and universities and how to start putting it right. London: The Tufnell Press.

Anderson, L. and N. Bennett, eds. (2003) Developing educational leadership. London: Sage.

Anderson, V. (2006) What's new and what's not. *Catalyst.* http://www.catalyst-chicago.org/news/index.php?item=1919&cat=51.

Anning, A. (2005) Investigating the impact of working in multi-agency service delivery settings in the UK on early years practitioners' beliefs and practices. *Journal of Early Childhood Research,* 3(1):19–50.

Anyon, J. (1997) Ghetto schooling—A political economy of urban educational reform. New York: Teachers College Press.

———. (2005) Radical possibilities. New York: Routledge.

Appadurai, A. (1996) Modernity at large. Cultural dimensions of globalisation. Minneapolis, London: University of Minnesota Press.

———. (2001) Grassroots globalization and the research imagination. In A. Appadurai ed. Globalisation. Durham: Duke University Press.

Apple, M. (2001) Educating the "Right" way. New York: Routledge.

Apple, M., and K. Buras. (2006) The subaltern speak. Curriculum, power and educational struggles. New York: Routledge.

Archer, L., M. Hutchings, and A. Ross. (2003) Higher education and social class: Issues of exclusion and inclusion. London: Routledge Falmer.

Archer, L. and H. Yamashita. (2003) Knowing their limits? Identities, inequalities and inner city school leavers' post-16 aspirations. *Journal of Education Policy.* 18(1):53–69.

Armstrong, F. (2007) Disability, education and space: some critical reflections. In K. Gulson and C. Symes, eds. Spatial theories of education: Policy and geography matters. New York and London: Routledge.

Ashford, S., J. Gray, and M. Tranmer. (1993) The introduction of GCSE examinations and changes in post-16 participation. Sheffield: Department for Education and Employment, Youth Cohort Report No. 23.

Atkinson, M., P. Doherty, and K. Kinder. (2005) Multi-agency working: Models, challenges and key factors for success. *Journal of Early Childhood Research.*3(1):7–17.

Australian Council of Social Services (August 2007) A fair go for all Australians: International Comparisons. Strawberry Hills, NSW: Australia Fair.

Australian Labor Party (2007) A digital education revolution. Election Campaign Launch.

Bagley, C., C.L. Ackerley, and J. Rattray (2004) Social exclusion, Sure Start and organizational social capital: Evaluating inter-disciplinary multi-agency working in an education and health work programme. *Journal of Education Policy.* 19(5):595–607.

Ball, S.J. (1990) *Politics and Policymaking in Education.* London: Routledge.

———. (1994) Education reform: A critical and post-structural approach. Buckingham: Open University Press.

———. (2003) Class strategies and the educational market: The middle class and social advantage. London: Routledge Falmer

———. (2008) The education debate. Bristol: Policy Press.

Ball, S.J., M. Maguire, S. Macrae. (2000) Choice, pathways and transitions post 16. New youth, new economies in the global city. London and New York: Routledge Falmer.

Barber, M. (2007) Instruction to deliver; Tony Blair, the public services and the challenge of achieving targets. London: Politico's Publishing.

Barnes, J. and H. Lucas. (1975) Positive discrimination in education: Individuals, groups and institutions. In J. Barnes, ed. Educational priority, Vol. 3. London: HMSO.

Barth, P., K. Haycock, H. Jackson, K. Mora, P. Ruiz, S. Robinson, and A. Wilkins. (1999) Dispelling the myth. High poverty schools exceeding expectations. Washington, DC: The Education Trust.

Bartlett, W. and J. Le Grand, (1993) Quasi-markets and social policy. Basingstoke: Macmillan Press.

Barton, D., and M. Hamilton. (1998) Local literacies. Reading and writing in one community, London and New York: Routledge.

Bash, L. and A Green, eds. (1995) Youth, education and work. London; Kogan Page.

Bauder, H. (2002) Neighbourhood effects and cultural exclusion. *Urban Studies.* 39(1):85–93

Beck, U. (1992) Risk Society: towards a new modernity. London: Sage

Behrman, J.R. And P. Taubman. (1989) Is schooling "mostly in the genes"? Nature-nurture decomposition using data on relatives. *Journal of Political Economy.* 97(6):1425–46

Bell, D. (2003) Access and achievement in urban education: Ten years on. Speech to the Fabian Society. London: OfSTED.

Bénabou, R., F. Kramarz, and C. Prost. (2005) The French zones d'éducation prioritaires: Much ado about nothing? CEPR discussion paper No. 5085. http://www.cepr.org/pubs/dps/DP5085.asp.

Bennett, L., N. Hudspeth, and P.A. Wright. (2006) A critical analysis of the ABLA redevelopment plan. In L. Bennett, J.L. Smith and P. A. Wright, eds. Where are poor people to live? New York: M.E. Sharpe.

Berends, M., S. Bodily, and S. Kirby. (2002) Looking back over a decade of whole-school reform: The experience of new american schools. *Phi Delta Kappan* 84(2):168–175.

Bernstein, B. (1961) Social class and linguistic development: A theory of social learning. In A.H. Halsey, J. Floud, and C.A. Andersons, eds. Education, economy and society. New York: Free Press.

Berthoud, R. (1998) Incomes of ethnic minorities. Essex, University of Essex: Institute for Social and Economic Research.

Blanden, J. and S. Machin. (2003) Educational inequality and the expansion of UK higher education. London: London School of Economics, Centre for Economic Performance, Mimeo.

———. (2007) Recent changes in intergenerational mobility in Britain. Report for Sutton Trust. http://www.suttontrust.com/reports/mainreport.pdf.

Bloom, B.S. (1965) Compensatory education for cultural deprivation. New York: Holt, Reinhart and Winston.

Bloom, B.A., A. Davis, R. Hess. (1967) Compensatory education for cultural deprivation. [A report] based on working papers contributed by participants in the Research Conference on Education and Cultural Deprivation. New York: Holt, Rinehart and Winston.

Blossfeld, H.P., E. Klijzing, M. Mills, and K. Kurz, eds. (2005) Globalization, uncertainty and youth in society. London: Routledge.

Blossfeld, H. and Y. Shavit. (1993) Persisting Barriers. Changes in educational opportunities in thirteen countries. In H. Blossfeld, and Y. Shavit, eds. Persistent inequality: Changing educational stratification in thirteen countries. Boulder, Colorado: Westview Press.

Bloustien, G. (2003) Girlmaking. A cross-cultural ethnography of the processes of growing up female. Oxford: Berghahn Books.

Blunkett, D. (2000) Influence or irrelevance: can social science improve government? Secretary of State's ESRC Lecture Speech. 2 February 2000. London: ESRC and DFEE.

Bobbitt, P. (2002) The shield of Achilles. London: Penguin.

Bond, R. & Saunders, P. (1999). Routes of success: influences on the occupational attainment of young British males. *British Journal of Sociology*, 50(2), 217–249.

Bourdieu, P. (1990) In other words. Cambridge: Polity Press.

Bourdieu, P. And J. Passeron. (1977) Reproduction in education, society and culture (Vol. 5). London: Sage.

Bowe, R. and S.J. Ball, with A. Gold. (1992) Reforming education and changing schools. London: Routledge.

Bowers, C.A. (2005) The false promises of constructivist theories of learning. A global and ecological critique. New York: Peter Lang.

Bowles, J. and H. Gintis. (1976) Schooling in capitalist America. London: Routledge and Kegan Paul.

Bradley, S and J. Taylor. (2002) The report card on competition in schools. London: ASI (Adam Smith Institute) Ltd.

Breen, R. and J.H. Goldthorpe, (1997) Explaining educational differences: Towards a formal rational action theory. *Rationality and Society*, 9(3):275–305.

———. (1999) Class, mobility, and merit: The experience of two British birth cohorts. *European Sociological Review*. 17:81–101.

———. (2001) Class, mobility and merit—The experience of two British birth cohorts. *European Sociological Review*. 17(2):81–101.

————. (2002) Merit, mobility, and method: Another reply to Saunders. *British Journal of Sociology.* 53:575–582.

Brenner, N. and N. Theodore. (2002) Cities and the geographies of actually existing neoliberalism. *Antipode.* 34(3):349–379.

Brighouse, T. (2007) The London challenge: A personal view. In T. Brighouse and L. Fullick, eds. Education in a global city: Essays from London. London: Institute of Education.

Bronfenbrenner, U. (1979) The ecology of human development: experiments by nature and design. Canbridge, Massachusetts: Harvard University Press.

Brooke, R., ed. (2003) Rural voices: place-conscious education and the teaching of writing. New York: National Writing Project and Teachers College Press.

Brooks-Gunn, J., G. Duncan, P. Klebanov, and N. Sealand. (1993) Do neighborhoods influence child and adolescent development? *American Journal of Sociology.* 99(2):353–395.

Brophy, J. (1992) Probing the subtleties of subject-matter teaching. *Educational Leadership.* 49(7):4–8.

Brown, P. (1999) Globalisation and the political economy of high skills. *Journal of Education and Work.* 12(3):233–252.

————. (2008) Are we witnessing the rise of a high skilled, low waged workforce? Cardiff: Teaching and Learning Research Programme (TLRC), Research Briefing No. 53. http://www.tlrp.org/dspace/retrieve/3686/BrownRB53final.pdfo.

Bryk, A.S., P.B. Sebring, D. Kerbow, S. Rollow, and J.Q. Easton. (1998) Charting Chicago school reform: Democratic localism as a lever for change. Boulder: Westview Press.

Burrell, G. and G. Morgan. (1979) Sociological perspectives and organisational analysis. Aldershot: Gower.

Butler, J. (1997) *The psychic life of power.* Stanford, CA: Stanford University Press.

Butler, T. and G. Robson. (2001) Social capital, gentrification and neighbourhood change in London: A comparison of three south London neighbourhoods. Urban Studies. 38(12):2145–62.

Bynner, J. (2001) British youth transitions in comparative perspective. *Journal of Youth Studies.* 4(1):5–23.

————. (2006) Rethinking the youth phase of the life-course: The case for emerging adulthood? *Journal of Youth Studies.* 9:367–384.

Bynner, J. and H. Joshi. (2002) Equality and opportunity in education: Evidence from the 1958 and 1970 birth cohort studies. *Oxford Review of Education.* 28(4):405–425.

Bynner, J. and S. Parsons. (1997) Getting on with qualifications. In J. Bynner, E. Ferri, and P. Shepherd, eds. Getting on, getting by, getting nowhere. Aldershot: Ashgate.

————. (2002) Social exclusion and the transition from school to work: The case of young people not in education, employment, or training (NEET). *Journal of Vocational Behavior.* 60(2):289–309.

Byrne, D. (2005) Social exclusion. Berkshire: Open University Press.

Callaghan, J. (1976) Towards a national debate (The full text of the speech by Prime Minister James Callaghan, at a foundation stone-laying ceremony at Ruskin College, Oxford, on October 18, 1976). *The Guardian.* October 15, 2001. http://education.guardian.co.uk/print/0,3858,4277858-109002,00.html.

Callahan, D. Gentler capitalism promises to redress economic inequality. *The Age.* February 5, 2008.

Cameron, S. (2003). Gentrification, housing redifferentiation and urban regeneration: 'Going for growth' in Newcastle upon Tyne. *Urban Studies.* 40(12):2367–82.

Carney, S. A policy that should teach us some lessons about opportunity. *The Age.* August 27, 2008.

Carr, W. and A. Hartnett. (1996) Education and the struggle for democracy. Buckingham: OUP.

Carrington, V. and M. Robinson. (2009) Digital literacies. Social learning and classroom practice. London: Sage.

Carter, P.L. (2003) "Black" cultural capital, status positioning, and schooling conflicts for low-income African American youth. *Social Problems.* 50(1):136–155.

Catalyst Chicago. (2007) Special Report: School autonomy all over the map. http://www.catalyst-chicago.org/news/index.php?item=2141&cat=23.

Cauce, A., A. Stewart, M. Rodriguez, B. Cochrane, and J. Ginzler. (2003) Overcoming the odds? Adolescent development in the context of urban poverty. in S. Luthar, ed. Resilience and vulnerability: Adaptation in the context of childhood adversities. Cambridge Massachusetts: Cambridge University Press.

Central Advisory Council for Education. (1967) Children and their primary schools. The Plowden Report. London: HMSO.

Chapman, C. and H.M Gunter, eds. Radical Reforms: public policy and a decade of educational reform. London: Routledge.

Childress, H. (2000) Landscapes of betrayal, landscapes of joy. Curtisville in the lives of its teenagers. New York: State University of New York Press.

Chitty, C. (2002) Education and social class. *The Political Quarterly.* 73(2):208–10.

Chubb, J.E. and T.M Moe. (1990) Politics, markets and America's schools. Washington, DC: Brookings Institute.

Clausen, J.A. (1993). *American lives: looking back at the children of the Great Depression.* Berkley: University of California Press.

Cleary, R. Helping *all* Australians. *The Age.* January 23, 2008.

Coe, R., K. Jones, J. Searle, D. Kokotsaki, A. Mohd Kosnin, and P. Skinner. (2008) Evidence on the effects of selective educational systems. A report for the Sutton Trust. Durham: CEM Centre, University of Durham, for the Sutton Trust.

Coffield, F. (2000) The necessity of informal learning. Bristol: Policy Press.

Coleman, J.S. (1966) Equality of educational opportunity study. Washington, DC: United States Department of Health, Education and Welfare, Office of Education.

Comber, B., H. Nixon, and J.A. Reid, eds. (2007) Literacies in place: teaching environmental communications. Newtown, New South Wales: Primary English Teachers Association.

Comber, B., P. Thomson, and M. Wells. (2001) Critical literacy finds a "place": Writing and social action in a low income Australian grade 2/3 classroom. *Elementary School Journal.* 101(4):451–64.

Committee of Inquiry into the Education of Children from Ethnic Minority Groups [Committee appointed by the Department of Education and Science under the chairmanship of Lord Swann]. (1985) Education for all: report of the Committee of Inquiry into the education of children from ethnic minority groups. London: HMSO.

Connell, J. and A.M. Klem. (2000) You can get there from here: Using a theory of change approach to plan urban education reform. *Journal of Educational and Psychological Consulting.* 11 (1):93–120.

Connell, J.P. and A.C. Kubisch. (1998) Applying a theory of change approach to the evaluation of comprehensive community initiatives: Progress, prospects and problems. In K. Fulbright-Anderson, A. C. Kubisch, and J.P. Connell, eds. New approaches to evaluating community initiatives. Vol. 2: Theory, measurement and analysis. Queenstown: The Aspen Institute.

Connell, N. (1996) Getting off the list: School improvement in New York City. New York: New York City Educational Priorities Panel.

Connell, R.W., V.M. White, and K.M. Johnston. (1992) An experiment in justice: The disadvantaged schools program and the question of poverty, 1974–1990. *British Journal of Sociology of Education*. 13(4):447–64.

Connors, L., ed. (2007) Making federalism work for schools: Due process, transparency, informed consent. Sydney: NSW Public Education Alliance.

Cooper, C.W. and C.A. Christie. (2005). Evaluating parent empowerment: A look at the potential of social justice evaluation in education. *Teachers College Record*. 107(10):2248–74.

Council of Australian Governments. (2006) COAG meeting 14 July communiqué. http://www.coag.gov.au/coag_meeting_outcomes/2006-0714/docs/coag140706.pdf.

Cox, R.W. (1981) Social forces, states and world orders: Beyond international relations theory. *Millennium: Journal of International Studies*. 10(2):126–55.

Creemers, B.P.M. (1994) The effective classroom. London: Cassell.

———. (1997) Effective schools and effective teachers: An international perspective. Coventry: Centre for Research in Elementary and Primary Education University of Warwick, UK.

Creemers, B.P.M. and L. Kyriakides. (2006) Critical analysis of the current approaches to modelling educational effectiveness: The importance of establishing a dynamic model. *School Effectiveness and School Improvement*. 17(3):347–66.

Crompton, R. (2006) Employment and the family: The reconfiguration of work and family life in contemporary societies. Cambridge: Cambridge University Press.

Crowder, K. and S.J. South. (2003) Neighborhood distress and school dropout: The variable significance of community context. *Social Science Research*. 32:659–698.

Cuban, L. and M. Usdan. (2003) Powerful reforms with shallow roots: Improving America's urban schools. New York: Teachers' College Press.

Cummings, C., A. Dyson, D. Muijs, I. Papps, D. Pearson, C. Raffo, L. Tiplady, L. Todd, and D. Crowther. (2007) Evaluation of the full service extended schools initiative: Final report. DfES Research Report No. 852. London: DCSF.

Cummings, C., A. Dyson, I. Papps, D. Pearson, C. Raffo, and L. Todd. (2005). Evaluation of the full service extended schools project: End of first year report. Nottingham: DfES Research Report, DfES Publications. Research Report No. RR680. http://www.dfes.gov.uk/research/data/uploadfiles/RR680.pdf.

Cunningham, M., J. Lopes, and P. Rudd. (2004) Evaluation of EiC/EMAG pilot project. DfES Research Report No. RR583. London, DfES.

Davidson, K. Free computers don't make an education revolution. *The Age*, September 4, 2008.

Davies, B. (2000) (in)Scribing body/landscape relations. Walnut Creek, California: Alta Mira Press.

———. (2006) Subjectification: The relevance of Butler's analysis for education. *British Journal of Sociology of Education*. 27(4):425–38.

Davies, P., K. Slack, A. Hughes, J. Mangan, and K. Vigurs. (2008) Knowing where to study? Fees, bursaries and fair access. Staffordshire University: Report for the Sutton Trust. http://www.suttontrust.com/reports/StaffordshireReportFinal.pdf.

Davis, M. (2006). Planet of slums. London: Verso.

———. (2008) Land of plenty. Melbourne: Melbourne University Press.

Dean, C., A. Dyson, F. Gallannaugh, A. Howes, and C. Raffo. (2007) Schools, governors and disadvantage. York: Joseph Rowntree Foundation.

De Broucker, P. and A. Sweetman, eds. (2002) Towards evidence-based policy for Canadian education. Montreal and Kingston: McGill-Queens University Press.

Demie, F., R. Butler, and A. Taplin. (2002) Educational achievement and the disadvantage factor: Empirical evidence. *Educational Studies*. 28(2):101–10.

Desforges, C., with A. Abouchaar. (2003) The impact of parental involvement, parental support and family education on pupil achievement and adjustment: A literature review. DfES Research Report No. 433. London: DfES.

DfEE. (1998) *Handbook for Education Action Zones*, London, DfEE.

———. (1999a) Schools plus: Building learning communities. Improving the educational chances of children and young people from disadvantaged areas: A report from the Schools Plus Policy Action Team 11. London: DfEE.

———. (1999b) Sure Start: Making a difference for children and families. London: DfEE.

———. (1999c) Excellence in cities. London: HMSO.

———. (2003a) Full-service extended schools planning documents. London: DfES.

———. (2003b) Report of the special schools working group. London: DfES.

———. (2005a) Ethnicity and education: The evidence on minority ethnic pupils. London: HMSO.

Dickens, R., P. Gregg, and J. Wadsworth. (2003) The labour market under new labour: The state of working Britain. Basingstoke: Palgrave Macmillan.

Dillabough, J.A., J. Kennelly, and E. Wang. (2007) Warehousing young people in urban Canadian schools: Gender, peer rivalry and spatial containment, In K. Gulson, and C. Symes, eds. Spatial theories of education: Policy and geography matters. New York and London: Routledge.

Diepstraten, I., M. du Bois-Reymond, and H. Vinken. (2006) Trendsetting biographies: Concepts of navigating through late-modern life and learning. *Journal of Youth Studies*. 9:175–93.

DiPietro, J.A. (2000) Baby and the brain: Advances in child development. *Annual Review of Public Health*. 21:455–71.

Dorsett, R. (1998) Ethnic minorities in the inner city. Bristol: The Policy Press.

Douglas, J.W.B. (1964) The home and the school. London: MacGibbon and Kee.

Driver, S., and A. Martell. (1997) New labour's communitarianisms. *Critical Social Policy*. 52(17):27–46.

Dryfoos, J. (1994) Full-service schools. San Francisco: Jossey-Bass.

Dryfoos, J., J. Quinn, and C. Barkin, eds. (2005) Community schools in action: Lessons from a decade of practice. Oxford: Oxford University Press.

Duckworth, K. (2008) The influence of context on attainment in primary school: Interactions between children, family and school contexts. London: Centre for Research on the Wider Benefits of Learning, Institute of Education.

Duncan, P. and S. Thomas. (2000) Neighbourhood regeneration: Resourcing community involvement. Bristol: The Policy Press.

Dunne, M, A. Dyson, F. Gallannaugh, S. Humphreys, D. Muijs, and J. Sebba. (2007) Effective teaching and learning for pupils in low attaining groups. Research Report No. DCSF-RR011. London: DCSF.

Dyson, A. and F. Gallannaugh. (2008) Disproportionality in special needs education in England. *The Journal of Special Education*. 42(1):36–46.

Dyson, A., and E.B. Kozleski. (2008) Disproportionality in special education: A transatlantic phenomenon. In L. Florian and M.J. Mclaughlin, eds. Disability classification in education. Thousand Oaks, California: Corwin Press.

Dyson., A and C. Raffo. (2007) Education and disadvantage: The role of community-oriented schools. *Oxford Review of Education*. 33(3):297–314.

Eamon, M.K. (2001) The effects of poverty on children's socio-emotional development: An ecological systems analysis. *Social Work*. (46)3:345–360.

Editorial The road to learning is paved with complexity. *The Age*. August 27, 2008.

Edmonds, R. (1979) Effective schools for the urban poor. *Educational Leadership* 37(1):15–27.

Education Committee of the Civic Committee. (2003) Left behind. Chicago: Commercial Club of Chicago.

Edwards, A. (in press) Understanding boundaries in inter-professional work ('The SERA Keynote'). *The Scottish Educational Review.*

Elder, G.H. (1968) Achievement motivation and intelligence in occupational mobility: A longitudinal analysis. *Sociometry.* 327–354.

Ellenbogen, M.A. and S. Hodgins. (2004) The impact of high neuroticism in parents on children's psychosocial functioning in a population at high risk for major affective disorder: A family-environmental pathway of intergenerational risk. *Development and Psychopathology.* 16:113–36.

Engestrom, Y. (2001) Expansive learning at work: Toward an activity-theoretical reconceptualisation. *Journal of Education and Work.* 14(1):133–56.

Erikson, R. and J.O. Jonsson. (1996) Explaining class inequality in education: The Swedish test case. In R. Erikson and J.O. Jonsson, eds. Can education be equalized? The Swedish case in comparative perspective. Bolder, Colorado: Westview Press.

Esping-Andersen, G. (2004) Social inheritance and equal opportunities policy. Paper presented at the Social Mobility and Life Chances Forum, Oxford.

Evans, G. (2006) Educational failure and working class white children in Britain. Basingstoke: Palgrave Macmillan.

Evans, N. (2003) Making sense of lifelong learning. Respecting the needs of all. London: Routledge Falmer.

Evans, S. and H. Boyte. (1986) Free spaces: The sources of democratic change in America. Chicago and London: University of Chicago Press.

Exworthy, M., M. Stuart, D. Blane, and M. Marmo. (2003) Tackling health inequalities since the Acheson Inquiry. Bristol: The Policy Press.

Fabian Society (Great Britain). Commission on Life Chances and Child Poverty (2006) Narrowing the gap: The final report of the Fabian Commission on life chances and child poverty. London: The Fabian Society.

Fairclough, N. (2000) New labour, new language. London: Routledge.

Farmer, H. (1997) Diversity and women's career development. London: Sage.

Feinstein, L., K. Duckworth, and R. Sabates. (2004) A model of the inter-generational transmission of educational success. Wider Benefits of Learning Research Report No. 10. London: Centre for Research on the Wider Benefits of Learning.

Feinstein, L. and J. Symons. (1999) Attainment in secondary school. *Oxford Economic Papers.* 51:300–21.

Fielding, M. (2006) Leadership, radical student engagement and the necessity of person-centred education. *International Journal of Leadership in Education.* 9(4):299–313.

Floud, J. (1961) Social class factors in educational achievement. in A.H. Halsey, ed. Ability and educational opportunity. Paris: OECD.

Floud, J.E., A.H. Halsey, and F.M. Martin. (1956) Social class and educational opportunity. London: Heinemann.

Forbes, J. and C. Watson, eds. (2009) Service integration in schools: Research and policy discourses, practices, and future prospects. Rotterdam: Sense Publishers.

Foster, M. (2007) Urban education in North America: Section editor's introduction. In G.W. Noblit and W.T. Pink, eds. International handbook of urban education. Dordecht, The Netherlands: Springer.

Franklin, W. (2000) Students at promise and resilient: A historical look at risk. In M.G. Sanders, ed. Schooling students placed at risk. New York: Lawrende Erlbaum Publishers.

Freedman, S. and S. Horner. (2008) School funding and social justice: A guide to the pupil premium. Policy Exchange, http://www.policyexchange.org.uk/images/publications.pdfs/School_Funding_and_Social_Justice.pdf.

Freire, P. (1970) Pedagogy of the oppressed. London: Continuum.

———. (1972) Pedagogy of the oppressed, Harmondsworth: Penguin.

Furbey, R., A. Dinham, R. Farnell, D. Finneron, G. Wilkinson, C. Howarth, D. Hussain, and S. Palmer. (2006) Faith as social capital. Connecting or diving? Bristol: The Policy Press.

Furlong, A. and F. Cartmel. (1997) Young people and social change. Buckingham: Open University Press.

Galindo-Rueda, F., O. Marcenaro Gutierrez, and A. Vignoles. (2008) The widening socio-economic gap in UK higher education. *National Institute Economic Review*. 190:75–88.

Galindo-Rueda, F. and A. Vignoles. (2002) Class ridden or meritocratic? An economic analysis of recent changes in Britain (Vol. IZA DP, No. 677). Bonn: Forschungsinstitut zur Zukunft der Arbeit (IZA).

———. (2005) The declining relative importance of ability in predicting educational attainment. *Journal of Human Resources*. 40(2):335–53.

Gallie, D. (2000). The labour force. In A.H. Halsey and J. Webb, eds. Twentieth century British social trends. London: Macmillan.

Gaskell, J. (2001). Creating the "public" in public schools: A school board debate. *Canadian Journal of Education*. 26(1):19–36.

Gewirtz, S. (2001) Cloning the Blairs: New labour's programme for the re-socialization of working-class parents. *Journal of Education Policy*. 16(4):365–78.

Giddens, A. (1991) Modernity and self-identity: Self and society in the late modern age. Cambridge: Polity Press.

Gillard, J. (2008a) Speech to the Australian Council for Educational Research conference. Brisbane, August 11, 2008.

———. (2008b) John Button memorial lecture. Melbourne, July 17, 2008.

Gillborn, D. (2005) Education policy as an act of white supremacy: Whiteness, critical race theory and education reform. *Journal of Education Policy*. 20(4):485–505.

Gillborn, D. and D. Youdell. (2000) Rationing education: Policy, practice, reform, and equity. Buckingham: Open University Press.

Goldstein, H. and G. Woodhouse. (2000) School effectiveness research and educational policy. *Oxford Review of Education*. 26(3&4):353–64.

Goodman, A. and S. Webb. (1994) For richer, for poorer; The changing distribution of income in the United Kingdom 1961–1991. London: Institute for Fiscal Studies.

Gonzales, N. and L. Moll. (2002). Cruzanda el puente: building bridges to funds of knowledge. *Educational Policy*. 16(4):623–41.

Gonzales, N., L. Moll, and C. Amanti. (2005). Funds of knowledge. Mahwah, New Jersey: Lawrence Erlbaum.

Gorard, S. (1997) Market forces, choices and diversity in education: The early impact. *Sociological Research Online*. 2(3). http://www.socresonline.org.uk/2/3/8.html.

Gorard, S., E. Smith, H. May, L. Thomas, N. Adnett, and K. Slack. (2006) Review of widening participation research: Addressing the barriers to participation in higher education. York: Higher Education Academy and Institute for Access Studies. http://www.york.ac.uk/depts/educ/equity/barriers.htm.

Gordon, J. Gillard wants business in schools. *Sunday Age*. July 27, 2008.

Gottfredson, L.S. (1981) Circumscription and compromise—A developmental theory of occupational aspirations. *Journal of Counselling Psychology*. 28(6):545–79.

Gough, D. Fears that rankings will lead to blame and shame game. *Sunday Age*. August 17, 2008a.

———. Lesson one: never be afraid to mix it up. *Sunday Age.* July 20, 2008b.

Gough, J., A. Eisenschitz, and A. McCulloch. (2006) Spaces of social exclusion. London: Routledge.

Grattan, M., F. Tomazin, and D. Harrison. School v school: PM's rule. *The Age.* August 28, 2008.

Grace, G., ed. (1984) Education and the city: Theory, history and contemporary practice. London: Routledge and Kegan Paul.

Grace, G. (1994) Urban education and the culture of contentment: the politics, culture and economics of inner-city schooling. In N. Stromquist, ed. Education in urban areas: Crossnational dimensions. Westport, Connecticut: Praeger.

Gray, J., D. Jesson, and M. Tranmer, (1993) Boosting post-16 participation in full-time education. A study of some key factors. Youth Cohort Report No. 20. Sheffield: Department for Education and Employment.

Green, A. (1996) Aspects of the changing geography of poverty and wealth. In J. Hills, ed. New inequalities: The changing distribution of income and wealth in the United Kingdom. Cambridge: Cambridge University Press.

Green, A. and R. White. (2007) Attachment to place: Social networks, mobility and prospects of young people. York: Joseph Rowntree Foundation.

Green, B. and W. Letts. (2007) Space, equity and rural education. In K. Gulson and C. Symes, eds. Spatial theories of education: Policy and geography matters. New York and London: Routledge.

Green, D. and J. Kesselman. (2006) Dimensions of inequality in Canada. Vancouver: UBC Press.

Greenlee, A., N. Hudspeth, P. Lipman, D.A. Smith, J. Smith. (2008) Investing in neighborhoods research paper #1: Examining CPS' plan to close, consolidate, turn-around 18 schools. Data and Democracy Project: University of Illinois-Chicago.

Gregory, E. and A. Williams. (2000) City literacies. Learning to read across generations and cultures. London and New York: Routledge.

Gruenewald, D.A. (2003) The best of both worlds: A critical pedagogy of place. *Educational Researcher,* 32(4):3–12.

Gruenewald, D.A. and G. Smith. (2008) Making room for the local. In D.A. Gruenewald and G. Smith, eds. Place-based education in the global age. Local diversity. Mahwah, New Jersey: Lawrence Erlbaum.

Gulson, K. (2005) Renovating educational identities: Policy, space and urban renewal. *Journal of Education Policy,* 20(2):141–58.

———. (2007) Mobilising space discourses: Politics and educational policy change. In K. Gulson and C. Symes, eds. Spatial theories of education: Policy and geography matters. New York and London: Routledge.

———. (2008) Urban accommodations: Policy, education and a politics of place. *Journal of Education Policy.* 23(2):153–63.

Gulson, K. and C. Symes. (2007) Spatial theories of education: Policy and geography matters. New York and London: Routledge.

Gunter, H.M. and T. Fitzgerald. (2008) The future of leadership research. *School Leadership and Management.* 28(3):263–80.

Gunter, H.M. and G. Forrester. (2008) New labour and school leadership 1997–2007. *British Journal of Educational Studies.* 55(2):144–62.

Gunter, H.M. and P. Thomson. (2006) Stories from the field of commissioned research. Paper presented to the British Educational Research Association Conference, University of Warwick, September 2006.

Haberman, M. (1991) The pedagogy of poverty vs good teaching. *Phi Delta Kappan.* 73(4):290–94.

Hackworth, J. (2007) The neoliberal city: Governance, ideology, and development in American Urbanism. Ithaca: Cornell University Press.

Hallinger, P. and J.F. Murphy. (1986) The social context of effective schools. *American Journal of Education.* 94(3):328–55.

Halsey, A.H., ed. (1972) Educational priority: EPA problems and practices. Vol. 1. London: HMSO.

Hanley, L. (2007) Estates: An intimate history. London: Granta.

Hargreaves, A. (2008) The coming of post-standardization: Three weddings and a funeral. In C. Sugrue, ed. The future of educational changes—International perspectives. London and NY: Routledge.

Hargreaves, D. (1996) Teaching as a research-based profession: Possibilities and prospects. Teacher Training Annual Lecture. London: TTA.

Harris, A. and S. Ranson. (2005) The contradictions of education policy: Disadvantage and achievement. *British Educational Research Journal.* 31(5):571–87.

Harvey, D. (1973) Social justice and the city. London: Edward Arnold.

———. (2001) Spaces of capital: Towards a critical geography. London: Routledge.

———. (2007) A brief history of neoliberalism. Oxford: Oxford University Press.

Hayes, D., M. Mills, P. Christie, and B. Lingard. (2005). Teachers and schooling: Making a difference. Productive pedagogies, assessment and performance. Sydney: Allen and Unwin.

Hastings, A., J. Flint, C. McKenzie, and C. Mills. (2005) Cleaning up neighbourhoods: Environmental problems and service provision in deprived neighbourhoods. Bristol: Policy Press.

Hattam, R., K. Brown, and J. Smyth. (1996) Sustaining a culture of debate about teaching and learning. Adelaide: Flinders Institute for the Study of Teaching.

Hattam, R., P. McInerney, J. Smyth, and M. Lawson. (1999a) Enhancing school-community dialogue. Adelaide: Flinders Institute for the Study of Teaching, Flinders University of South Australia.

———. (1999b) Promoting student voices. Adelaide: Flinders Institute for the Study of Teaching, Flinders University of South Australia.

Hattie, J. (2003) Teachers make a difference: What is the research evidence? Paper Presented at the Australian Council for Educational Research Annual Conference on Teacher Quality.

Hayek, F. (1976) Law, legislation and liberty. Vol. 2. The mirage of social justice. Chicago: University of Chicago Press.

Haymes, S.N. (1995) Race, culture and the city. Albany: SUNY Press.

Health, Commission on Social Determinant of. (2008) Closing the gap in a generation: Health equity through action on the social determinants of health. Geneva: World Health Organization.

Henchey, N. (2001) Schools that make a difference: Final report. Twelve Canadian secondary schools in low-income settings. Kelowna, BC: Society for the Advancement of Excellence in Education.

Henig, J., R. Hula, M. Orr, D. Pedescleaux. (1999) The color of school reform: Race, politics and the challenge of urban education. Princeton: Princeton University Press.

Henry, M., B. Lingard, F. Rizvi, and S. Taylor. (2001) The OECD, globalisation, and education policy. Oxford: Pergamon.

Herman, R.E. (1999) An educators guide to schoolwide reform. Washington, DC: American Institutes for Research.

Herrnstein, R. and C. Murray. (1994) The bell curve. New York: Simon and Schuster.

Hess, Frederick M., ed. (2005) Urban school reform: Lessons from San Diego. Cambridge, Massachusetts: Harvard University Press.

Hillage, J., R. Pearson, A. Anderson, and P. Tamkins. (1998) Excellence in research in schools. London: DfEE.

Hills, J., J. Le Grand, and D. Piachaud. (2002) Understanding social exclusion. Oxford: Oxford University Press.

Hills, J., T. Sefton, and K. Stewart. (2009) Towards a more equal society? Poverty, inequality and policy since 1997. Bristol: The Policy Press.

Hirsch, D. (2004) Strategies against poverty: A shared road map. York: Joseph Rowntree Foundation.

HM Government. (2005) Higher standards, better schools for all: More choice for parents and pupils. Cm6677. London: HMSO.

Hodkinson, P., A.C. Sparkes, and H. Hodkinson. (1996) Triumphs and tears: Young people, markets and the transition from school to work. London: David Fulton Publishers.

Hoggart, L. and D. Smith, (2004) Understanding the impact of *Connexions* on young people at risk. DfES Research Report No. 607. London: DfES.

Holligan, C. (2008) Politics and peer review. *Research Intelligence.* 2008(105):26–27.

Holtzman, N.A. (2002) Genetics and social class. *J Epidemiol Community Health.* 56:529–35.

Holzman, L. (1997) Schools for growth: Radical alternatives to current educational models. Mahwah, New Jersey: Lawrence Erlbaum.

Hopkins, D. and D. Reynolds. (2001) The past, present and future of school improvement: Towards the third age. *British Educational Research Journal.* 27:459–76.

Houtveen, A.A.M., W.J.C.M. van de Grift, and B.P.M. Creemers. (2004) Effective school improvement in mathematics. *School Effectiveness and School Improvement.* 15(3–4):337–77. 93.

Hughes, G. and G. Mooney. (1998). Imagining welfare futures. London: Routledge.

Hulchanski, J.D. (2007) The three cities within Toronto: Income polarization among Toronto's neighbourhoods. 1970–2000. Research Bulletin 41. Toronto, Ontario: University of Toronto, Centre for Urban and Community Studies.

Hursh, D. (2008) High-stakes attesting and the decline of teaching and learning. Lanham: Rowman and Littlefield.

Hyman, H.H. (1967) The value systems of different classes. In R Bendix and S.M. Lipset, eds. Class, status and power. London: RKP.

ILO and I.L. Organization. (2008). Labour market trends and globalization's impact on them. http://www-old.itcilo.org/actrav/actrav-english/telearn/global/ilo/seura/mains.htm.

Interactive Illinois Report Card (2008) Illinois State Board of Education. http://iirc.niu.edu/District.aspx?districtID=150162990.

Ireland, E., S. Golden, and M. Morris. (2006) Evaluation of integrated Aimhigher: Tracking surveys of young people. DfES Research Brief No. RB811. Nottingham: DfES.

Jackson, B. and D. Marsden. (1962) Education and the working class. London: Routledge and Kegan Paul.

Jencks, C. (1972) Inequality: An assessment of the effect of family and schooling in America. New York: Basic Books.

Jensen, A.R. (1984) Test validity: G versus the specificity doctrine. *Journal of Social and Biological Structures.* 7:93–118.

Jones, C. and T. Novak. (1999) Poverty, welfare and the disciplinary state. London and New York: Routledge.

Jones, G. (2009) Youth. Cambridge: Polity Press.

———. (in press) From paradigm to paradox: Parental support and transitions to independence. In I. Schoon and K.R. Silbereisen, eds. Transitions from school to work: Globalisation, individualisation, and patterns of diversity. New York: Cambridge University Press.

Joyce, B., Calhoun, E. and Hopkins, D. (1999) *The new structure of school improvement: Inquiring schools and achieving students*, Buckinghamshire, Open University Press.

Kadlec, A. (2006) Reconstructing Dewey: The philosophy of critical pragmatism. *Polity*, 38(4):519–42.

Kahlenberg, R.D. (2001) All together now: The case for economic integration of the public schools. Washington, DC: Brookings Institution Press.

Kalmijn, M. and G. Kraaykamp. (1996) Race, cultural capital, and schooling: An analysis of trends in the United States. *Sociology of Education*. 69:22–34.

Kao, G. and M. Tienda. (1998) Educational aspirations of minority youth. *American Journal of Education*. 106:349–84.

Kelly, A. (1995) *Free school meal contextualisation of GCSE examination results*. Report. Stockport: National Consortium for examination results, Stockport LEA.

Kelly, P. Rudd's courageous gamble. *Weekend Australian (Inquirer)*. August 30–31, 2008.

Kelly, R. (2005) Education and social progress. London: DfES.http://www.dfes.gov.uk/speeches/speech.cfm?SpeechID=242.

Kemp, P., J. Bradshaw, P. Dornan, N. Finch, and E. Mayhew. (2004) Routes out of poverty: A research review. York: Joseph Rowntree.

Kendall, L., L. O'Donnell, S. Golden, K. Ridley, S. Machin, S. Rutt, S. McNally, I. Schagen, C. Meghir, S. Stoney, M. Morris, A. West, and P. Noden. (2005). Excellence in cities: The national evaluation of a policy to raise standards in urban schools 2000–2003. DfES Research Report No. RR675A. Nottingham: DfES, http://www.dfes.gov.uk/research/data/uploadfiles/RR675A.pdf.

Kendall, S., A. Johnson, C. Gulliver, K. Martin, and K. Kinder. (2004) Evaluation of the vulnerable children grant. National Foundation for Educational Research, DfES Research Report No. RR592. London: DfES

Kingdon, J. (1994) Agendas, ideas and policy change. In L. Dodd, C. Jillson, eds. New perspectives on American politics. Boulder, Colorado: Westview Press.

———. (2003) Agendas, alternatives and public policies (2nd Ed.). New York: Longman.

Kirkness, V. and S. Bowman. (1992) First nations and schools: Triumphs and struggles. Toronto, Ontario: Canadian Education Association.

Kohl, H. (1994) "I won't learn from you" and other thoughts on creative maladjustment. New York: The New Press.

Kozol, J. (1991) Savage inequalities. Children in America's schools. New York: Crown.

Ladson-Billings, G. (1998) Just what is critical race theory and what's it doing in a *nice* field like education? *Qualitative Studies in Education*. 11(1):7–24.

Ladson-Billings, G. and W.F. Tate. (1995) Towards a critical race theory of education. *Teachers College Record*. 97:47–68.

Ladson-Billings, G. and W.F. Tate, eds. (2006) Education research in the public interest. New York: Teachers College Press.

Lamb, S. and K. Mason. (2008) How young people are faring '08. Report for the Foundation for Young Australians. Centre for Post-Compulsory Education and Lifelong Learning, University of Melbourne.

Lareau, A. (1987) Social class differences in family-school relationships: The importance of cultural capital. *Sociology of Education*. 60(April):73–85.

Lash, S. and J. Urry. (1994) Economies of signs and space. London: Sage.

LaVeist, T.A. and K. Bell McDonald. (2002) Race, gender, and educational advantage in the inner city. *Social Science Quarterly.* 83(3):832–852.

Lawson, M.A. (2003) School-family relations in context. Parent and teacher perceptions of parent involvement. *Urban Education.* 38(1):77–133.

Lebfevre, H. (1991) *The Production of Space.* Oxford: Blackwell.

Ledoux, G. and M. Overmaat. (2001) Op Zoek Naar Succes. Een onderzoek naar Basisscholen die Meer en Minder Succesvol Zijn voor Autochtone en Allochtone Leerlingen uit Achterstandsgroepen. Amsterdam: SCO-Kohnstamm Instituut.

Leete, R. and J. Fox. (1977) Registrar general's social classes: Origins and users. *Population Trends.* 8:1–7.

Lein, L., J.F. Johnson, and M. Ragland. (1996) Successful Texas schoolwide programs: Research study results. Austin, TX: The University of Texas at Austin, The Charles A. Dana Center.

Leithwood, K., and R. Steinbach. (2002) Successful leadership for especially challenging schools. *Journal of Leadership in Education.* 79(2):73–82.

Levačić, R. and P.A. Woods. (2002) Raising school performance in the league tables (part 1): Disentangling the effects of social disadvantage. *British Educational Research Journal.* 28(2):207–26.

Levin, B. (2009) Enduring issues in urban education. *Journal of Comparative Policy Analysis.* 11(2):181–195.

Levin, B. and C. Ungerleider. (2007) Accountability, funding and school improvement in Canada. In T. Townsend, ed. International handbook of school effectiveness and improvement. Dordrecht, NL: Springer.

Levitas, R. (2004) Let's hear it for Humpty: Social exclusion, the third way and cultural capital. *Cultural Trends.* 13(2):1–15.

Lingard, B. and J. Ozga. (2007) Introduction. Reading education policy and politics. In B. Lingard. and J. Ozga, eds. The Routledge Falmer reader in education policy and politics, London: Routledge.

Lipman, P. (2004) High stakes education: Inequality, globalization, and urban school reform. London: Routledge Falmer.

———. (2008) Mixed-income schools and housing: Advancing the neoliberal urban agenda. *Journal of Education Policy.* 23(2):119–34.

Lipman, P. and N. Haines. (2007). From education accountability to privatization and African American exclusion—Chicago public schools' 'Renaissance 2010.' *Educational Policy.* 21(3):471–502.

Lipman, P., A. Person., and Kenwood Oakland Community Organization. (2007) Students as collateral damage? A preliminary study of Renaissance 2010 school closings in the Midsouth. Chicago: Kenwood Oakland Community Organization.http://www.uic.edu/educ/ceje/index.html.

Lipsky M. (1983) Street level bureaucrats: The dilemmas of individuals in public services. New York: Russell Sage Publications.

Lister, R. (2004) Poverty. Cambridge: Polity Press.

Lloyd, J. (1999) A new style of governing. *New Statesman,* October 4, 1999.

Locurto, C. (1988) On the malleability of IQ. *The Psychologist II—The Bulletin of the British Psychology Society.* 14:275–92.

Lohman, M. (2006) An aptitude perspective on talent: Implications for identification of academically gifted minority students, *Journal for Education of the Gifted,* 28(3–4), 333–360.

Love, J., E.E. Kisker, C.M. Ross, P.Z. Schochet, J. Brooks-Gunn, D. Paulsell, K. Boller, J. Constantine, C. Vogel, A.S. Fuligni, C. Brady-Smith. (2002) Making a difference in the lives of infants and toddlers and their families: The impacts of Early Head Start, Vol. 1: Final Technical Report. Princeton, New Jersey: Mathematica Policy Research Inc. http://www.mathematica-mpr.com/PDFs/ehsfinalvol1.pdf.

Lupton, R. (2003) Neighbourhood effects: Can we measure them and does it matter. CASE paper No. 73. London: CASE.

———. (2004) Schools in disadvantaged areas: Recognising context and raising performance. CASE paper No. 76. London: CASE.

———. (2005) Social justice and school improvement: Improving the quality of schooling in the poorest neighbourhoods. *British Educational Research Journal.* 31(5):589–604.

Luthar, S. and L. Zelazo. (2003) Research on resilience: An integrative review. In S. Luthar, ed. Resilience and vulnerability: Adaptation in the context of childhood adversities. Cambridge Mass: Cambridge University Press.

Machell, J. (1999). The lost boys or the great unwashed? Collaborative strategies to address disaffection. Paper presented at the BERA Annual Conference. University of Sussex at Brighton, September 2–5.

Machin, S. (2003) Unto them that hath. . . . *Centre Piece.* 8:4–9.

Machin, S., and A. Vignoles. (2004) Education inequality. *Fiscal Studies.* 25:107–128.

Maden, M. (2001) *Success against the odds: Five years on*, London, Routledge Falmer.

Maden, M. and Hillman, J. (Eds) (1993) *Success against the odds: Effective schools in disadvantaged areas*, London: Routledge.

Madoka, S. (2003) Amartya Sen's capability approach to education: A critical exploration. *Journal of Philosophy of Education.* 37(1):17–33.

Maguire, M. (2006) Education and poverty: A matter of complexity. Paper presented at University of Manchester International Seminar on Education and Poverty. Manchester, March 2006.

Mandelson, P. and R. Liddle. (1996) The Blair revolution. London: Faber and Faber.

Marcus, G. (1998) Ethnography through thick and thin. Princeton, New Jersey: Princeton University Press.

Marcus, J. (2008) From campus to capitol and back again. *Times Higher Education.* November 6, 2008.

Marshall, G., A. Swift, and S. Roberts. (1997) Against the odds? Social class and social justice in industrial societies. Oxford: Clarendon Press.

Martell, G., ed. (1974) The politics of the Canadian public school. Toronto: James Lewis and Samuel.

Massey, D. A global sense of place. *Marxism Today.* June 24–29, 1991.

———. (1994) Space, place and gender. Cambridge: Polity Press.

———. (2007) World city. Cambridge: Policy Press.

Massey, D. and P. Jess. (1995). Places and cultures in an uneven world. In D. Massey and P. Jess, eds. A place in the world? Places, cultures and globalisation. London: Sage/Open University.

Matthews, H. (2003) Children and regeneration: Setting an agenda for community participation and integration. *Children and Society.* 17(4):264–76.

McCaskell, T. (2005) Race to equity: Disrupting educational inequality. Toronto: Between the Lines Press.

McCrone, D. (1994) Getting by and making out in Kirkaldy. In M. Anderson, F. Bechhofer, and J. Gershunny, eds. The social and political economy of the household. Oxford: Oxford University Press.

McHugh, B. and S. Stringfield. (1998) Implementing a highly specific curricular, instructional and organisational high school design in a high poverty urban elementary school: Three year results. Baltimore: Johns Hopkins University, Centre for Research on the Education of Students Placed At Risk

McInerney, P. (2003) Renegotiating schooling for social justice in an age of marketisation. *Australian Journal of Education.* 47(3):251–64.

————. (2004) Making hope practical: School reform for social justice. Flaxton, Qld: Post Pressed.

McInerney, P., R. Hattam, J. Smyth, and M. Lawson. (1999) Making socially just curriculum. Adelaide: Flinders Institute for the Study of Teaching, Flinders University of South Australia.

McMorrow, J. (2008) Reviewing the evidence: Issues in Commonwealth funding of government and non-government in the Howard and Rudd years. Sydney: Australian Education Union.

McVicar, D. and P. Rice. (2001) Participation in further education in England and Wales: An analysis of post-war trends. *Oxford Economics Papers.* 53:47–66.

Meen, G., K. Gibb, J. Goody, T. McGrath, and J. Mackinnon. (2005) Economic segregation in England: Causes, consequences and policy. Bristol: The Policy Press.

Meinhof, U. and K. Richardson, eds. (1994) Text, discourse and context: Representations of poverty in Britain. London: Longman.

Megalogenis, G. One baby in seven prey to poverty. *The Australian.* August 15, 2007.

Melhuish E., J. Belsky, and A. Leyland. (2005) Early impacts of Sure Start local programmes on children and families: Report of the cross-sectional study of 9-and 36-Month old childrens and their families. DfES Research Report No. NESS/2005/FR/013. London: DfES.

Mello, Z.R. (2008) Gender variation in developmental trajectories of educational and occupational expectations and attainment from adolescence to adulthood. *Developmental Psychology,* 44(4):1069–80.

Mendell, D. and D. Little. (2002) Rich '90s failed to lift all. *Chicago Tribune.*www. chicagotribune.com/business/local/monday/chi-0208200185aug20,0,3773589.

Middleton, S., K. Perren, S. Maguire, J. Rennison, E. Battistin, C. Emmerson, E. Fitzsimons. (2005) Evaluation of education maintenance allowance pilots: Young people aged 16 to 19 years. DfES Report No. RR678. London: DfES.

Milbourne, L., S. Macrae, and M. Maguire. (2003). Collaborative solutions or new policy problems: Exploring multi-agency partnerships in education and health work. *Journal of Education Policy.* 18(1):19–35.

Miletic, D. Two million Australians below poverty line. *The Age.* August 30, 2007.

Millar, J. (2000) Keeping track of welfare reform: The new deal programme. York: Joseph Rowntree Foundation.

Ministerial Council on Education, Employment, Training and Youth Affairs. (2008) Melbourne declaration on educational goals for young Australians. Melbourne: Ministerial Council on Education, Employment, Training and Youth Affairs.

Mirón, L. (2006) A response to the education and poverty working paper. University of Manchester International Seminar on Education and Poverty. March 2006, Manchester.

Montgomery, A., R. Rossi, N. Legters, E. McDill, J. McPartland, and S. Stringfield. (1993) Educational reforms and students placed at risk: A review of the current state of the art. Washington: US Department of Education, OERI.

Moreno Herrara, L. (2008) Highlights about priority education policies in Sweden. paper presented to School of Education University Manchester. November 17, 2008.

Morris, M. and S. Golden. (2005) Evaluation of Aimhigher: Excellence challenge interim report 2005. http://www.dcsf.gov.uk/research/data/uploadfiles/RR648.

Morrow, R.A. and C.A. Torres. (2000) The state, globalisation, and educational policy. In N.C. Burbules and C.A. Torres, eds. Globalisation and education, critical perspectives. New York: Routledge.

Morrow, V. (2005) Social capital, community cohesion and participation in England: A space for children and young people. *Journal of Social Sciences*, 9:57–69.

Mortimore, P. (1991) Bucking the trends: Promoting successful urban education. Paper presented at the Times Educational Supplement Greenwich Annual Lecture, London.

———. (2009) Ignoring bad news is politically naïve. *EducationGuardian*, January 6, 2009.

Mortimore, P. and G. Whitty. (1997) Can school improvement overcome the effects of disadvantage? London: Institute of Education, University of London.

Moss, P., P. Petrie, and G. Poland. (1999) Rethinking school: Some international perspectives. Leicester: Youth Work Press for the Joseph Rowntree Foundation.

Moynagh, M. and R. Worsley. (2005) Working in the twenty-first century. Leeds: Economic and Social Research Council: The Tomorrow Project.

Muijs, D. (2006) New directions for school effectiveness research: Towards school effectiveness without schools? *Journal of Educational Change*, 7(3):141–60.

———. (2007) Leadership in full-service extended schools: Communicating across cultures. *School Leadership and Management*. 27(4):347–62.

Muijs, D., A. Harris, C. Chapman, L. Stoll, and J. Russ. (2004) Improving schools in socio-economically disadvantaged areas: An overview of research, school effectiveness and school improvement. 15(2):149–76.

Muijs, D. and D. Reynolds. (2000) School effectiveness and teacher effectiveness: Some preliminary findings from the evaluation of the mathematics enhancement programme. *School Effectiveness and School Improvement*. 11(3):247–63.

———. (2001) *Effective teaching: Evidence and practice*. London: Sage.

———. (2002) Teacher beliefs and behaviors: What matters. *Journal of Classroom Interaction*. 37(2):3–15.

———. (2003) Student background and teacher effects on achievement and attainment in mathematics, educational research and evaluation, 9(1):21–35.

———. (2005) *Effective teaching: evidence and practice* (2nd Edition), London: Routledge.

Müller, W. (1996) Class inequalities in educational outcomes: Sweden in comparative perspective. In R. Erikson and J.O. Jonsson, eds. Can education be equalized?: the Swedish case in comparative perspective. Boulder, Colorado: Oxford, Westview Press.

Müller, W. and M. Gangl, eds. (2003) Transitions from education to work in Europe. The integration of youth into EU labour markets. Oxford: Oxford University Press.

Nason, D. Gillard's supreme teacher. *Weekend Australian (Inquirer)*. August 23–24, 2008.

National Center for Education Statistics (NCES). (2007). Digest of education statistics 2007. Washington, DC: Government Printing Office.

National Strategy for Urban Renewal. (2000) Policy action team report summaries: A compendium. London: Office of the Deputy Prime Minister, England

Native Indian Brotherhood. (1972) Indian control of Indian education. Ottawa: Native Indian Brotherhood.

Nayak, A. (2003) Boyz to men: Masculinities, schooling and labour transitions in de-industrial times. *Educational Review*. 55(2):147–59.

Newmann, F. and Associates. (1996). Authentic achievement. Restructuring schools for intellectual quality. San Francisco: Jossey Bass.

Nicholson, T. Child poverty is booming, like the economy. *The Age*. June 22, 2007.

Noble, M. and G. Smith. (1996) Two nations? Changing patterns of income and wealth in two contrasting areas. In J. Hills, ed. New inequalities: The changing distribution of income and wealth in the United Kingdom. Cambridge: Cambridge University Press.

Novak, T. (1988) Poverty and the state: An historical sociology. Milton Keynes: Open University Press.

Nutley, S., H. Davies, I. Walter. (2002) Briefing note 1: What is a research synthesis? University of St Andrews, Research Unit for Research Utilisation. http://www.st-andrews.ac.uk/~ruru/Conceptual%20synthesis.pdf.

OECD. (2001) Knowledge and skills for life: First results from PISA 2000. Paris: OECD.

———. (2008a) Education at a glance. available at http://www.oecd.org/dataoecd/21/15/41278761.pdf.

———. (2008b) Growing unequal? Income distribution and poverty in OECD countries. Paris: OECD.

———. (2008c) Ten steps to equity in education. Paris: OECD Publishing.

———. (2009) Education today: The OECD perspective. Paris: OECD.

Office of the Deputy Prime Minister. (2005) Mainstream public services and their impact on neighbourhood deprivation. London: ODPM. http://www.neighbourhood.gov.uk/document.asp?id=1044.

OfSTED (2000), *Evaluating Educational Inclusion - Guidance for inspectors and schools*, London: OfSTED. http://www.ofsted.gov.uk/Ofsted-home/Forms-and-guidance/Browse-all-by/Other/General/Evaluating-Educational-Inclusion-Guidance-for-Inspectors-and-Schools.

O'Higgins, N. (2004), Recent trends in youth labour markets and youth employment policy in Europe and Central. *Asia Journal of Economics*. 107(2):439–79.

Olszewski, L. and C. Sandovi. (2003) Rebirth of schools set for south side. *Chicago Tribune*. Sec. 1. December 19, 2003.

Opdenakker, M.C. and J. Van Damme. (2000) Effects of schools, teaching staff and classes on achievement and well-being in secondary education. *School Effectiveness and School Improvement*. 11(2):165–96.

Orfield, G. (1990) Wasted talent, threatened future: Metropolitan Chicago's human capital and Illinois public policy. In L.B. Joseph, ed. Creating jobs, creating workers: Economic development and employment in metropolitan Chicago. Chicago: University of Chicago Center for Urban Research and Policy Studies.

Ornstein, M. (2006) Ethno-racial groups in Toronto, 1971–2001: A demographic and socio-economic profile. Toronto, ON: York University, Institute for Social Research.

Osborn, A.F. (1990) Resilient children: A longitudinal study of high achieving socially disadvantaged children. *Early Child Development and Care*. 62:23–47.

Ozga, J. (2000) Policy research in educational settings. Buckingham: Open University Press.

———. (2002) Education governance in the UK: The modernisation project. *European Educational Research Journal*. 1(2):331–41. 175

———. (2005) Modernizing the education workforce: A perspective from Scotland. *Educational Review*. 57(2):207–19.

Ozga, J. and R. Dale. (1991) Module 1. Introducing education policy: principles and perspectives. Milton Keynes: Open University Press.

Ozga, J. and R. Jones. (2006) Travelling and embedded policy: The case of knowledge transfer. *Journal of Education Policy*. 21(1):1–17.

Pathak, S. (2000) Race research for the future ethnicity in education, training and the labour market. DfEE Research Topic Paper No. RTP01. Nottingham: DfEE.

Payne, J. (2003) The impact of part-time jobs in years 12 and 13 on qualification achievement. *British Educational Research Journal*. 29(4):599–610.

Payton A. (2006) Investigating cognitive genetics and its implications for the treatment of cognitive deficit. *Genes, Brain and Behavior.* 5(1):44–53

Peck, J. and Tickell, A. (2002). Neoliberalizing space. In N. Brenner and N. Theodore, eds. Spaces of neoliberalism: Urban restructuring in North America and Western Europe. Oxford: Blackwell.

Philips, J. (1996) Culture, community and schooling in delta county: State assistance and school change in schools that would never change. Paper presented at the Annual Meeting of the American Educational Research Association. Montreal, Quebec.

Pinch, S. (1979) Territorial justice in the city: A case study of the social services for the elderly in Greater London. In D. Herbert and D. Smith, eds. Social problems and the city: Geographical perspectives. Oxford: Oxford University Press.

Plewis, I. (1998) Inequalities, targets and zones: Current policies to raise education standards could raise inequality. *New Economy.* 5(2):104–8.

Plewis, I. and C. Kallis. (2008) Changing economic circumstances in childhood and their effects on subsequent educational and other outcomes. London: Department of Work and Pensions.

Plug, E. and W. Vijverberg. (2003) Schooling, family background, and adoption: Is it nature or is it nurture? Journal of Political Economy. 111(3):611–41.

Pollitt, C. (2007) New labour's re-disorganisation. *Public Management Review.* 9(4):529–43.

Power, L. League tables can't measure a school's true worth: principals. *Sunday Age.* September 7, 2008.

Power, M. I audit, therefore I am. *Times Higher Education Supplement.* October 18, 1996.

Power, S. and S. Gewirtz. (2001) Reading education action zones, *Journal of Education Policy.* 16(1):38–51.

Power, S., G. Rees. and C. Taylor. (2005) New Labour and educational disadvantage: the limits of area-based initiatives. *London Review of Education.* 3(2):101–16.

Power, S., S. Warren, D. Gillborn, A. Clark, S. Thomas, and C. Kelly. (2003) *Education in deprived areas. Outcomes, inputs and processes.* London: Institute of Education, University of London. 128.

Pratt, G. and S. Hanson. (1994) Geography and the construction of difference. *Gender, Place and Culture.* 1(1):5–29.

Pring, R. (2000) Editorial: Educational research. *British Journal of Educational Studies.* 48(1):1–9.

Pritchard, S. Why the language of poverty is a sensitive issue. *The Observer.* November 9, 2008.

Purcell, K. (2002) Qualifications and careers: Equal opportunities and earning among graduates. Manchester: EOC: Working Paper Series 1.

Raffel, J.A., L.R. Denson, D.P. Varady, and S. Sweeney, (2003) Linking housing and public schools in the HOPE VI public housing revitalization program: A case study analysis of four developments in four cities. http://www.udel.edu/ccrs/pdf/LinkingHousing.pdf.

Raffo, C. (2003) Disaffected young people and the work-related curriculum at key stage 4: issues of social capital development and learning as a form of cultural practice, *Journal of Education and Work.* 16(1):69–86.

Raffo, C., A. Dyson, H. Gunter, D. Hall, L. Jones, and A. Kalambouka. (2007) Education and poverty: A critical review of theory, policy and practice. York: Joseph Rowntree Foundation.

Raffo, C. and M. Reeves. (2000) Youth transitions and social exclusion: Developments in social capital theory. *Journal of Youth Studies.* 3(2):147–166.

Ranson, S. (1993) Markets or democracy for education. *British Journal of Educational Studies.* 41(4):333–52.

Reay, D., M.E. David, and S.J. Ball. (2005) Degrees of choice. Social class, race and gender in higher education. Stoke on Trent: Trentham Books.

Reay, D. and H. Lucey. (2000) 'I don't like it here but I don't want to live anywhere else': Children living on inner London council estates. *Antipode: A Radical Journal of Geography.* 32(4):410–28.

Rees, G., S. Power, and C. Taylor. (2007) The governance of educational inequalities: The limits of area-based initiatives. *Journal of Comparative Policy Analysis.* 9(3):261–74.

Reindal, S.M. (2009) Disability, capability, and special education: towards a capability-based theory. *European Journal of Special Needs Education.* 24(2):155–68.

Reitzle, M., F.W. Vondracek, and R.K. Silbereisen. (1998) Timing of school-to-work transitions: A developmental-contextual perspective. *International Journal of Behavioral Development.* 22:7–28.

Research Intelligence (2008) Profile: Philip Cowley: Your man in the Treasury. *Research Intelligence.* November 2008, Issue 105.

Ribbins, P., R. Bates, and H.M. Gunter. (2003) Reviewing research in education in Australia and the UK: evaluating the evaluations. *Journal of Educational Administration.* 41(4):423–44.

Rizvi, F. and B. Lingard. (2000) Globalisation and education: Complexities and contingencies. *Education Theory.* 50(4):419–26.

Roberts, K. (1980) Schools, parents and social class. In M. Craft, J. Raynor, and L. Cohen, eds. Linking home and school (3rd Ed.). London: Harper and Row.

Robertson, R. (1992) Globalisation, social theory and global culture. London: Sage.

Roe, E. (1994) Narrative policy analysis: Theory and practice. Durham, NC: Duke University Press.

Roker, D. (1998) Worth more than this: Young people growing up in family poverty. London: Children's Society.

Romano, R. and Glascock, C. (2002) Hungry minds in hard times. Educating for complexity for students of poverty. New York: Peter Lang.

Rose, N. (1999) Powers of freedom: Reframing political thought. Cambridge: Cambridge University Press.

Rothstein, R. (2004) Class and schools: Using social, economic and educational reform to close the black-white achievement gap. Washington: Economic Policy Institute.

Royal Commission on Aboriginal Peoples. (1996) Final report. Ottawa: Indian and Northern Affairs Canada.

Rudd, P. (1997) From socialisation to postmodernity: A review of theoretical perspectives on the school-to-work transition. *Journal of Education and Work.* 10(3):257–80.

Rudduck, J. and D. McIntyre, eds. (1998) Challenges for educational research. London: PCP.

Rumberger, R.W. and K.A. Larson. (1998) Student mobility and the increased risk of high school drop out. *American Journal of Education.* 107:1–35.

Rutledge D. (1988). Institutionalizing change: The problem of system beliefs. In M. Lightfoot and N. Martin, eds. The word for teaching is learning: Essays for James Britten. Portsmouth: Heinemann Educational Books.

Rutter, M. (2003) Genetic influences on risk and protection: Implications for understanding resilience. In Suniya Luthar, ed. Resilience and vulnerability: Adaptation in the context of childhood adversities. Cambridge Mass: Cambridge University Press.

Sacker, A., I. Schoon, and M. Bartley. (2002) Social inequality in educational achievement and psychosocial adjustment throughout childhood: Magnitude and mechanisms. *Social Science and Medicine.* 55(5):863–80.

Sammons, P. (2007) School effectiveness and equity: Making connections. London: CfBT.

Sassen, S. (2006) Cities in a world economy, 3rd Ed. Thousand Oaks, California: Pine Forge Press.

Saunders, P. (2002) Reflections on the meritocracy debate in Britain: A response to Richard Breen and John Goldthorpe. *British Journal of Sociology.* 53:559–74.

Savage, M. (2009) Labour's record on poverty in tatters. *The Independent,* May 8, 2009.

Schneider, B. and D. Stevenson. (1999) The ambitious generation: America's teenagers, motivated but directionless. New Haven: Yale University Press.

Schools Analysis and Research Division, Department for Children Schools and Families. (2009) Deprivation and education: The evidence on pupils in England. Foundation stage to key stage 4. London: DCSF.

Schoon, I. (2006) Risk and resilience. Adaptations in changing times. Cambridge: Cambridge University Press.

———. (2008) A transgenerational model of status attainment: The potential mediating role of school motivation and education. *National Institute Economic Review.* 205:72–82.

Schoon, I., P. Martin, and A. Ross. (2007) Career transitions in times of social change. His and her story. *Journal of Vocational Behavior.* 70(1):78–96.

Schoon, I., A. McCulloch, H. Joshi, R.D. Wiggins, and J. Bynner. (2001) Transitions from school to work in a changing social context. *Young.* 9:4–22.

Schoon, I., and S. Parsons. (2002) Teenage aspirations for future careers and occupational outcomes. *Journal of Vocational Behavior.* 60(2):262–288.

Schoon, I., A. Ross, and P. Martin. (in press). Sequences, patterns, and variations in the assumption of work and family related roles. Evidence from two British birth cohorts. In I. Schoon and K.R. Silbereisen, eds. Transitions from school to work: Globalisation, individualisation, and patterns of diversity. New York: Cambridge University Press.

Schoon, I. and K.R. Silbereisen, eds. (in press) Transitions from school to work: Globalisation, individualisation, and patterns of diversity, New York: Cambridge University Press.

Schweinhart, L.J., J. Montie, J. Xiang, W.S. Barnett, C.R. Belfield, and M. Nores. (2005) Lifetime effects: The high/scope Perry preschool study through age 40. (Monographs of the High/Scope Educational Research Foundation, 14). Ypsilanti, Michigan: High/Scope Press.

Scott, J. (2004) Family, gender, and educational attainment in Britain: A longitudinal study. *Journal of Comparative Family Studies.* 35:565–90.

Scott, J., S. Dex, H. Joshi, K. Purcell, and P. Elias, eds. (2008) Women and employment: Changing lives and new challenges. Northampton: Edward Elgar.

Scott, S., T. O'Connor, and A. Futh. (2006) What makes parenting programmes work in disadvantaged areas? The PALS trial. York: Joseph Rowntree Foundation.

Seaman, P., K. Turner, M. Hill, A. Stafford, and M. Walker. (2006) Parenting and children's resilience in disadvantaged communities. York: Joseph Rowntree Foundation.

Searle, C. (1998) None but our words. Critical literacy in the classroom. Buckingham: Open University Press.

Sen, A. (1999) Development as freedom. Oxford: Oxford University Press.

———. (2000) Social exclusion. Manila: Asian Development Bank.

Sennett, R. (2003) Respect. London: Allen Lane.

Sewell, W.H. and V.P. Shah. (1968) Social class, parental encouragement, and educational aspirations. *American Journal of Sociology.* 73:559–72.

Seymour, D. (2008) Reporting poverty in the UK. York: Society of Editors, Media Trust and the Joseph Rowntree Foundation. http://www.jrf.org.uk/bookshop/details.asp?pubID=977.

Shain, F. and J. Ozga. (2001) Identity crisis? Problems and issues in the sociology of education. *British Journal of Sociology of Education.* 22(1):109–120.

Shavit, Y. and W. Müller. (1998) From school to work: A comparative study of educational qualifications and occupational destinations. Oxford: Clarendon Press.

Shields, C. (2004) Dialogic leadership for social justice: Overcoming pathologies of silence. *Educational Administration Quarterly.* 40(1):109–32.

Siemiatycki, M. and E. Isin. (1997) Immigration, diversity and urban citizenship in Toronto. *Canadian Journal of Regional Science.* 20(1–2):73–102.

Silberman, M. (2007) The handbook of experiential learning. San Francisco, California: John Wiley and Sons.

Silverman, E., R. Lupton, and A. Fenton. (2005) A good place for children? Attracting and retaining families in inner urban mixed income communities. Coventry: Chartered Institute of Housing for the Joseph Rowntree Foundation.

Shonkoff, J.P. and D.A. Phillips, eds. For the Committee on Integrating the Science of Early Childhood Development (2000) From neurons to neighbourhoods. The science of early childhood development. Washington D.C.: National Academy Press.

Sibley, D. (1995) Geographies of exclusion. London: Routledge.

Skinner, C. (2004) The changing occupational structure of large metropolitan areas: Implications for the high school educated. *Journal of Urban Affairs.* 26(1):67–88.

Slee, R., G. Weiner, and S. Tomlinson, eds. (1998) School effectiveness for whom? Challenges to the school effectiveness and school improvement movements. London: Falmer Press.

Smith, C. and A. Turley. Our forgotten poor. *The Age.* October 29, 2007.

Smith, G. (1987) Whatever happened to educational priority areas? *Oxford Review of Education.* 13(1):23–37.

———. (2002) Place-based education. Learning to be where we are. *Phi Delta Kappan.* 83(8):584–595.

Smith, G., T. Smith, and T. Smith. (2007) Whatever happened to EPAs? Part 2: Educational priority areas–40 years on. *Forum.* 49(1 and 2):141–56.

Smith, N. (2002) New globalism, new urbanism: Gentrification as global urban strategy. *Antipode.* 34(3):427–50.

Smith, T. and M. Nobel. (1995) Education divides–poverty and schooling in the 1990s. London: Child Poverty Action Group (CPAG) Ltd.

Smyth, J. (2003a) Engaging the education sector: A policy orientation to stop damaging our schools. *Learning Communities: International Journal of Learning in Social Contexts.* 1(1):22–40.

———. (2003b) Undamaging 'damaged' teachers: an antidote to the 'self-managing school'. *Delta: Policy and Practice in Education.* 55(1 and 2):15–42.

———. (2005) Modernizing the Australian education workplace: A case of failure to deliver for teachers of young disadvantaged adolescents. *Educational Review.* 57(2):221–33.

———. (2006) Researching teachers working with young adolescents: Implications for ethnographic research. *Ethnography and Education.* 1(1):31–51.

———. (2007a) Teacher development against the policy reform grain: An argument for recapturing relationships in teaching and learning. *Teacher Development: An International Journal of Teachers' Professional Development.* 11(2):221–36.

————. (2007b). Toward the pedagogically engaged school: Listening to student voice as a positive response to disengagement and 'dropping out'. In D. Thiessen and A. Cook-Sather, eds. International handbook of student experience of elementary and secondary school. Dordrecht, The Netherlands: Springer Science Publishers.

————. (2008) Australia's great disengagement with public education and social justice in educational leadership. *Journal of Educational Administration and History.* 40(3):221–33.

Smyth, J., L. Angus, B. Down, , and P. McInerney. (2008) Critically engaged learning: Connecting to young lives. New York: Peter Lang Publishing.

————. (2009) Activist and socially critical school and community renewal: Social justice in exploitative times. Rotterdam, The Netherlands: Sense Publishers.

Smyth, J., B. Down, and P. McInerney. (2008) 'Hanging in with kids' in tough times: Engagement in contexts of educational disadvantage in the relational school. Ballarat: School of Education, University of Ballarat.

Smyth, J. and L. Fasoli. (2007) Climbing over the rocks in the road to student engagement and learning in a challenging high school in Australia. *Educational Research.* 49(3):273–95.

Smyth, J., R. Hattam, J. Cannon, J. Edwards, N. Wilson, and S. Wurst. (2000) Listen to me, I'm leaving: Early school leaving in south Australian secondary schools. Adelaide: Flinders Institute for the Study of Teaching; Department of Employment, Education and Training; and Senior Secondary Assessment Board of South Australia.

————. (2004) 'Dropping out', drifting off, being excluded: Becoming somebody without school. New York: Peter Lang Publishing.

Smyth, J., R. Hattam, and M. Lawson, eds. (1998a) Schooling for a fair go. Sydney: Federation Press.

Smyth, J., R. Hattam, P. McInerney, and M. Lawson. (1999) School culture: The key to school reform (Investigation Series, Teachers' Learning Project). Adelaide: Flinders Institute for the Study of Teaching.

Smyth, J. and H. Gunter. (2009) Debating new labour education policy. In C. Chapman. and H. Gunter, eds. Radical reforms: Public policy and a decade of educational reform. London: Routledge.

Smyth, J. and P. McInerney. (2007a) "Living on the edge": A case of school reform working for disadvantaged adolescents. *Teachers College Record.* 109(5):1123–70.

————. (2007b) Teachers in the middle: Reclaiming the wasteland of the adolescent years of schooling. New York: Peter Lang Publishing.

Smyth, J., P. McInerney, R. Hattam, and M. Lawson. (1998b) Teacher learning: the way out of the school restructuring miasma. *International Journal of Leadership in Education: Theory and Practice.* 1(2):95–110.

————. (1999a) Critical reflection on teaching and learning. Adelaide: Flinders Institute for the Study of Teaching.

————. (1999b) A culture of reform for social justice: The Pines School. Adelaide: The Flinders Institute for the Study of Teaching.

Smyth, J., and G. Shacklock. (1998) Re-making teaching: Ideology, policy and practice. London and New York: Routledge.

Sobel, D. (2004) Place-based education: Connecting classrooms and communities. Greater Barrington, Massachusetts: The Orion Society.

Social Exclusion Unit. (1998) Bringing Britain together: A national strategy for neighbourhood renewal. Cm4045. London: The Stationery Office.

————. (2001a) Preventing social exclusion. London: Social Exclusion Unit.

Soja, E. (1996) *Thirdspace: Journeys to Los Angeles and other real and imagined places.* Oxford: Blackwell.

Sorenson, M. (2008) STAR. Service to all relations. In D.A. Gruenewald and G. Smith, eds. Place-based education in the global age. Local Diversity, Majwah, New Jersey: Lawrence Erlbaum.

Spicker, P. (2007) The idea of poverty. Bristol: Policy Press.

Steedman, H. (2004) How to motivate (demotivated) 14-16 year olds, with special reference to work related education and training. London: Centre for Economic Performance, London School of Economics.

Steedman, H. and S. Stoney. (2004) Disengagement 14–16: Context and evidence. CEP Discussion Paper No. 654, London: London School of Economics.

Stone, C.N., J. Henig, B.D. Jones, C. Pierannunzi. (2001) Building civic capacity: The politics of reforming urban schools. Lawrence: University of Kansas Press.

Stone, D. (2002) *Policy paradox: The art of political decision-making* (2nd Ed.). New York: W.W. Norton Co. 152.

Strand, S. (2007) Minority ethnic pupils in the longitudinal study of young people in England (LSYPE). London: Department for children, schools and families (DCSF). Research Report No. RR002. http://www.dfes.gov.uk/research/data/uploadfiles/DCSF-RR002.pdf.

Strauss, H. and C. de la Maisonneuve. (2007) The wage premium on tertiary education: New estimates for 21 OECD countries. OECD Working Paper No. 589, 49(Dec 07), http://www.olis.oecd.org/olis/2007doc.nsf/linkto/eco-wkp.

Swyngedouw, E. (1997). Neither global nor local. "Glocalisation" and the politics of scale. In K. Cox, ed. Spaces of globalisation. Reasserting the power of the local. New York: The Guilford Press.

Sylva, K., E. Melhuish, P. Sammons, I. Siraj-Blatchford, and B. Taggart. (2008) Final report from the primary phase: Pre-school, school and family influences on children's development during key stage 2 (age 7–11). London: DCSF.

Szirom, T., R. Jaffe, and D. MacKenzie (Strategic Partners in association with the Centre for Youth Affairs and Development). (2001) National evaluation report. Full service schools program 1999 and 2000. Canberra: Commonwealth Department of Education, Training and Youth Affairs.

Teddlie, C. and D. Reynolds. (2000) The international handbook of school effectiveness research. London: Falmer Press.

Teddlie, C., and S. Stringfield. (1993) School matters: Lessons learned from a 10-year study of school effects. New York: Teachers College Press.

Teddlie, C., S. Stringfield, R. Wimpelberg, and P. Kirby. (1989) Contextual differences in models for effective schooling in the USA. Paper presented at the International Congress on School Effectiveness and School Improvement.

Terzi, L. (2005) Beyond the dilemma of difference: The capability approach on disability and special educational needs. *Journal of Philosophy of Education.* 39(3):443–59.

The National Educational Research Forum. (n.d.) Research and development in education. Nottingham: NERF.

Thomson, P. (2002) Schooling the rustbelt kids—Making the difference in changing times. Stoke-on-Trent: Trentham Books.

———. (2006) Miners, diggers, ferals and showmen: School community projects that unsettle identities? *British Journal of Sociology of Education.* 27(1):81–96.

Thomson, P. and C. Hall. (2008) Opportunities missed and/or thwarted? 'Funds of knowledge' meets the English national curriculum. *Curriculum Journal.* 19(2):87–103.

Thomson, P., V. McQuade, and K. Rochford. (2005) "My little special house": Reforming the risky geographies of middle school girls at Clifftop College. In G. Lloyd, ed. Problem girls. Understanding and supporting troubled and troublesome girls and young women. London: Routledge Falmer.

Thrift, N. (1996) Spatial formations. London: Sage.

Thrupp, M. (1999) Schools making a difference: Let's be realistic! School mix, school effectiveness and the social limits of reform. New York: Taylor and Francis.

Thrupp, M. and R. Willmott. (2003) Education management in managerialist times: Beyond the textual apologists. Maidenhead: Open University Press.

Tomazin, F. Brightest and best to help difficult schools. Recruitment drive for uni graduates *The Age*. August 23, 2008.

Tomazin, F. and D. Rood. Fast-food giants may be welcomed in schools. *The Age*. September 3, 2008.

Tomazin, F. and B. Smith. Gillard wants to put top graduates into the toughest classrooms. *The Age*. July 18, 2008.

Tomlinson, S. (2005) Education in a post-welfare society. Maidenhead: Open University Press.

Tooley, J. with D. Darby. (1998) Educational research: A review. London: OFSTED.

Tooley, J., P. Dixon, and J. Stanfield. (2003) Delivering better education: Market solutions for educational improvement. London: ASI (Adam Smith Institute) Ltd.

Toronto Board of Education. (1976) Draft report of the subcommittee on multiculturalism. Toronto, Ontario: Levin.

Townsend, P. (1979) Poverty in the United Kingdom. Harmondsworth: Penguin.

Toynbee, P. and D. Walker. (2008) Unjust rewards. Exposing greed and inequality in Britain today. London: Granta.

Tucker, C.J., J. Marx, and L. Long. (1998). Moving on: Residential mobility and children's school lives. *Sociology of Education*. 71:111–29.

Tunstall, R. and R. Lupton. (2003) Is targeting deprived areas an effective means to reach poor people? An assessment of one rationale for area-based funding programmes. CASE paper No. 70. London: CASE.

US Government Department of Education (2005) How no child left behind benefits African Americans. http://www.ed.gov/nclb/accountability/achieve/nclb-aa.pdf.

Van Veen, D. and P. van den Bogaert. (2006) LCOJ-monitor: leerlingenzorg en zorgadviesteams in het voortgezet onderwijs. Leuven: Garant.

Venkatesh, S.A., I. Celimli, D. Miller, A. Murphy, B. Turner. (2004) Chicago public housing transformation: A research report. New York: Center for Urban Research and Policy, Columbia University.

Verma, G.J. (1985) The Swann report and ethnic achievement: A comment. *New Community*. 12(3):470–75.

Walker, M. and E. Unterhalter. (2007) The capability approach: Its potential for work in education. In M. Walker and E. Unterhalter, eds. Amartya Sen's capability approach and social justice in education. Basingstoke: Palgrave Macmillan.

Walker, M. and E. Unterhalter, eds. (2007) Amartya Sen's capability approach and social justice in education. London: Palgrave.

Weindling, D. (2004) Funding for research on school leadership. Nottingham: NCSL http://www.ncsl.org.uk.

Weiner, L. (2006) Urban teaching: the essentials. New York: Teachers College Press.

Wexler, P. (1992) Becoming somebody: Towards a social psychology of school. London: Falmer Press.

Whalen, S. (2002) Report of the evaluation of the Polk Bros. Foundation's full service schools initiative. Executive summary. Chicago, Illinois: Chapin Hall Center for Children at The University of Chicago for the Polk Bros Foundation.

Whitty, G. (2002) Making sense of education policy. London: PCP.

Whitty, G., S. Power, and D. Halpin. (1998) Devolution and choice in education: The school, the state and the market. Buckingham: Open University Press.

Wigginton, E. (1986) Sometimes a shining moment: The Foxfire experience. Twenty years teaching in a high school classroom. New York: Anchor Press, Doubleday.

Wilkinson, R. and K. Pickett. (2009) The spirit level: Why more equal societies almost always do better. London: Penguin Books.

Williams, R. (1973) The long revolution (3rd Ed.). London: Pelican Books.

Willis, P. (1977) Learning to labour: How working class kids get working class jobs. Aldershot: Gower.

Wilson, J. (1987) The truly disadvantaged: The inner city, the underclass, and public policy. Chicago: University of Chicago Press.

Winnipeg School Division (2005). *Aboriginal education policy.* Downloaded Sept 7, 2009 from http://www.sd1.org/board/policies_pdf/Policy_IGABA.pdf.

W.K. Kellogg Foundation. (2004) Logic model development guide. Battle Creek, MI: W.K. Kellogg Foundation.

Woodhead, C. (2000) Old values for the new age. *Times Educational Supplement,* 7/1/2000. p. 13.

Woods, P.A. and R. Levačić. (2002) Raising school performance in the league tables (part 2): Barriers to responsiveness in three disadvantaged schools. *British Educational Research Journal.* 28(2):227–48.

Yau, M. (1996) Moving toward the year 2000: Rethinking the inner city project school model and mandate. Toronto: Toronto District School Board, Research and Information Department.

Youdell, D. (2006) Subjectivation and peformative politics—Butler thinking Althusser and Foucault: Intelligibility, agency and the raced-nationed-religioned subjects of education. *British Journal of Sociology of Education.* 27(4):511–28.

Younger, M., M. Warrington, J. Gray, J. Rudduck, R. McLellan, E. Bearne, R. Kershner, and P. Bricheno. (2005) Raising boys' achievement. DfES Research Report No. RR636. London: DfES.

Zellmann, G. and J. Waterman. (1998) Understanding the impact of parent school involvement on children's educational outcomes. *Journal of Education Research.* 91:370–80.

Index